www.congregationalresources.org

www.congregationalresources.org

a guide to resources for building congregational vitality

Richard Bass, editor

THE
ALBAN
INSTITUTE

Herndon, Virginia
www.alban.org

The Alban Institute
2121 Cooperative Way, Suite 100
Herndon, VA 20171-5370
www.alban.org

Library of Congress Control Number: 2002104642
ISBN 1-56699-266-4

08 07 06 05 04   VG   1 2 3 4 5

CONTENTS

110954

CONTRIBUTORS

RICHARD BASS is director of publishing at the Alban Institute. He was formerly the project director of the Congregational Resource Guide.

PAUL C. CHAFFEE is executive director of the Interfaith Center at the Presidio in San Francisco, California. He is the author of *Accountable Leadership: A Resource Guide to Sustaining Legal, Financial, and Ethical Integrity in Today's Congregations* (Jossey-Bass, 1997).

THOMAS F. FISCHER, director of ministryhealth.net, is an active clergyman of the Michigan District of the Lutheran Church–Missouri Synod.

RYAN D. HAZEN is a Congregational Services Specialist with the Board of Church Extension of the Disciples of Christ and is the editor of its quarterly newsletter, *Cutting Edge.*

DAN HOTCHKISS is a Senior Consultant at the Alban Institute. He is the author of *Ministry and Money: A Guide for Clergy and Their Friends* (Alban Institute, 2002).

JOHN JANKA, the former director of consulting and education at the Alban Institute, is currently serving First Presbyterian Church of Howard County in Columbia, Maryland.

JACQUELINE J. LEWIS is associate collegiate minister at Middle Collegiate Church in New York City. She is a former Senior Consultant at the Alban Institute.

G. LEE RAMSEY, JR., is an associate professor at Memphis Theological Seminary, where he teaches pastoral care and preaching. He is the author of *Care-full Preaching: From Sermon to Caring Community* (Chalice Press, 2000).

AMY L. SHERMAN is Senior Fellow at the Hudson Institute, where she directs the Faith in Communities Initiative. She also serves as Urban Ministries Advisor at Trinity Presbyterian Church in Charlottesville, Virginia. She is the author of *Restorers of Hope: Reaching the Poor in Your Community with Church-based Ministries That Work* (Crossway Books, 1997).

JEAN MORRIS TRUMBAUER is a consultant, trainer, and author of *Sharing the Ministry: A Practical Guide for Transforming Volunteers into Ministers* (Augsburg Fortress, 1995, 1999) and *Created and Called: Discovering Our Gifts for Abundant Living* (Augsburg Fortress, 1998).

JOHN WIMMER is a program officer in the religion division of Lilly Endowment Inc. He was the founding director of the Indianapolis Center for Congregations.

PREFACE

In April 1998 the Alban Institute—in partnership with the Indianapolis Center for Congregations and the support of a generous grant from Lilly Endowment Inc.—began to develop a guide to the best resources to help congregations address the most pressing and critical issues they face. The Congregational Resource Guide, as it came to be known, began as a simple listing of what congregations have found to be the most useful resources (books, Web sites, organizations, videos, consultants, and other congregations) on the dozen issues we found that congregations ask about most often. Since 1998 this guide has grown to include over 900 resources in 116 topic areas, shared with the public through an interactive Web site at www.congregationalresources.org. Yet, in spite of this growth, the Congregational Resource Guide has retained its purpose: to recommend to congregations the best resources—from whatever source—on those issues congregations tell us are most pressing to them and to help guide congregations in the use of those resources.

We came to realize, however, that while a collection of individual resources is helpful, it is equally important to bring these resources into conversation with each other in the context of a particular topic. To this end we commissioned essays from a diverse group of nine experts who were knowledgeable about key issues facing congregations. We asked them to provide an introduction to the issue and to review the resources that would be most helpful to someone wanting to learn more. We hoped that they would provide insights into both the topic and the resources, while also introducing readers to new perspectives on issues that may be outside the scope of their everyday interests.

When there are as many resources in as many categories as there are in the Congregational Resource Guide, the choice of which topics to focus on in a collection such as this is quite difficult. Rather than create a tightly focused collection, we decided instead to attempt to mirror the broad spectrum of voices and of topics in the guide itself. As a result, the chapters in the book may appear to be only loosely connected. But when viewed from a greater distance, the topics addressed here are those that congregational leaders face regularly: building issues, money, evaluation, leadership, cultural diversity, the role of lay persons, congregational conflict, community ministry, and preaching. We hope that these essays bring not only new ideas and new resources, but also exposure to new ways of thinking about the issues that face us today.

All of the authors were encouraged to write about the topic from their own perspectives rather than from some "objective" position. They are, however, responsible only for the essays in each chapter. The "Resources from the Congregational Resource Guide" section that accompanies each essay were selected by me from the resources included in the guide. Some of these resources from the guide are addressed in the essays while others are not. The guide is continually updated, so please be sure to visit www.congregationalresources.org for the most current resources on these and other topics.

I want to thank the authors of the essays. All were generous with their time and the attention they gave this project. Some are current or former employees of the Alban Institute, while others are working with us here for the first time. I also want to thank the Congregational Resource Guide team, past and present, who together have helped make the guide the comprehensive collection that it is today: Ian Evison, Claudia Greer, Anne Van Dusen, and Lou Nistler from the Alban Institute and Nancy DeMott, Brent Bill, Aaron Spiegel, John Wimmer, and Tim Shapiro from the Indianapolis Center for Congregations. Without the vision and generous support of the religion division of Lilly Endowment Inc. for the Congregational Resource Guide, this project would not have been possible. I thank them all for their patience, confidence, and support.

INTRODUCTION

CONNECTING TO SOURCES OF WISDOM AND HELP

John Wimmer

Congregations have always used outside resources in one form or another. Even though congregations exist in particular contexts (a neighborhood, community, county, state or province, nation, or even an empire), they have also almost always possessed the need and desire to connect with sources of help, wisdom, and direction beyond their own walls and people. Biblical texts, understood in this way, are resources that reflect the earliest way in which congregational leaders sought and received help, wisdom, and direction. (The apostle Paul *did*, after all, have a few things to say about the way the congregation in Corinth, for example, should behave toward one another and how God's love should be made manifest in community.) The writings and teachings of the "church fathers"—such as Augustine's works on preaching or Hippolytus' exemplary eucharistic prayer—similarly were resources that provided instruction to congregational leaders on important facets of organizing congregational life and worship. The construction of medieval cathedrals—breathtaking structures that continue to glorify God even today—demanded the participation of artisans, stonemasons, engineers, and architects. Today, denominations, publishing houses, seminaries, professors, church-related agencies, and many more types of people and institutions provide curriculum and training materials, books, and consultants that help lay and clergy leaders think in practical as well as theological terms about congregational life and service.

In every period of history and every place where people of faith have gathered to worship, pray, teach, learn, and serve their neighbors, congregational leaders have sought and benefited from being

1

connected to resources that tap into the collected (and collecting) knowledge, wisdom, and expertise of their faith tradition, as well as to the best of contemporary thought.

Congregations in our time are heirs to this tradition of resource development, and they are contemporary participants in the ongoing process of producing and using resources that help strengthen people of faith. The Congregational Resource Guide is an attempt to help congregational leaders connect with sources of wisdom and help. Resources reconnect us to the wisdom of the ages as well as spirit of God.

Before moving on to the essays that point to excellent resources in areas of central concern for congregational leaders, this chapter surfaces and examines some of the convictions, diagnoses, and theological assumptions that gave rise to the Resource Guide.

The Congregational Resource Guide grows out of a distinctive diagnosis about the nature of congregational life in our time and the ways resources are or are not available. It also reflects a set of key convictions about what this diagnosis means about the ways congregations find and utilize resources. Let's first examine the diagnosis.

A Changed and Changing Religious Landscape

It is no secret that the landscape of religious life in America has changed dramatically over the last generation. The long list of societal influences and cultural factors contributing to our radically changed environment is familiar to any thoughtful congregational leader who attempts to deal with and find ways to thrive in this context of change. The rise of entertainment-driven consumer culture, the technological/digital revolution, the changing role of the federal government in social services, broadening and deepening cultural expressions, widening gaps between rich and poor, the lessening of denominational loyalty among the young, the advent of "mega church" models of congregating, the liturgical renewal movement, Vatican II—the list is exhausting! Some of these changes have affected parishes chiefly as they relate to (and in some ways compete in) the cultural environment around them. Other changes, however, have been much more direct in their impact.

Take, for example, the changing role of denominations in relation to congregations over the last 40 years or so. On the one hand, changing denominational fortunes—increasing numbers of adherents for some and decreasing numbers for others—have had a dramatic impact on congregations. Congregations affiliated with denominations that were once relatively larger have experienced a general tightening or diminution of resources available to them from their general and judicatory levels. Judicatory or general church staff positions, publications, and related institutions (such as church-related colleges, hospitals, seminaries, mission societies) have all radically changed in their relationships with congregations.

This change in denominational connections seems to involve more than reduced denominational and judicatory wherewithal, however. We are more and more in a time of choice and voluntary associations. That is partly because we are in a time when denominational resources just cannot meet or satisfy the diverse resource needs of a denomination's congregations.

It is hard to say which came first, the denominational disconnect or reduced denominational offerings. Regardless, they both are a part of modern congregational life. And they impact the way resources are discovered and made available.

CHANGED PATHWAYS TO SOURCES OF HELP AND WISDOM

There have been massive alterations in the *pathways* to sources of help and wisdom for congregations resulting from the changed relationships of congregations with resources and resource providers. There is a line in a popular song by Dan Fogelberg that says, "Gone are the pathways the child followed home, gone like the sand and the foam." It is much like that for the paths from congregations to resources. The old pathways are simply not there or have radically changed.

The combination of a changing landscape and altered pathways has left churches, parishes, and synagogues oftentimes on their own to fend for themselves in finding resources.

NEW RESOURCES AND RESOURCE PROVIDERS HAVE MULTIPLIED

In the midst of all of this, the resources available to congregations have, curiously, not diminished—but increased! Probably resulting from the vacuum created in the wake of diminished and changed resource pathways that left some congregations disconnected, there has been a virtual explosion in the number of other kinds of agencies and resources arising to help congregations.

There is no better example of this phenomenon than the Alban Institute itself. Alban was created in 1974 partly in response to the phenomena I am describing. It provided a kind of help and resource to congregations that was becoming (and remains) very difficult for denominational and other agencies to provide. Consulting services, new types of research, books, and other resources for congregational leaders on topics such as conflict, clergy transition, and strategic planning arose from the new needs and demands of congregations to find helpful resources amid changing circumstances and altered pathways.

While the Alban Institute is an excellent example of the new kind of institution surfacing in this time frame, it is not alone. Organizations like Leadership Network, Shalem Institute, Interim Ministry Network, and the National Association of Church Business Administration, publications such as *Net Results, The Clergy Journal, Rev., Worship Leader, Group*, and fund raising consultants (RSI, Cargill, Genesis Group, to mention only a few) all provide services, information, and help that was not available a generation ago!

In the midst of the sea changes to culture, society, and denominations, the result is not too few resources but almost too many! Congregational leaders are often faced with the difficulty of picking out the best resources from a lengthy list of possibilities.

It is the daunting reality of our time that congregational leaders are faced, on the one hand, with a *diminishing set of resources* provided by denominations, and, on the other, an *explosion of resources* available to them!

This precarious predicament is one reason we believe the Congregational Resource Guide is valuable.

CONVICTIONS

In addition to these diagnoses, the resource guide is also based on a set of convictions.

Congregations Can Always Use Help

We are convinced that all kinds of congregations—big and small, urban and rural, denominational and independent, Protestant and

Catholic, Evangelical and Jewish, mainstream and ethnic—can benefit from the help and wisdom that outside resources provide. We sometimes labor under the misconception that, for example, very large "mega churches" have so much going for them that they need no resources. Correspondingly, it is sometimes believed that very small membership congregations are so far gone that they are beyond help. (Similar observations could be made about the other pairs mentioned.) I do not believe that any of these assertions are true. Our experience has proved otherwise. Churches, parishes, and synagogues can and do benefit from the help of resources, no matter their size or circumstance.

Congregations, Left on Their Own, Do Not Always Know Where to Turn for Help

The result of the circumstances I have outlined is that congregational leaders are not always sure where to turn for the resources and help they need. No wonder! These circumstances are worsened by our culture's false impression that resources are *unlimited*! Resources presumed available in the area of computer technology and ministry is one example. Software and hardware vendors often say things like, "The possibilities are limited only by your imagination!" *Wrong!* There are in fact all manner of limitations to how computer resources can be used for ministry. Limited computer memory (RAM and ROM, if you understand the difference—and I don't), pre-programmed software features, your operating system (is it updated?), and the sheer limits of the ability of the computer operator (which in my case are significant!) are *all* factors that can significantly limit your imagination. If you are a congregational leader, given these realities, where do you turn to select the best congregational management software package for your church? I suggest that software vendors—not unlike sales people for any particular product—are not always the best place to turn for reliable information!

So, if you are faced with making the decision about a software package, where do you turn? This question can, of course, be applied to almost every area of congregational life in our time: given the long list of available resources, where do we go for reliable advice?

This larger question about "where to turn" is the most important reason that the Congregational Resource Guide was developed.

While this book contains helpful information in a only a few areas of congregational life, please be sure to reference the online version that is being continually updated.

Here a word is appropriate about the Indianapolis Center for Congregations, which was pivotal in accumulating the information in this resource guide. The Indianapolis Center was created in 1997 by a grant from Lilly Endowment to Alban Institute. The purpose of the Center was to create a new kind of agency in a local setting that could take into account the diagnosis and convictions we have just visited. We were given permission to form a mediating institution designed to help connect or reconnect congregations to excellent resources that address their important challenges. The Center's staff meets face to face with Indianapolis-area congregational leaders and, in conjunction with Alban Institute staff, attempts to find excellent resources that can help address the needs our congregations identify. Many of the resources listed in the Congregational Resource Guide are the result of this process.

By placing this information on the World Wide Web and in the publication you hold in your hand we hope to expand this beyond Indianapolis and embrace congregations everywhere. This is a never-finished work. We need your help continually to uncover, evaluate, and recommend excellent resources to help strengthen congregational life.

WHAT DO WE MEAN BY RESOURCES?

You may be asking yourself what we mean by *resources?* I asked myself that every day at the Indianapolis Center for Congregations, whose mission is to help congregations find excellent resources. When we say *resources*, we mean those sources of help, expertise, and wisdom that come to a congregation from beyond itself. This is a subtle, and in some ways false, distinction. We are all aware that many of the best "resources" available to a congregation are the people, talents, materials, funds, and other treasures from within a congregation itself. Our process and our product, however, assumes that congregational leaders probably already know a great deal about the resources available from within their own flock. (Although there have been more than a few instances in our conversations with particular congregations where we recommend a person as a resource from within their own congregation that they neither

know about or think to ask! There may be a lesson here for you. . . .)
We cannot, of course, presume to know the best resources from *within*
your congregation. But there is a wealth of resources available to
you from *without*—and that is the realm of the Congregational Resource Guide.

Granted these assumptions, then, by "resources" we mean:
printed materials (books, articles, research papers, the list is long),
newsletters, agencies, Web sites, denominational and judicatory offices, government agencies, colleges, seminaries, consulting firms,
architects, consultants, funding sources, fund raising services—the
list can be as lengthy as you like! There are two elements that are
common to the term *resource* as we are using it here. One element is
connecting and the other is *networking*.

Connecting

I want to advance the claim that the use of resources by congregational leaders is a process of *connecting* to the larger wisdom of an
ongoing and developing faith tradition. As I stated at the beginning, congregations have always used resources from outside themselves. This has been true for the entire history of the Christian faith.
In two thousand years of Christian tradition—and even longer for
Jewish congregating—faith traditions have learned and accumu-
lated wisdom, by means of both revelation and experience, that need
not be lost on our generation even as change in our time is compared to shooting whitewater rapids in a raft.

Connecting with a historic theological text as a resource, for example, means we do not have the burden of "reinventing the wheel"
for every issue we face in contemporary congregational life. Over
the last two thousand years—and maybe even in the last few years—
another congregation, community of faith, or thoughtful leader has
faced a situation similar to yours. They probably produced some
resource that can not only help save you some pain and frustration
but can also help your congregations be more faithful and effective.
In addition, there are some crucial and common questions that congregations across a broad spectrum (theologically, denomination-
ally, and experientially) face as special challenges in our own time:
worship, organizational structures, size transitions, community ministry, passing the faith along to the next generation, the changing
relationship between clergy and laity. These are only a few. To help

address all these challenges (and many more), excellent resources from both the past and the present are already available to you. Connecting to them can comfort and help you as a leader facing change and challenge!

Networking

Connecting with resources necessarily carries with it the second element, which is *networking*. While congregations are indeed communities of faith, they are also part of the larger Community of Faith. For Christian congregations that means the Church. For synagogues, it means Judaism. One of the chief things we have learned in Indianapolis is how strongly congregations desire, and benefit from, networking with each other. Congregations within the larger community of faith are probably the very best resources that are available. By this I do not necessarily mean cooperative ecumenism. Rather, I am talking about congregations simply being in touch with, communicating with, sharing with, and advising each other on issues of faith, order, and practice. This networking to gain help and wisdom can be through neighborhood associations of congregations, ministerial alliances, districts, synods, presbyteries, suburban-urban partnerships, or relationships with sister congregations . My point is that congregations can, do, and need to *network* with one another as *resources*.

Facilitating these connections is not easy to do by just reading a book, perusing a Web site, or any other of the communication means of we have these days. The goal of reading, perusing and communicating is to inform our connections and the conversations that occur within that context. One-to-many resources are valuable. So, too, are one-on-one resources. When you put them together, they provide a source of help and inspiration that has rarely been available in congregational life. We hope that the resources explored in this guide reflect and represent a form of networking between and among congregations and with many of the sources of help that are available to them.

RECONNECTING TO THE SOURCE

Finally—and above all—there is an important theological point to make as we define and recommend resources. Let me state it in the form of a credo: *I believe that resources connect and re-connect us to the Source of all help, wisdom, and treasure—the spirit of God.*

I was struck by this when reading the *Merriam-Webster Dictionary's* definition for the word *resource.* It spoke of "a source of supply or support" and "a natural source of wealth or revenue" and "a source of information or expertise." That's about what I expected. But what struck me was the etymology for the word *resource.* The Old French word was *ressourse,* which is derived from the verb *resourdre,* which means "to relieve or, literally, to rise again." This old French verb *resourdre* in turn came from the Latin *resurgere*—a term that was used in Latin as synonymous with the English word *resurrection.*

Though I seldom find myself spiritually edified by reading the dictionary, this changed me! Suddenly, I came to understand that congregations connecting to resources are participating in a theological reconnection to the *source* of all wisdom, hope, and help. In Christian terms, utilizing a resource to help our community of faith face a particular challenge connects us to the Resurrection itself— the power and hope of Christian people and congregations to "rise again" from their death-like inefficiencies, ineffectiveness, and unfaithfulness toward lives of hope, help, healing, and faithfulness. Surely people of any faith, Christian or not, see God as the source of all wisdom and strength. So, even if not understood in such a specific Christian theological term as "resurrection," the use of resources can be understood theologically as connection to divine forces. Using *resources* can *revive* (add new life!), *resuscitate* (*reawaken*), and *renew* a congregation by *reconnecting* it to the Source of faith and hope. May you find such a renewal through the resources of the Congregational Resource Guide.

1

A Building Project:
From Dream to Dedication

Ryan D. Hazen

Mission and Ministry Come First

A congregation that is not clear about its mission is a floundering congregation. At first glance, the mission of a particular Christian congregation should be the same as the Christian congregation across the street and across town: we are called by the Great Commission to spread the Gospel of Jesus Christ. The mission of which I speak, however, is not *what* we are called to do but *how* we are called to do it. Carrying out the Great Commission may look very different in the rural countryside of Iowa than it does in downtown Los Angeles. We often quote the passage from 1 Corinthians (1 Cor. 12: 4–6) that talks about the different gifts and different abilities anytime we want to highlight the value of diversity in individuals. The same passage can be used to talk about groups of individuals or congregations. A congregation must understand the particular gifts that uniquely enable it to spread the Gospel before embarking on a building project. Kennon Callahan, in his book *Building for Effective Mission*, encourages congregations to first develop a Mission Action Plan that "includes at least one specific mission focus; builds on the congregation's gifts, strengths, compassion, and hope; maximizes the effectiveness of the specific mission resources to be shared; and lives itself out through all areas of the congregation's witness."[1]

Congregations cannot be all things to all people. The first task, even when the need for building or renovation seems clear, is to have a mission that is fully understood and mostly supported by the congregation and consistent with the needs of the neighborhood of the church. For example, most congregations want a strong youth group or children's ministry, but it is rather unlikely that such a mission is compatible with the congregation in Florida that is surrounded by a retirement community. Another common occurrence happens when shifting demographics leaves a once prominent downtown congregation in the midst of a transitional area where even city leaders struggle for solutions to blight and decay.

Tools are available to help a congregation understand their particular mission—how they might participate in spreading the Gospel in their own unique way. A vision committee or long range planning task force can best shepherd this initial process. As with any functional committee, a group of seven to ten people representing the "face" of the congregation is ideal for achieving meaningful work. First and foremost, the committee, supported by the congregation as a whole, should pray for the enlightenment of the Holy Spirit, study scripture together, and take time to listen for God's call to their congregation.

Understanding current demographic information is a good next step; congregations and neighborhoods that have changed dramatically in the past decade may have on blinders about what has happened because it has happened slowly over time. Other people, more aware of the change, will be struck to see factual rather than anecdotal information about the area surrounding the church, otherwise known as the target area. Many committees have a sudden realization after seeing hard demographic information and a prediction of trends that the congregation is confronted with hard choices—usually either to stay and minister to and with the community, thus allowing the face of the congregation to change, or to move to an area where their current face can be preserved. Understanding what is unique about a congregation, knowing or researching the needs and gaps in neighborhood services, and developing a plan for programming will begin to give definition to the mission and ministry of the congregation.[2]

Good communication and the buy-in of the congregation will be most important to subsequent steps in a successful building project. Any serious talk about building or renovation should begin only after the mission and ministry question has been answered and the relocation question, if it has surfaced, has been addressed squarely and forthrightly. In short, every possible building change or addition (or relocation) should be considered only when it speaks directly to helping the mission of the congregation. The vision committee or long range planning task force should end up with a simple, well-defined plan for ministry. A good plan will provide benchmarks and will name groups or individuals responsible for action, thereby increasing accountability over other mission statements that may otherwise gather dust.

Understanding Needs, Balancing Wants

With a ministry plan in place and work in full swing on making it happen, the congregation (represented either by the existing vision committee or a new short-term task force) can then begin to understand the possibilities and needs for the site and facilities that can best serve the mission.

It may be helpful to divide the analysis of the facilities into five areas—worship, education, administration, fellowship/recreation, and general property. Each area should be examined in detail as to what is currently available, what is currently needed, and what is likely needed (again based on the mission) over the next five to seven years. Each of the above areas can be examined by one or two people on the committee, utilizing the members of the congregation who work in the respective areas as resources. For example, when looking at the needs of education, it only makes sense to ask the Sunday School teachers, Bible Study instructors, Vacation Bible School teachers, and mid-week program people what ideas they have for improved space in light of the mission. In addition to giving "expert" input, such a process also begins to broaden the ownership of any possible recommendation of the committee.

Many times, the perceived needs or wants of the congregation as they are identified by the committee far exceed the current financial ability of the congregation. The committee will need to keep the congregation's ability in perspective throughout the process. If the identified needs or wants are unrealistic based on the financial potential of the congregation, the committee will have to look at phasing projects in over a period of time or scaling projects down. The financial potential of the congregation should be analyzed and considered early in the process, not to limit the committee's thinking but rather to provide a benchmark so that dreaming can be tempered with reality.

Congregations choose to fund a potential building project in a variety of ways based upon the tradition of the congregation, size of project, culture, and locale. Most Anglo congregations conduct capital fund campaigns over and above the congregation's operating budget while many African American and Hispanic congregations have surplus funds from the "tithes and offerings" that will be tapped for a building project. If a capital campaign is conducted in an intentional way with broad support, it is likely that the congregation can raise in three-year pledges about one and one-half times the annual operating income. For less glamorous projects like roof or boiler replacement, three-year pledges equal to the annual operating income may be more realistic.

If borrowing is to be considered for a project, the borrowing potential should be based directly on a congregation's ability to repay (from initial and future campaigns) and *not* on the assets of the congregation. The congregation's borrowing potential is approximately two times the initial three-year campaign total for a fifteen-year loan. Such borrowing would require follow-up campaigns for the purpose of debt retirement. Congregations should not be talked into going beyond fifteen-year loans for anything other than sanctuary construction, and then only loans with a maximum amortization of twenty years should be considered.

A quick way to understand the congregation's financial potential for a building project is to answer the following questions and add the three amounts.

- What is the cash on hand now that can be used for this project?
- What will be the additional cash on hand by the completion of the project (from the capital campaign)?
- How much can we realistically borrow for this project?

Keep in mind that the total of these three answers represents funds available for *all* costs related to the project, including nontangible costs like design fees, permits, insurance, title costs, and loan and legal fees. For a major project, these "soft" costs can represent 25 to 30 percent of the project. Other often forgotten costs such as landscaping and furnishings must be considered as well.[3]

BRINGING THE CONGREGATION ALONG

A project will go nowhere in most congregations without broad congregational support. The planning committee that is developing a recommendation should outline the need and general parameters of the project by answering key questions: Why (how will it help our mission)? When? How much might it cost? How can we afford it? The answers to these questions, along with the recommendation itself, are best presented to the membership in small group meetings of ten to twelve people, held in an informal setting. People need the opportunity to ask questions without the pressure of an impending vote. In this way, people will have most questions answered by the time the recommendation reaches the point of approval by either the governing board or the congregation.

Because this is a key decision in the future of the church, the congregation at this point is usually asked to support the recommendation and approve the formation of a building committee, which will work with a design professional to move the project forward. Members should be reminded that this is not an approval of a design but only the approval of a recommendation to move to the next step of the process. If approved, the building committee will bring preliminary plans (with associated costs) back to the congregation for consideration at a later date.

Seeking Professional Help

The building committee should be a group of 6 to 12 people (depending on size of congregation and project) who can meet regularly and who are open to a variety of solutions that might be presented. It is not necessary that all of the "building people" in the congregation be on the building committee. Knowledge of design or building is not a prerequisite of a committee member. The committee, however, should agree at the outset to at least four operating criteria. They include:

1. Keep Christ at the center of the meetings; bathe the process with prayer and study scripture as a part of the process.
2. Don't try to design the project; that's the architect's job for which he or she is being well paid. If preconceived notions are in place about the outcome, the architect's gifts are taken out of the picture.
3. Don't revisit decisions because of the absence of one or two members. A covenant early on will help move the process along. Good meeting records distributed soon after each meeting will help keep everyone on the same page.

4. Be of one voice after decisions are made. It is expected and hoped that each member of the committee will speak his or her mind about important decisions; however, once a decision is made, it should be seen as a decision of the whole group. Nothing can derail a project more quickly than "parking lot" dissension by a member of the committee.

Employing the services of a design professional is necessary on all but the smallest of projects. This person, usually an architect, can insure that the building or addition is efficient and safe and that it meets the exact needs of the congregation both now and into the future. Architects are best found like a good doctor is found—on the recommendation of a friend—in this case, other churches that have recently completed projects. Listings of architects who work with churches are available through Interfaith Forum on Religion, Art and Architecture, a part of the American Institute of Architects (AIA).[4]

Most architects charge between 7 and 12 percent of the construction cost for their services, and this fee is payable in phases as the work progresses. Phone and personal interviews with potential firms will help the committee find a good match. The suggested questions on page 21 offer topics you will want to cover with any prospective architect. [5]

To formalize the relationship between the architect and congregation, a contract is needed. The American Institute of Architects has standardized contracts that provide protection for both parties. It is suggested that an amendment be added to any contract that allows for redesign of the project at no cost to the congregation if bids are over the predetermined budget by a set percentage (usually 10 percent).

The building committee will then have to decide, with input from the architect, whether to select the general contractor at this point (sometimes called design-build or pre-selected contractor) or wait for the projects to be sent out to bid later in the process. One clear advantage to selecting the contractor at this point is to keep costs in line; an experienced contractor will know ways to achieve similar results at less cost. Only the first phase of an architect's work—the preliminary or conceptual drawings—should be completed before taking the information back to the congregation (again in small group meetings) for ultimate go-ahead of the plan and for approval to conduct a capital fund campaign.

RAISING THE MONEY

With preliminary plans and congregational approval in hand, the congregation has enough information to begin to raise funds. The preliminary plans will provide the drawings and probable costs necessary to communicate to the members and motivate their giving to a building fund campaign. As stated above, most congregations will have to conduct a campaign that is over and above operational expenses in order to raise funds for a building project. This campaign is best conducted at a time apart from the emphasis on the operational budget. For example, a congregation that operates on a calendar year for the operational budget will usually be raising operational funds in the fall. The best time for a building campaign for these congregations is the spring. This separation eliminates confusion that arises when people are asked to make two pledges at the same time, usually for two different time periods. It also makes clear that the building fund is over and above the operating budget and not a different slicing of the same pie.

A group separate from the building committee will be organized to lead the fund raising effort. A clear process should be followed in such a campaign and outside professional counsel is strongly recommended. Many denominational offices have such resources and there are also companies dedicated to helping congregations through the process. Both will charge for these fund raising services, but such programs contribute greatly to the successful raising of significant capital funds. Usually two to six months should be allowed for the fund raising effort, followed by a two- to three-year payout or pledge period. It is not advisable that the pledge period go beyond three years. The drop in pledge income due to those who have paid in advance and due to those who have moved or passed away greatly diminish any income beyond the three-year time frame. If funding is needed beyond the initial campaign, for debt retirement for example, a new campaign should be conducted as the initial pledge period is about to expire.

A SECOND LOOK AT INCOME AND EXPENSES

The period immediately following the capital fund campaign is the perfect time to examine the projected costs of the building with the funding that is available from all sources by using the building costs worksheet on pages 22 and 23. A much clearer picture of the financial situation is available after the results of fund raising are known. With the focus of the work now beginning to point to actual construction, it is most important at this stage to consider *all* costs of the project, including "soft" costs. The congregation will need to keep in mind that it may not have all of the funds from the campaign in by the time the building is complete and that only funds that will be in hand by completion should be counted as cash toward the project. For example, about 40 percent of the funds pledged in a three-year campaign will come in during the first year of the payout period. Any remaining pledges on the campaign will be used to make loan payments if money is borrowed to complete the project.

DETAILED DRAWINGS

With a clear grasp of the financial ability of the congregation that is based on the results of a capital campaign, the building committee can return to work with the architect to modify the drawings, if necessary, to meet the financial criteria. Once modified, the architect can move to subsequent phases of the planning process known as design development and construction documentation. The construction documentation phase is the most costly phase of the architect's contract and the plans are much more difficult (and costly) to change after this phase is complete. It will be these drawings that contractors (or subcontractors if a general contractor was selected earlier in the process) will use to prepare bids to submit to the architect and the building committee for consideration. The bid process should be done by invitation only (versus an open bid where anyone can bid) to determine the qualifications of the contractors in advance of the bid. In this way, the decision at bid opening has to do with cost and not whether a bidder can actually perform the work.

INSURING SUCCESS

It is strongly recommended (and required by many lenders) that a performance and payment bond be required of the successful bidder(s) on all but the smallest of projects. Such an expectation should be explained in the bid documents so that the cost of the bond can be included in the bid. The performance and payment bond is essentially an insurance policy taken out by the contractor (but paid for by the congregation) that insures that the project will be completed as expected and that subcontractors will be paid in a timely manner for work completed. Horror stories abound of congregations that had no such protection and were left scrambling to complete a building or with liens from subcontractors against the project. Neither situation makes for good feelings about the project.

PAPERWORK

With a bid in place that is in line with expectations, all of the contractual documentation can be implemented for both the loan (if needed) and for the construction itself. If a loan is needed, time will be needed for approval, title work, documentation, signatures, and so forth before funds are available. Checking with lenders and title companies can give the committee an idea about how long to allow for this process.

CONSTRUCTION!

After waiting and planning and raising funds and waiting and planning some more, the day will finally arrive when a shovel can hit the ground both ceremonially and actually. One person must be identified as the point person on the building committee through which all questions can be directed from the contractor, architect, and anyone else needing information about the project. The building committee will have to put significant trust in this individual as there will be times that decisions must be made on the spot without waiting for the next building committee meeting to roll around.

On most building projects, there will be a general contractor who will coordinate all subcontractors for the various facets of the project, including electrical, plumbing, and HVAC (heating, ventilation and air conditioning). The contractor should communicate with the architect who will communicate with the point person from the building committee. If there are changes (additions or deletions) to the original design plans, a change order must be executed to change the scope of work. These change orders will almost always affect the cost as well, raising the price if something must be added to the plans or lowering the price if something is deleted. On larger projects, it may be wise for the building committee to employ a construction manager. This person oversees the entire project for a fee, usually a percentage of the contract.

Building committees who begin the construction phase of a project thinking that everything has been decided and that all costs are known up front are usually disappointed. Those who expect surprises and treat them as opportunities to make the project better will feel better when the project is over. Keeping the congregation informed of the project status along the way will promote their understanding and continued support.

DEDICATE THE PROJECT TO THE GLORY OF GOD

Whether a new sanctuary or a new boiler or a new roof, it is appropriate to dedicate the project to the glory of God. A time to celebrate accomplishment will recognize the real work that a building project is for all involved. A dedication service will put the project in proper perspective and focus the work of the congregation beyond itself to a greater good and tie the project again to the mission and ministry of the congregation.

NOTES

1. Kennon Callahan, *Building for Effective Mission: A Complete Guide for Congregations on Bricks and Mortar Issues* (San Francisco: Jossey-Bass, 1995), p. 9.
2. Resources include the U.S. Census at www.census.gov, local school administrators, Department of Transportation officials, and community Chambers of Commerce. In addition, demographic providers such as Percept at www.link2lead.com can be very helpful.
3. See the Building Cost Worksheet on pages 22 and 23.
4. A listing of IFRAA (Interfaith Forum on Religion, Art and Architecture) architects is available from the American Institute of Architects at www.aia.org or by contacting IFRAA at 1735 New York Ave., NW, Washington, DC 20006, (800) 364-9364.
5. Planning Guides on a variety of subjects related to building are available on the Church Extension of Disciples of Christ Web site at www.churchextension.org.

QUESTIONS TO ASK AN ARCHITECT

- Describe your firm (personnel, size, and experience of the organization).
- What memberships do you hold in professional organizations? Awards received?
- What schools were attended by the staff and what general training requirements are expected of the staff?
- What is your philosophy or understanding of church design? Are there particular styles or approaches to church architecture you like or dislike?
- What are your thoughts on cooperation between architect and church and building committee? Specifically: What is the congregation's job? What is the job of the committee? What is the architect's job?
- What is your method of assigning design responsibilities?
- Do you provide design and help in the selection of furnishings? What is the fee for this service?
- What is your responsibility for the engineering of the project?
- Who will supervise the construction? How will it be supervised? Do you provide supervisory services? How much is the fee, and how much onsite supervision do you provide?
- Questions about preliminary design for the building: What method will be used to secure approval from the building committee? What method will be used to secure approval from the congregation? How do you prepare the estimated cost of the project? Are you committed to working within the congregation's budget? Do you help prepare a brochure (with a sketch) that can be used in presenting the project to the congregation?
- What type of bidding is preferred? Separate or one general? Open or invitational? And what is your knowledge of local and area markets?
- Describe your prior work including churches and educational facilities for churches. What were the estimated costs and actual costs? Will you suggest churches for which you have worked that we can contact for recommendations?
- Is preparation of comprehensive and schematic studies included in your service?
- What is your firm's record in meeting time schedules?
- Describe your fee structure and contract: AIA standards, amounts for new and remodeling jobs, termination opportunities, responsibility and procedure when bid overages occur, model or rendering (a drawing or miniature model) included? What extras?
- What construction delivery methods have you used/do you prefer?
- What questions do you, the architect, have for the committee?
- Other questions or comments.

BUILDING COST WORKSHEET

Projected project costs

1. Site purchase/preparation costs
   a. Site purchase $_____
   b. Sewer/water/gas (tap in fees, sewer/septic) _____
   c. Site preparation & improvements (parking, landscape, turn-lanes, etc.) _____

2. Professional fees
   a. Architectural and engineering fees _____
   b. Attorney fees, title insurance, survey, mortgage filing fees _____
   c. Testing fees (soil borings/environmental tests, etc.) _____

3. Building costs
   a. General contract _____
   b. HVAC (heat/air-conditioning) _____
   c. Plumbing _____
   c. Electrical _____
   d. Other _____

   Building total _____

4. Furnishings and equipment _____

5. Miscellaneous items
   a. Fund raising costs _____
   b. Construction loan interest during construction _____
   c. Contingency (10% of building total above) _____
   d. Loan closing fee (allow 1% of funds drawn) _____
   e. Performance and payment bond (allow 2% of building total above) _____

   Total building costs (total of items 1 through 5) _____

6. Balance of existing loan(s) (if included in new project financing) _____

   Total of all costs (total of items 1 through 6) $_____

BUILDING COST WORKSHEET

Resources available for project

1. Cash paid to date on costs included
   above (architectural, etc.) $_____

2. Cash on hand now   _____

3. Additional cash raised by completion of project   _____

4. Other sources, such as sale of property (list sources)   _____

5. Loan requested   _____

   Total resources $_____

Note: Total resources should equal or exceed total of all costs to proceed
with project as planned.

Resources on Building Issues from the Congregational Resource Guide

Callahan, Kennon L. **Building for Effective Mission: A Complete Guide for Congregations on Bricks and Mortar Issues.** San Francisco: Jossey-Bass, 1997.

> Callahan asserts that although we are no longer living in a "churched culture," we can rejoice that God now calls us to mission—to serve, using our individual and congregational strengths, and to work for justice and peace. Mission grows with compassion and community, and the mission field is the world. A congregation is a mission outpost to the people beyond its walls. In accordance with these principles, this book describes concrete actions congregations may take to discover a mission and a focus for it, and to plan for accomplishing it. Later chapters discuss the physical plant that furthers a chosen mission, evaluating possible sites for location, mission potential, property characteristics, and financial considerations; describing facilities that allow efficient staffing, scheduling, and leadership; and showing how to develop a schedule for completing building plans. Other concrete advice concerns creating a building team and selecting an architect. Finally, suggestions for funding a building project that will include money for mission are given. Whether or not a congregation plans to move or renovate, it will find this book's emphasis on mission thought provoking.

Church Architecture: A Resource Network
Dixon Arts Guild, Inc., www.churcharchitecture.net

> This Web site, begun as a guide to resources for church building and renovation, has developed into a fine guide to resources about church architecture, with articles, organizations, and other re-

24

sources. It is well organized and nicely done, with many links for church building enthusiasts to explore.

Dean, Peggy Powell, and Susanna A. Jones. **The Complete Guide to Capital Campaigns for Historic Churches and Synagogues.** Philadelphia: Partners for Sacred Places, 1998.

Capital campaigns to restore historic buildings offer opportunities to seek grants and gifts that are not ordinarily available to congregations. This comprehensive, 200-page looseleaf guide carries the reader from preliminary restoration plans through plans to extend relationships built during the campaign into the congregation's future. It includes an outline of the capital campaign process that would be useful to any congregation, plus advice on involving community leaders not affiliated with the congregation and seeking grants from foundations and government sources. Any congregation needing to raise funds to renovate historic buildings should obtain a copy of this guide.

Giles, Richard. **Re-Pitching the Tent: Reordering the Church Building for Worship and Mission.** Collegeville, MN: Liturgical Press, 1999.

This comprehensive historical and theological treatise on the nature of worship spaces includes dozens of photographs and sketches. The book was written in England, but has usefulness in many cultural contexts, in part because of its argument that liturgical action should be the primary concern in designing liturgical spaces. The book concludes with helpful appendices on appointing an architectural consultant, landscaping, fundraising, lighting schemes, and floor surfaces.

Holliman, Glen N., and Barbara L. Holliman. **With Generous Hearts: How to Raise Capital Funds for Your Church, Church School, Church Agency or Regional Church Body.** Harrisburg, PA: Morehouse Publishing, 1997.

This book is an excellent overview of capital campaigns. The Hollimans, who are capital campaign consultants, emphasize the importance of a thorough feasibility study and the need for advanced gifts. They present six steps of effective fundraising: (1) identify the urgent and compelling need for which funds are required; (2) identify the potential donors who are able to respond financially to the need; (3) communicate the need to those potential donors; (4) ask for a donation to address the urgent and compelling need; (5) say "thank you" to those who have made donations; then (6) continue the process of identifying needs and donors, sharing information, and inviting people to participate. The book also includes a helpful chapter on "What to Expect from Your Church Architect" and others on judicatory and church school campaigns.

Mauck, Marchita B. **Places for Worship: A Guide to Building and Renovating.** Collegeville, MN: Liturgical Press, 1995.

This 70-page booklet provides expert advice for such practical matters as forming a building committee, selecting a liturgical consultant and an architect, pre-designing and programming, developing a master site plan, and overseeing the entire renovation project. The book is written by one of the leading experts in the field, and provides a very accessible overview appropriate for all congregational leaders involved in a building process.

McCormick, Gwen E. **Planning and Building Church Facilities.** Nashville: Broadman Press, 1992.

Produced within the Baptist tradition, *Planning and Building Church Facilities* is a comprehensive guide to the building process. Special attention is given to organizing committees, property and financial issues, working with an architect, and attending to accessibility issues. Relatively little is said about the function of worship and the ways that worship will shape the space, but the advice on process is helpful.

Money and Ideas: Creative Approaches to Congregational Access. Bethesda, MD: Alban Institute, 2001.

Congregations seeking greater accessibility for people with disabilities often find that a key challenge is the availability of resources. How does a congregation find money, materials, or labor for a ramp, an elevator, or accessible restrooms? *Money and Ideas*, a booklet published jointly by the Alban Institute and the National Organization on Disability, takes a two-fold approach to encouraging creative thinking on this issue. First, it tells brief stories of how fifty congregations around the country became more accessible. Examples include the pastor who ran a fund-raising marathon, the Eagle Scouts who built a church ramp, and the youth program that raised money by "renting kids" to do odd jobs. Second, *Money and Ideas* features an annotated "Selected Resources" section that includes helpful books, periodicals, organizations, and Web sites. Congregations aiming at greater accessibility, but feeling stymied by a lack of resources, will find this booklet useful and inspiring. Available free online as an Adobe Acrobat file at www.congregationalresources.org/MoneyAndIdeas.pdf.

Partners for Sacred Places
1700 Sansom Street, Tenth Floor
Philadelphia, PA 19103
(215) 567-3234
partners@sacredplaces.org
www.sacredplaces.org

Partners for Sacred Places is a nonprofit organization devoted to helping Americans care for and make good use of older and historic religious properties. Its Web site provides free information and advice about property maintenance, fundraising, and professional references. It also features information about Partners' Professional Alliance, a membership program aimed at for-profit practitioners—including architects, engineers, stained glass restorers, specialized contractors (such as roofers and masons), and fundraising consultants—that specialize in historic religious property restoration. The user can purchase publications online and learn about advocacy and research efforts on behalf of older religious properties. The newsletter, *Partners' Update,* includes information on events from around the country.

Warren, Jackqueline T. **Open the Doors, See All the People: A Guide to Serving Families in Sacred Places.** Philadelphia: Partners for Sacred Places, 2001.

This resource considers systematically how religious buildings can be seen as an asset to ministry with children and families, combining success stories with solid, specific advice for making programs work. It takes the reader through a process beginning with assessment of needs and resources and refining your congregation's vision. Stories include: a Kids' Cafe for children in an afterschool program created by St. Phillip's United Methodist Community Church in Philadelphia; the Resurrection Project, a community center formed by a group of Catholic parishes in a closed church in Chicago; and a program in Maryland in which congregations serve as sites for child custody transfers. Available free online as an Adobe Acrobat file at www.sacredplaces.org/guide_srv_fam.html.

2

Faith and Money

Dan Hotchkiss

At least since Moses smashed the golden calf, the borderland between the realms of faith and money has not been an altogether
comfortable place to live. Religious leaders know that mammon still
competes with God for the loyalty of even the most devout. At the
same time, religious institutions need money for virtually all of their
activities. Spiritual exercises require space, preferably quiet space
whose landscaping, architecture, and acoustics favor and support
inward deepening, joyous celebration, and an inspiring sense of wide
connection. Such spaces are increasingly expensive. So are the services of clergy and other workers. Religious leaders' dual relationship with money—as bearers of the message that "the love of money"
(in Paul's phrase) can distract the faithful from what is most important and as fundraisers for their own, presumably good, causes—
puts churches and synagogues at risk of being, or of seeming to be,
hypocritical. Especially in a culture that hawks consumer goods from
street corners while keeping personal finances in the closet, it is
easy for a congregation to say nothing to its members about money
except "give us some of yours." It is dissatisfaction over this dual
relationship of faith to money that motivates much of the recent
surge of writing on the subject.

SOCIOLOGY

For sociologists, most conversations about faith and money begin,
or at least touch base, with Max Weber's writings, especially *The
Protestant Ethic and the Spirit of Capitalism*, first published in 1905.
Weber seeks to explain the fact that the industrial and commercial
revolutions of the eighteenth and nineteenth centuries came first to

those European lands most influenced by the Protestant Reformation, especially in its Calvinistic form. Calvin's doctrine of predestination, Weber argued, moved the core of spirituality out of the social and ecclesial realm and made it a matter of private self-examination and prayer. While his historical argument is much debated, Weber's analysis of the tension created by the Calvinist's "deep spiritual isolation" and the resultant "restless, systematic struggle with life"[1] still rings true. So does the connection Weber drew between spiritual anxiety and the striving for material betterment that is the most powerful engine of the capitalist economy. Weber lamented the diminishment of social life that seemed to be the price of capitalist prosperity: "The more the world of the modern capitalist economy follows its own immanent laws," he wrote, "the less accessible it is to any imaginable relationship with a religious ethic of brotherliness."[2]

Another classic of American sociology that addresses the relation of money to religion is Alexis de Tocqueville's *Democracy in America*. Tocqueville, a French visitor to the United States in the 1830s, made many trenchant observations, among them that he found it difficult to tell whether American preachers thought that "the principal object of religion is to procure eternal felicity in the next world or prosperity in this."[3]

Finally, while it has received more attention from literary critics and economists than from religious leaders, Thorstein Veblen's *The Theory of the Leisure Class: An Economic Study of Institutions* contains valuable (and very funny) observations and analysis of how religion can function as a form of "conspicuous consumption" whose value lies not in the direct benefits to the consumer but in the envy and admiration it arouses in others.

The Social Sources of Denominationalism by H. Richard Niebuhr is so influential it forms an important basis for the thinking of thousands of people who have never read it. Building on Weber's distinction between state-sponsored churches and autonomous sects, Niebuhr argues that the division of American churches by denomination is a "moral failure" to achieve the unity demanded by the gospel in favor of "conformity to the order of social classes and castes."[4] If mainline Protestants are embarrassed when they try to talk about money, Niebuhr has given them plenty to be embarrassed about!

More recent analyses of American society, especially those that touch on the relation of religion and economic life, address Weber's concern about the diminishment of social resources, or "social capital," as Robert D. Putnam calls it in a much-read study, *Bowling Alone: The Collapse and Revival of American Community*. Another post-Weberian work of sociology of much interest to leaders of congregations is Robert N. Bellah, et al., *Habits of the Heart: Individualism and Commitment in American Life*. Putnam and Bellah share Weber's concern for the decay of noncommercial forms of association in the face of rapid economic growth.

In the last 10 or 15 years a number of sociologists have looked specifically at the role of money in religious attitudes and institutions. Robert Wuthnow has produced a body of data and analysis that will feed such study for a long time. In *God and Mammon in America*, Wuthnow draws a portrait of contemporary attitudes about religion and economic behavior. Using his own survey data, he shows that Americans have yet to reconcile their inherited religious and moral traditions with the radical changes brought about by the Industrial Revolution and the accompanying migration of the workforce from farms and small towns to cities and by unprecedented economic growth since World War II.

In *Poor Richard's Principle: Recovering the American Dream through the Moral Dimension of Work, Business, and Money*, Wuthnow uses new survey research to describe the moral quandary of modern Americans drawn by materialistic pursuits but also restrained by higher values of which many of them are only vaguely aware. Wuthnow advocates that we reclaim and build on moral traditions exemplified for him by the philosophy expressed in Benjamin Franklin's *Autobiography* and *Poor Richard's Almanack*. Turning specifically to religious institutions in *The Crisis in the Churches: Spiritual Malaise, Fiscal Woe*, Wuthnow gives evidence that many churches succeed neither at providing guidance for their members nor at making a convincing case for their own financial support. While finding "ample reason to be hopeful about the future of Christianity,"[5] Wuthnow makes a convincing case that clergy and congregations can no longer afford to treat money as a topic too delicate to be faced directly.

Even more directly focused on religious institutions is the work of Dean Hoge and his collaborators, whose *Money Matters: Personal Giving in American Churches* provides the closest analysis to date of the motives that influence people to give (or not to give) to churches. Setting out to test 22 hypotheses about money, the authors offer a convincing, if somewhat laborious, exposition. Luckily the same material is available in a much more accessible form in the aptly named *Plain Talk about Churches and Money* by Dean Hoge, Patrick McNamara, and Charles Zech.

Mark Chaves and Sharon Miller have edited a useful collection of writings, *Financing American Religion*. Ranging in subject matter from Calvin O. Pressley and Walter V. Collier's "Financing Historic Black Churches" to Michael O'Neill's "Religious Nonprofits in Illinois," the collection lacks editorial polish and a clear unifying purpose. But perhaps it is enough to collect and make available some recent work in what, to date, has been a field rich in conviction but poor in evidence and clear analysis.

THEOLOGY AND SPIRITUALITY

Any resume of theological writings related to money will be selective and idiosyncratic. As a nonspecialist, I am certain that there are many excellent books relating the religious to the economic life that I have never heard of, much less read. I offer the following comments on my favorites in the hope that it will inspire readers to seek out works that speak to their own souls.

Herman E. Daly and John B. Cobb's *For the Common Good: Redirecting the Economy toward Community, the Environment, and a Sustainable Future* critiques the assumptions of capitalist economics from the standpoint of process theology. Fortunately, given the importance of the topic, Daly and Cobb largely eschew the jargon that has kept process thinking from entering the mainstream thought of seminarians and the clergy. But seriously religious people of all faiths should read *For the Common Good*, not to accept all of the specific proposals (some of which, appropriately for process thought, have been substantially revised since the original edition in 1989), but for its stimulating interplay of theology and economics.

A younger process theologian, Carol Johnston, has published an evocative study of the origins and contradictions of today's conventional economic thinking in *The Wealth or Health of Nations: Transforming Capitalism from Within*. Focusing on the canonical figures of Anglo American economics—Smith, Ricardo, Malthus, Mill, Marx, Marshall, Keynes, and Friedman—Johnston restates with fresh argument familiar criticisms against this tradition's individualism and amorality. Johnston also provides helpful ways to use an ecological philosophy to challenge and temper capitalism's excesses.

A recent treatment of the Christian scriptures' teachings about money is Sondra Ely Wheeler's *Wealth as Peril and Obligation: The New Testament on Possessions*. Wheeler finds no simple code of economic behavior in the teachings of Jesus and the early church but rather a complex awareness that money and other forms of wealth pose "dangers of distraction and entanglement, of misplaced trust and loyalty" while at the same time providing the means to fulfill the duty of "provision for oneself and one's family." [6]

A variety of original thinkers have contributed to *Rethinking Materialism: Perspectives on the Spiritual Dimension of Economic Behavior*, edited by Robert Wuthnow. The first half of the book includes historical and sociological essays, such as Wilfred M. McClay's "Where Have We Come Since the 1950s? Thoughts on Materialism and American Social Character" and Marsha G. Witten's "'Where Your Treasure Is': Popular Evangelical Views of Work, Money, and Materialism." The latter half moves toward constructing a critical alternative to materialism and features Nicholas Wolterstorff's "Has the Cloak Become a Cage? Charity, Justice, and Economic Activity" and Albert Bergeson's "Deep Ecology and Moral Community." It is clear that scholarly reflection on this subject is at an early, formative stage, and *Rethinking Materialism* contains much of the best thinking up to its publication in 1995.

In a more popular vein, *Money and the Meaning of Life* by Jacob Needleman rambles delightfully as it follows the course of one of Needleman's seminars in the University of California's extension program. As he grapples with his own ideas and the questions posed by adult learners steeped in various backgrounds and vocations, Needleman is refreshing in his honest confrontation of the real but hidden loyalties that interfere with those we are prepared to acknowledge and nourishing in his eclectic probing of his own tradition (Judaism) and others for guidance useful to the serious inquirer.

A more prescriptive work is George Kinder's *Seven Stages of Money Maturity: Understanding the Spirit and Value of Money in Your Life*. While I confess that I am put off by Kinder's system of "stages," including "Knowledge I" and "Knowledge II," I think this book is a useful challenge to much of what is said in congregations about "spirituality"—for Kinder, the test of everything is not in the correctness of the thinking but the rightness of the action that proceeds from it.

While it is not explicitly religious, *Your Money or Your Life: Transforming Your Relationship with Money and Achieving Financial Independence* by Joe Dominguez and Vicki Robin can help those who suspect they may be caught in a cycle of get-and-spend that eclipses their commitment to truer centers of loyalty. This highly practical guide (and the other books, seminars, and tape recordings that go with it) shows how to scale down your rate of spending so that you can achieve financial independence—the freedom to spend your "life energy" as you feel called to spend it.

Congregation members interested in pursuing such radical alternatives to American middle-class values will probably get farther doing it in groups than as individuals. For evangelicals a useful resource for this is John and Sylvia Ronsvalle's *At Ease: Discussing Money and Values in Small Groups*. While *At Ease* will discomfort readers who dislike road maps with a predetermined destination ("The Cross of Gold and the Cross of Christ"), it contains useful scripture citations and a good guide to running a small group discussion.

A wider range of Christians will be able to use the discussion guide from Ministry of Money, a group that "encourages all persons to become free from their attachment to cultural values regarding money and to live out joyfully God's call for their lives and resources." A guide, *Ministry of Money: Exploring Money and Spirituality* by Jan Sullivan Dockter, can be ordered from the Ministry of Money Web site (www.ministryofmoney.org).

A resource for Jews interested in exploring themes related to money, ethics, and social justice is Lawrence Bush and Jeffrey Detko's *Jews, Money, and Social Responsibility: Developing a "Torah of Money" for Contemporary Life*, which covers such seemingly diverse topics as shopping, investing, philanthropy, and social justice advocacy. The idea of a "Torah of money" has been picked up by Rabbi Shawn Zevit of the Jewish Reconstructionist Federation (JRF) in his curriculum by that name, which is available at present only to those involved in JRF training but no doubt will take new forms in the future.

RELIGIOUS HISTORY

Surprisingly little has yet been published on the history of American churches as economic entities. A tantalizing start is James Hudnut-Beumler's *Generous Saints: Congregations Rethinking Ethics and Money*. Though lacking the endnotes that would make it a more useful resource, *Generous Saints* provides much-needed perspective on some of the ideas and practices—tithing, stewardship, pledging—that we now take so much for granted that it seems they must date from before the Flood.

Robert Wood Lynn has spoken and written widely on the history of finance in American Protestant churches; unfortunately his work, scattered in articles and speeches, is not yet readily available. Precisely because congregational fundraising is stuck in some rather dated ruts, it will be helpful to open our minds to the wide range of practices that have qualified as Christian (or Jewish) through the centuries.

CONGREGATIONAL LEADERSHIP

The nuts and bolts of money and the church (or synagogue) is found in the works of Richard R. Hammar, whose *Pastor, Church, and Law* has been the standard textbook in its field for many years. Hammar's briefer but still weighty annual *Church and Clergy Tax Guide* gives the most complete and authoritative coverage of tax laws, IRS policies, and court decisions. Together with Hammar's Web site (www.iclonline.com) and monthly newsletter, these works provide much more than most clergy and lay leaders want to know about finances, taxation, payroll, incorporation, accounting, liability, insurance, and a long list of other topics that are more important to us than we like to think.

Too little has been written about the leadership role clergy play and could play in the money realm. Loren B. Mead, in his *Financial Meltdown in the Mainline?*, lays much of the blame for mainline churches' financial plight on clergy who learn in seminary how to preach and counsel but not to connect their vision to the budget, fundraising, or the management of property and endowments. One small step toward filling this lacuna is my book *Ministry and Money: A Guide for Clergy and Their Friends*.

Still valiantly filling the comparative dearth of humorous writing for congregational leaders is a forgotten classic from 1965, *How to Become a Bishop without Being Religious* by Charles Merrill Smith. Smith points out that the lack of an authoritative book on the theology of church finance is understandable. As Smith points out, "You can't find any published information on 'The Philosophy of Fee Setting for Medical Doctors' either."

FUNDRAISING

More has been published about fundraising than on any other topic in the faith-and-money category, and most of what is written has some merit. The fundraising literature, like most how-to writing, tends to absolutize each author's special methods and perspective. This is natural—people put in charge of a fund drive want direction, not philosophy—but it is unfortunate as well, because in fundraising as I have experienced it only one generalization has proved consistently practical: everyone is different. The donors to any church or synagogue all give for their own reasons, and they each respond to different kinds of appeals. Moreover, no technique works forever; one reason fundraising consultants succeed is that each one brings a unique twist to the process, and the novelty helps focus people's attention, at least temporarily.

One writer who understands this is Kennon Callahan, whose *Effective Church Finances: Fund-Raising and Budgeting for Church Leaders* suggests choosing a different "strategic objective" for each year's campaign. In one year, the goal might be to increase the number of giving households; in the next, it might be to increase the giving of a specific segment of the congregation. Callahan's readable, orderly prose encourages the reader to focus on the congregation's underlying mission and its programmatic vision. The same message—packaged for what Callahan calls "the grass roots"—is found in his companion volume *Giving and Stewardship in an Effective Church: A Guide for Every Member*.

A perennial classic, Lyle E. Schaller's *44 Ways to Expand the Financial Base of Your Congregation* is useful for the congregation stuck in the tiresome mud of a stale fundraising style. In his trademark list-making style (I once heard Schaller respond to an audience question by announcing, "I have 14 answers for that question" and then ticking them off!), Schaller covers the bases from generational changes of attitude to effective reminder mailings to the role of the pastor.

Patrick H. McNamara reinforces the idea of variety in *More Than Money: Portraits of Transformative Stewardship*. McNamara, a sociologist who collaborated with Dean Hoge on the study mentioned above, selected 11 churches that have had unusual success in stewardship. Ranging from a liberal Congregational church in suburban Massachusetts to an African American Baptist congregation in

Phoenix, the congregations approach—and even define—steward-ship in different ways. Because they are so different, these churches' approaches to fundraising, social outreach, and the identification of spiritual gifts will open almost any reader's eyes to undiscovered possibilities.

Perhaps the best all-around fundraising guide for congregations and religious charities is *Ask and You Shall Receive: A Fundraising Training Program for Religious Organizations and Projects*, with both leader and participant manuals. The author, Kim Klein, is a veteran fundraiser who has consulted widely both in secular and religious organizations. Her guide is designed to be used as a training course and would be useful to a congregation interested in revamping its fundraising practices from the ground up.

Of the many "stewardship" guides written for churches, two of my favorites are *The Desires of Your Heart: A Guide to Stewardship and the Annual Giving Campaign*, published by Christian Community, Inc., and *Asking Makes a Difference: A Guide for Stewardship Teams* by Jerald L. King. *Desires of Your Heart* has a pietistic approach and includes a process for creating a booklet of devotions. *Asking Makes a Difference* is more pragmatic and will appeal to congregations whose language is more secular. Both works stress face-to-face so-licitation as the main method of seeking contributions. Despite the recent popularity of "Consecration Sunday" campaigns where pledges are requested and presented at a worship service, the most effective way to raise money still is to ask for it person to person.

For capital campaigns, the standard textbook is Kent E. Dove's *Conducting a Successful Capital Campaign*. While this book is written for secular nonprofits, its tested methods will be a helpful corrective to some of the bad habits that creep into congregational practice. Another good capital campaign guide, *The Complete Guide to Capital Campaigns for Historic Churches and Synagogues* by Peggy Powell Dean and Susanna A. Jones, contains both invaluable specifics for seeking historic preservation grants from government and foundation sources and a concise guide to running a capital campaign that would be helpful regardless of the age of the reader's building.

Every few years John and Sylvia Ronsvalle publish a new edition of *The State of Church Giving*. The current edition, published in 2004, contains data through 2002. This book is an invaluable compilation of statistics drawn from the National Council of Churches' yearbook. The picture it paints is a bit gloomy, as they portray the decline of the "mainline" denominations that once were the American elite at prayer. What this analysis does not capture is the movement of religious dollars into unaffiliated churches and the rainbow of new and unconventional forms of religious organization and expression, showing that religion (if not the old-fashioned steepled church) is alive and well.

Looking ahead, *Growing Up Generous: Engaging Youth in Giving and Serving* by Eugene C. Roehjlkepartain, Elanah Dalyah Naftali, and Laura Musegades gives guidance for those interested in building a philanthropic spirit in young people. This thoughtful and thoroughly researched book covers both the theory and the practice of nurturing teenagers' impulses toward charitable giving and voluntary service. While not a simplistic how-to guide (who needs more of those?), it is essential reading for youth ministers and leaders interested in moving with the young from faith to caring action.

Notes

1. Max Weber, *The Protestant Ethic and the Spirit of Capitalism,* translated by Talcott Parson (Los Angeles: Roxbury Publishing, 1930), 107–108.
2. H. H. Gerth and C. Wright Mills, eds., *From Max Weber: Essays in Sociology* (New York: Oxford University Press, 1946), 331.
3. Alexis de Tocqueville, *Democracy in America,* edited by Phillips Bradley, translated by Henry Reeve (New York: Alfred A. Knopf, 1945), part 2, chapter 9, 135.
4. H. Richard Niebuhr, *The Social Sources of Denominationalism* (New York: Henry Holt, 1929), 25.
5. Robert Wuthnow, *The Crisis in the Churches: Spiritual Malaise, Fiscal Woe* (New York: Oxford University Press, 1997), 8.
6. Sondra Ely Wheeler, *Wealth as Peril and Obligation: The New Testament on Possession* (Grand Rapids, MI: Eerdmans, 1995), 134.

Bibliography

Bellah, Robert N., et al. *Habits of the Heart: Individualism and Commitment in American Life.* Berkeley, CA: University of California Press, 1985.

Bush, Lawrence, and Jeffrey Detko. *Jews, Money, and Social Responsibility: Developing a "Torah of Money" for Contemporary Life.* Philadelphia: The Shefa Fund, 1993.

Callahan, Kennon L. *Effective Church Finances: Fund-Raising and Budgeting for Church Leaders*. San Francisco: Jossey-Bass, 1992.

———. *Giving and Stewardship in an Effective Church: A Guide for Every Member*. San Francisco: Jossey-Bass, 1992.

Chaves, Mark, and Sharon Miller, eds. *Financing American Religion*. Walnut Creek, CA: AltaMira Press, 1999.

Christian Community, *The Desires of Your Heart: A Guide to Stewardship and the Annual Giving Campaign for Congregations*. Fort Wayne, IN, 1996.

Daly, Herman E., and John B. Cobb. *For the Common Good: Redirecting the Economy toward Community, the Environment, and a Sustainable Future*, 2nd ed. Boston: Beacon Press, 1994.

Dean, Peggy Powell, and Susanna A. Jones. *The Complete Guide to Capital Campaigns for Historic Churches and Synagogues*, 2nd ed. Philadelphia: Partners for Sacred Places, 1998.

Dockter, Jan Sullivan. *Ministry of Money: Exploring Money and Spirituality*. Germantown, MD: Ministry of Money, 2001.

Dominguez, Joe, and Vicki Robin. *Your Money or Your Life: Transforming Your Relationship with Money and Achieving Financial Independence*. New York: Penguin, 1992.

Dove, Kent E. *Conducting a Successful Capital Campaign*, 2nd ed. San Francisco: Jossey-Bass, 2000.

Gerth, H. H., and C. Wright Mills, eds. *From Max Weber: Essays in Sociology*. New York: Oxford University Press, 1946.

Hammar, Richard R. *Church and Clergy Tax Guide*. Matthews, NC: Christian Ministry Resources, annual.

———. *Pastor, Church, and Law*, 3rd ed. Matthews, NC: Christian Ministry Resources, 2000.

Hoge, Dean, et al. *Money Matters: Personal Giving in American Churches*. Louisville: Westminster John Knox Press, 1996.

Hoge, Dean, Patrick McNamara, and Charles Zech. *Plain Talk about Churches and Money*. Bethesda, MD: Alban Insitute, 1997.

Hotchkiss, Dan. *Ministry and Money: A Guide for Clergy and Their Friends*. Bethesda, MD: Alban Institute, 2002.

Hudnut-Beumler, James. *Generous Saints: Congregations Rethinking Ethics and Money*. Bethesda, MD: Alban Institute, 1999.

Johnston, Carol. *The Wealth or Health of Nations: Transforming Capitalism from Within*. Cleveland: Pilgrim Press, 1998.

Kinder, George. *Seven Stages of Money Maturity: Understanding the Spirit and Value of Money in Your Life*. New York: Dell, 1997.

King, Jerald L. *Asking Makes a Difference: A Guide for Stewardship Teams*. Lansing, MI: King and Associates, 2000.

Klein, Kim. *Ask and You Shall Receive: A Fund Raising Training Program for Religious Organizations and Projects*, Leader and Participant Manuals. San Francisco: Jossey-Bass, 2000.

Lynn, Robert Wood. "An Interview with Robert Wood Lynn on Christian Giving in America." Available online at the Resources for American Christianity Web site, www.resourcingchristianity.org/interviews.asp.

McNamara, Patrick H. *More Than Money: Portraits of Transformative Stewardship*. Bethesda, MD: Alban Institute, 1999.

Mead, Loren B. *Financial Meltdown in the Mainline?* Bethesda, MD: Alban Institute, 1998.

Needleman, Jacob. *Money and the Meaning of Life*. New York: Doubleday, 1991.

Niebuhr, H. Richard. *The Social Sources of Denominationalism*. New York: Henry Holt, 1929.

Putnam, Robert D. *Bowling Alone: The Collapse and Revival of American Community*. Carmichael, CA: Touchstone Books, 2001.

Roehjlkepartain, Eugene C., Elanah Dalyah Naftali, and Laura Musegades. *Growing Up Generous: Engaging Youth in Giving and Serving*. Bethesda, MD: Alban Institute, 2000.

Ronsvalle, John, Sylvia Ronsvalle, and U. Milo Kaufmann. *At Ease: Discussing Money and Values in Small Groups*. Bethesda, MD: Alban Institute, 1998.

————. *The State of Church Giving through 2002*. Champaign, IL: Empty Tomb, 2004.

Schaller, Lyle E. *44 Ways to Expand the Financial Base of Your Congregation*. Nashville: Abingdon, 1989.

Smith, Charles Merrill. *How to Become a Bishop without Being Religious*. New York: Doubleday, 1965.

Tocqueville, Alexis de. *Democracy in America*, edited by Phillips Bradley, translated by Henry Reeve. New York: Alfred A. Knopf, 1945.

Veblen, Thorstein. *The Theory of the Leisure Class: An Economic Study of Institutions*. New York: MacMillan, 1899; reprint New York: New American Library, 1953.

Weber, Max. *The Protestant Ethic and the Spirit of Capitalism*, translated by Talcott Parson. Los Angeles: Roxbury Publishing, 1930.

Wheeler, Sondra Ely. *Wealth as Peril and Obligation: The New Testament on Possessions*. Grand Rapids, MI: Eerdmans, 1995.

Wuthnow, Robert. *God and Mammon in America*. New York: MacMillan, 1994.

———. *Poor Richard's Principle: Recovering the American Dream through the Moral Dimension of Work, Business, and Money*. Princeton, NJ: Princeton University Press, 1996.

———. *The Crisis in the Churches: Spiritual Malaise, Fiscal Woe*. New York: Oxford University Press, 1997.

———, ed. *Rethinking Materialism: Perspectives on the Spiritual Dimension of Economic Behavior*. Grand Rapids, MI: Eerdmans, 1995.

RESOURCES ON FAITH AND MONEY
FROM THE CONGREGATIONAL RESOURCE GUIDE

Durall, Michael. **Creating Congregations of Generous People.** Bethesda, MD: Alban Institute, 1999.

This view of stewardship asserts that continued generous giving to one's congregation comes about from individual satisfaction and consequent spiritual growth, not from a duty to help meet the budget. The author provides statistics showing that giving in most congregations is far below what most congregants could afford. He then offers detailed strategies for involving nonpledgers and for encouraging large and regularly increased pledges. Congregations whose pledge drives produce less than thrilling results may find here an approach that could eventually mean true community for congregants and opportunities for increased ministry.

Frank, Robert. **Luxury Fever: Why Money Fails to Satisfy in an Era of Excess.** New York: The Free Press, 1999.

According to economist and author Robert Frank, spending on luxury goods has grown four times as fast as overall spending in the United States. Meanwhile, our roads, water supply, air quality, and social programs are worsening, and we are spending more hours at work and fewer on restorative leisure or relationships. After pointing to behavioral science studies that show how little our happiness is enhanced by conspicuous consumption, Frank suggests we engage in it because of the social cues and contexts that make such consumption more compelling. The author's observations on our consumerist behavior, its causes, and its consequences suggest creative possibilities for reflection in congregational small group or adult education settings.

Hoge, Dean R., Patrick H. McNamara, Charles Zech, and Michael J.
Donahue. **Money Matters: Personal Giving in American Churches.**
Louisville: Westminster John Knox Press, 1996.

> Seeking to identify the factors that encourage or discourage indi-
> vidual giving, the authors present the results of extensive research
> on trends in congregational giving. Designed for practical use by
> congregational leaders, the book takes into account theological and
> sociological variables among churches, and offers guidelines for
> improving stewardship. Of special interest is the testing of 22
> hypotheses about stewardship, some of which are validated and
> others revealed to be myths. Denominational stewardship leaders,
> pastors, and any others charged with raising the giving sights of
> church members will want this very thorough study near at hand.

Hoge, Dean R., Patrick H. McNamara, and Charles Zech. **Plain Talk
about Churches and Money.** Bethesda, MD: Alban Institute, 1997.

> This book gives an overview of the types of financial programs
> used by churches and explores issues concerning stewardship and
> fundraising, including the reasons people give what they give, the
> issue of whether pastors should know about congregants' pledges,
> pastors' attitudes toward talking about money, and helpful
> fundraising strategies for mainline churches. The plain talk con-
> tained in this book will stimulate discussions among church leaders
> who may otherwise be reluctant to bring up this touchy subject.

Hotchkiss, Dan. **Ministry and Money: A Guide for Clergy and Their
Friends.** Bethesda, MD: Alban Institute, 2002.

> There is perhaps no topic that creates more discomfort in contem-
> porary congregations than money, a discomfort the author con-
> tends arises from clergy's lack of training in economics and the split
> between faith and money in American culture. The author com-
> bines economic theory and practical theology to address these
> issues. Reminding us that Jesus spoke more often about money
> than about any other topic, Hotchkiss encourages a biblical per-
> spective on finances. He also raises financial concerns for all faith
> communities to consider—such as linking the congregational
> budget with its values and perceived mission, advocating and

determining fair compensation for clergy, and providing guidelines for fundraising. This is a useful resource for everyone involved in the financial leadership of congregations.

Hudnut-Beumler, James. **Generous Saints: Congregations Rethinking Ethics and Money.** Bethesda, MD: Alban Institute, 1999.

Author James Hudnut-Beumler shifts notions of parish finance from budget-balancing to perennial religious questions undergirding mission and life. This book calls us to responsive tending to what has been placed in our care. We are enriched by our possessions, by our capacities, but mostly by what God and others have entrusted to us. *Generous Saints* does not waste your time or effort. Its calm but challenging analysis and its insightful exercises belong in the hands of a stewardship committee months before a stewardship campaign is designed and launched. And if clergy and boards read it too, more than a church's financial circumstances may benefit.

McNamara, Patrick H. **More Than Money: Portraits of Transformative Stewardship.** Bethesda, MD: Alban Institute, 1999.

Christian stewardship is the individual and corporate response to the gift of life and creation; it arises from a model of abundance rather than scarcity. According to Patrick McNamara, to see stewardship as only fundraising, or only the management of nonmonetary resources, is to miss the mark. In *More Than Money,* McNamara used qualitative research methods to report on 11 American Protestant churches that have held an intentional focus on stewardship over time. This volume is rich with encouraging examples of the personal and churchwide changes brought about by a commitment to a lifestyle of stewardship.

Mead, Loren B. **Financial Meltdown in the Mainline?** Bethesda, MD: Alban Institute, 1998.

In this book, Loren Mead sets out compelling financial challenges for today's churches: the failure of seminaries to provide training to future clergy in financial matters; changing giving patterns; the lack of short- and long-range planning; the need for knowledge of sound financial techniques; an over-reliance on "restructuring" to fix problems; and the lack of defensive planning for operational costs. He then covers the principles for rebuilding the financial condition of congregations, connecting the financial crisis in the churches to a spiritual crisis in the country—an addiction to money and the reluctance of congregations to talk about it. As its title makes clear, this book does not pull its punches, and provides much food for thought for those who hope for better in our religious institutions.

Naylor, Thomas H., John de Graaf, and David Wann. **Affluenza: The All-Consuming Epidemic.** San Francisco: Berrett-Koehler Publishers, 2001.

While Americans of all creeds have become consummate consumers, the feeling that life is empty and meaningless has accompanied increases in material wealth. *Affluenza* shows how our lives demonstrate the truth of such sayings as "it does no good to gain the world but lose your soul." For instance, we often hear about the importance of "family values," but as more adults work harder and longer to meet their families' and their own swelling material expectations, they and their families ultimately suffer. Calling "affluenza" a "disease," the authors discuss the disease's three facets (symptoms, causes, and treatment) and provide a strong vehicle for dialogue about our values, our consumer decisions, and our future.

Ronsvalle, John, Sylvia Ronsvalle, and U. Milo Kaufmann. **At Ease: Discussing Money and Values in Small Groups.** Bethesda, MD: Alban Institute, 1998.

This book by faith and money experts John and Sylvia Ronsvalle, with U. Milo Kaufmann, presents, in an evangelical tone, a method for making people comfortable discussing the difficult issues of linking money with values. Based on congregational small-group discussions that create support and trust, the method helps individuals identify their fears and worries, as well as their attitudes on stewardship and support of the church. A series of questions leads participants to new and increasingly probing conversations about these issues.

Ronsvalle, John, and Sylvia Ronsvalle. **Behind the Stained Glass Windows: Money Dynamics in the Church.** Grand Rapids, MI: Baker Book House, 1996.

> Congregations are often reluctant to talk about money, especially if the level of giving meets budgetary needs each year. But, according to John and Sylvia Ronsvalle, this maintenance orientation is preventing the church from living into its responsibilities for mission. Their book, which is based on a three-year study of attitudes toward money in 14 denominations, contains a mix of statistics, interviews with laypeople, clergy, denominational officers, and experts, and the authors' own analysis of stewardship practices. The picture it paints is not pretty, but it gives reasons to hope that the emerging church will find ways to link stewardship with discipleship rather than finance.

Wuthnow, Robert. **The Crisis in the Churches: Spiritual Malaise, Fiscal Woe.** New York: Oxford University Press, 1997.

> Wuthnow argues that the financial crisis in congregations today—declining giving and increased demands—is also a spiritual crisis arising from the failure of congregations to meet the spiritual needs of their middle-class members. Based on 2,000 interviews, Wuthnow finds that members of the clergy often don't like to talk about money, but that it is crucial that they and their congregations learn to address this topic boldly and directly. This book contains valuable insights for all who want to understand the intersection of spirituality and stewardship, and provides hope for the future of Christianity.

3

SPIRITUAL WINDSURFING:
EXPLORING THE CONTEXT FOR EVALUATION

John Janka

The Alban Institute receives a steady stream of requests and inquiries regarding resources for clergy and congregational evaluation. Congregations often face the challenge of wanting to conduct an evaluation but finding they are ill equipped for the task. It is usually the case that congregations are looking for the "magic bullet" instrument or survey and have not taken time to examine some of the deeper subtleties of the purpose and process for the evaluation nor the assumptions out of which the evaluation is launched. There are dimensions of clergy evaluation that make this process unique and distinct from techniques commonly found in the corporate world. If this process is not approached thoughtfully, it can result in frustration, alienation, or conflict.

When considering the evaluation of the clergy leader and assessing the ministry of the congregation, there are significant foundational issues to be explored. Calling, self-knowledge, and the clergy and faith community's prophetic role are central to shaping identity. It is important that the lay leadership of the congregation understands these issues and how they factor into the way clergy image and live out their role, and it is equally important that the clergy understand how these issues inform congregational ministry. An exploration of these issues influences how the congregation and the clergy frame the evaluation process and even helps in the shaping of questions to be asked.

CALLING

Ministry has often been defined as categorically different from occupational choice or even vocational pursuit. Rooted not in cultural expectations for productivity but in ancient religious story and metaphor, ministry is entered into as a "calling." This calling is born of the tradition of priest and prophet, of one chosen to speak for God, to protect and administer the moral code of personal and corporate conduct, to define the believer's relationship to the Holy, and to articulate revealed truth as a way to advance human community.

Our calling is to believe in the revealed truth so deeply that we are fundamentally changed by it and compelled to invite others to live as though this truth is the only reality of consequence in their lives.

We experience this calling so profoundly that we have no choice but to say "yes" to it even when we feel inadequate to the task, even when doing so could jeopardize our security, our peace of mind, and our physical comfort.

With this calling comes a vision so persistent that we feel no alternative but to pursue it full force, convinced of its power to remake the human heart and create a new world. It is a vision we feel we must manifest in deeds of love and mercy, to call for justice and work for peace, to speak for those without a voice, to claim that the lost have been found. Living out this call, pursuing this vision, is likely to place us in the breach between hope and despair, longing and fulfillment, the demonic and the sacred, the partial and the complete.

To engage in the act of claiming this calling and being claimed by it is to experience a profound encounter with the Holy. It is to experience the utter defeat of personal agendas and private aspirations, it is to experience and touch a spiritual dimension of reality that can never be adequately described or explained, not even to one's closest friend. Our response to this call results in making commitments capable of depleting the very soul that yesterday it caused to soar.

To honor this calling is to be alternately blessed and stretched, affirmed and challenged, nurtured by renewing waters and driven into the desert. It is to live with absolute certainty one moment and complete vulnerability the next. It is to identify oneself with the greatest of all hopes in the face of the greatest of all possible disillusionments. The archetypal story of this kind of calling is found in the story of Jeremiah. His calling, so beautifully and poetically set forth in the book's first chapter, turns dark by chapter 20. By that point in his career he is not only struggling with his calling ("I have become a laughingstock all day long") but has reached such depths of despair that he curses the day on which he was born. To live out this calling is to journey on the coattails of a promise as illusive as the evening mist.

Such a calling as this possesses a power and a mystery that can dominate the landscape of one's life and become the filter through which one sees and interprets all else. The very idea of this kind of mystery can be a foreign concept in a cynical world. We tend to be intolerant of the notion of mystery. We think of it as something we just don't know yet rather than as something fundamentally unknowable. We assume that anything viewed in the cold light of day, subjected to rational thought, will yield up its secrets. After all, in an information age what is there that we cannot know by simply pushing the correct key on the computer?

It is this element of mystery that makes living out our calling an experience in spiritual windsurfing, mastering and balancing ourselves by alternately tensing and yielding to the wind, developing a relationship with the wind that allows responsiveness to its shifting and moving. We skip across living waters with exhilarating freedom and are astounded by our agility, barely earthbound. It is the power and mystery of such profound calling that tethers us for life to this work. Once tethered in this way we should expect to ride the wind, to be both caressed and buffeted by it, to experience times of dead calm and typhoon.

It is not common practice in congregations that they speak the language of call. It is far more common to find congregations who are working to develop vision and mission statements and meeting annually for goal setting. It is the language of call, however, that sets before the faith community a new way of thinking. It allows them to move away from a "business model" and tap into the deep spiritual reservoir of their own faith tradition. It is in the context of call that the congregation is challenged in a new way to find its unique identity and to struggle with its role at a particular time and in a particular place.

This is not to say that there should not be goals for ministry in the congregation. Rather, it is to advocate for a focus on the congregation's sense of call as primary. It is this focus that moves the leaders of the congregation to explore larger questions of meaning and purpose. Goals then emerge out of this framework. When the congregation's call is central to its identity, the capacity for risk taking is expanded and the bar for expectations is raised.

SELF-KNOWLEDGE

Those who seek to know God and fail to know themselves deeply are likely on a fool's errand, for this is a journey into relationship. We cannot truly know the "Other" deeply without knowing ourselves. Spiritual leadership requires tending to one's own inner life. Exploring fearlessly what Parker Palmer calls the "shadow side" of ourselves and bringing to the surface our interior life is the path to spiritual depth. Understanding how our inner life shapes our public role—possessing the self-awareness to understand the inner forces that motivate and constrain us—is a vital leadership capacity. Being connected to the deeper places within us opens the possibility for congruence and authenticity in our relationships and in our role as spiritual leader. Palmer states in his pamphlet, *Leading from Within*,[1] "A leader is a person who must take special responsibility for what's going on inside him or her self, inside his or her consciousness, lest the act of leadership create more harm that good." To possess this self-knowledge is the greatest safeguard against posing behind the many masks we are tempted to wear. It allows for maintaining a proper balance between vulnerability and control and fends off self-deception.

The more access we have to our shadow side the more realistic our self-perceptions and the more our creative energies will be available to us in our work. This does not necessarily mean that we exorcise our demons, but it can mean we discover ways to divert their power for more creative, purposeful outcomes. Without self-knowledge we provide a hiding place for our guilt and regrets, for unresolved grief or anger, and thereby give these demons status and influence they do not deserve. Providing this hiding place is to commit the creative energies of our spirit to the holding action of control and containment when what is needed is acknowledgement, ownership, confession, and awareness of how these work and play against a full and fulfilling life. Self-knowledge is the key to freedom. It is what loosens our shackles and allows us to be self-affirming and engage others authentically.

Self-knowledge also allows us to engage in meaningful self-assessment. The more we are able to see within ourselves the more accurate our assessment of our true capacities and limitations. Accurate self-assessment is the counterbalance to the nearly constant feedback clergy experience. Knowing ourselves allows us to measure the feedback we receive and invite conversation with others about their perceptions and experience of us.

The ability to be deeply self-aware allows the leader to process data and monitor his or her own feelings while in the midst of stress. It is an asset in maintaining a nonanxious leadership presence and appropriate self-control in highly conflicted situations. Self-awareness is the starting point for setting relational boundaries and establishing behavioral covenants (agreements about our conduct in relationship to others). Such self-knowledge allows us to understand and accept our influence and power in relationship to others and to exercise that influence ethically.

While there is this "shadow side" in us, there is also in us the place where light resides. Knowing ourselves also means claiming and giving voice to our unspoken hopes, embracing the vision that won't let us go, that haunts our sleep and challenges our disbelief. Such self-knowledge can carry us beyond the constraints of our fears and allow us to traverse the open ground of experimentation and be both holy and wholly vulnerable.

Acquiring self-knowledge is not simply an exercise in introspection. We come to deep self-knowledge through the sometimes rough-and-tumble engagement with the world around us.

Howard Friend, in his book *Recovering the Sacred Center,* notes that there is a paradoxical quality to the journey toward the inner life. "It is the ironic paradox of traveling outward in order to journey inward. The quest that traverses sea and mountain, that encounters danger and discouragement, is yet a movement downward and inward at the same time." As a young pastor, I would visit a bedridden parishioner, a stroke victim named Edna. It took a few visits before I was able to develop an ear for her slurred speech. As we sat together she would talk on and on about how grateful she was for the all the ways God had blessed her. I confess that at first I was skeptical, but in time I learned this was authentically Edna. On some of my most difficult days, "shadow side days," in the parish, I discovered that a visit to Edna was a way for me to regain my balance and reconnect with my spiritual center. Getting outside myself was a way to rediscover and reintegrate myself, traveling outward in order to journey inward.

It is not enough, however, to confront the shadow side. We must also live in the light. It is this latter task that can be the most terrifying of all. To step out and announce the dream in the midst of the community requires uncommon courage. It requires a capacity for risk taking and a tolerance for failure. It is a mark of spiritual leadership that we have the capacity to confront the "dream stealers" among us, those who pick the spiritual pockets of the faith community, who limit its vision and diminish its resources. When spiritual leaders allow the inappropriate behavior of others to go unchecked and unchallenged, they lose their power and credibility. It is important that we have the spiritual strength to issue a challenge to the faith community and that we are sufficiently self-differentiated to stand against the fears of others and not be overcome by them. Jesus was not crucified because he confronted the demons in the desert. He was crucified for announcing the dream and living as though it was an accomplished fact. Our "living the dream" can exact a high cost. If we are not well centered, aware of our limitations and weaknesses as well as our strengths, or if we are unfamiliar with and unpracticed about our dream, we will be easily unbalanced.

Research into the field of emotional intelligence has concluded that self-knowledge, an awareness of one's emotions and their impact on others, is a key factor in giving exceptional leadership in any organization. Without this self-knowledge it is virtually impossible to empathize with another person. It is this capacity for empathy, for reading the feelings of others, that creates what *Primal Leadership* authors Daniel Goleman, Richard Boyatzis, and Annie McKee call "resonant leadership."

When the members of a group or community (or congregation) work with an emotionally intelligent leader, they connect with each other at an emotional level, form significant bonds, and can stay focused on their mission even in the face of disorienting change and stress. Their energy and investment are high and they feel free to exercise creativity and take appropriate risks. In the case of what these authors describe as "discordant leadership," the group or congregation can be hobbled by a lack of trust. The discordant leader's negative tone is manifested as barbed humor, cynicism, manipulation, and subtle judgements. When the leader is either unaware of his or her negative impact on others or unconcerned for their well-being, the community dynamic can become toxic.

According to Goleman, Boyatzis, and McKee, emotionally intelligent leaders will exhibit competencies in four key areas: self-awareness, self-management, social awareness, and relational management.

Self-awareness refers to leaders' ability to have ready access to their own feelings and understand how these feelings influence their relationships and their performance. This self-awareness also permits accurate self-assessment. Emotionally intelligent leaders have a realistic view of themselves and are able to be self-affirming as well as to identify their growing edges and work on them.

Self-management is the ability to manage strong emotions and impulses during highly stressful situations. It is the ability to stay focused on the issues at hand and not be driven inappropriately by strong feelings, which may compound the problems. Self-management refers to one's ability to state one's feelings clearly and proportionately in a given situation. It also means possessing the ability to set one's immediate strong feelings aside in order to hear the other deeply. Without self-management our feelings can become the agenda of the conversation and we risk missing the broader dynamic in the situation.

Social awareness is described as the leader's ability to read, understand, and relate to the social networks, power relationships, and political forces at work within the organization. It is the ability to relate creatively to individual representatives of various networks as well as to the groups as a whole and to exhibit the degree of empathy necessary to grasp the other person's point of view.

Relationship management includes the ability to nurture and mentor others in maximizing their contributions. Emotionally intelligent leaders are also able to give timely and constructive feedback and help others embrace a common vision. Additionally, they are change catalysts who advocate for change and motivate others by building buy-in. They present change as a reasonable and healthy risk and describe the change as achievable. They create a sufficiently safe environment for risk taking and an atmosphere of shared ownership, and they balance the attendant conflict and resistance.

It is as important that the congregation possesses this emotional intelligence as it is for the clergy leader. Knowing its history, understanding the values that shape its corporate life, and "owning" its shadow side—its fears, temptations, and self-imposed constraints—make possible the accurate self-assessment of its ministry. The ability to identify the way in which the congregation needs to grow and mature, the ability to name its demons and in some cases its secrets, will help release new energy for ministry, whether these demons represent constraining attitudes toward money, resistance to growth, or fear in the face of a racially transitional community.

Along with a clearheaded understanding of its shadow side, the congregation must also be articulate about its dream, the risks it is willing to take to accomplish that dream, and the spiritual and behavioral covenants that must be kept along the way. Establishing norms for how the congregation will live out its life together and working intentionally to honor those norms is a sign of congregational health.

THE PROPHETIC ROLE

Most often it is the prophet's role to speak the truth at the very moment it is least welcomed. It is the prophet who provides the corporate corrective and brings "the word of the Lord" to bear upon the community's misdirection. It is the prophetic role to read the dominant culture in the light of the faith tradition and to describe the discord and disconnect between them. The prophetic voice is not employed to announce revisions in the current reality but to announce a new reality altogether. In his book *The Prophetic Imagination*, Walter Brueggemann states, "The task of prophetic ministry is to nurture, nourish, and evoke a consciousness and perception alternative to the consciousness and perception of the dominant culture around us."[2] It is out of this alternative consciousness that the faith community finds its identity and defines its purpose.

The prophetic role is played out in the space between the faith community and the dominant culture where the battle for the soul of the faith community is waged. Ever wooed by the conveniences and contrivances of the dominant culture, the faith community is easily distracted and quickly diluted. It is the prophet who rehearses the promise and hope that is at the center of the faith community's identity and simultaneously challenges the values and injustices of the dominant culture. The further along the road to its own destruction the faith community has traveled, the more likely it will be to reject the prophet's message and alienate the prophet.

Illustrating this is one pastor's story of being appointed to a congregation situated in a racially transitional community. Perhaps half the members of the congregation had already moved out of the neighborhood in "white flight" by the time this pastor arrived, while the members remaining in the community had adopted a fortress mentality. As the pastor began to work with this congregation and raise questions such as, "Where will this congregation's new members come from in the future?" the congregational leaders became more anxious and reactive. The pastor, realizing that the congregation had avoided the issue for too long, felt that there was precious little time for a process of renewal. The church board grudgingly approved a request by the pastor to establish a study task force. The work of the task force resulted in a report with recommendations for a plan of revitalization, which placed a strong emphasis on reaching out to the local community. The congregational meeting at which the report was presented drew a packed house, including long inactive members who had been organized to defeat the proposal. Not only was the plan soundly defeated, but the pastor, in this case the messenger, was subjected to the harshest of treatments and directed to cease and desist on the matter. It was of little consequence that the pastor diagnosed the situation correctly. The congregation was well beyond the point of looking objectively at the issues. A few short years later the congregation turned its building over to a local Hispanic ministry.

By its very nature the prophetic role requires the prophet to be fully immersed in the life of the community and fully immersed in the tradition. It is this complete identification with both the community and the tradition that subjects the prophet to the grief and anguish of a faith community distanced from God and at the same time qualifies him or her as the authentic voice of hope. It is the prophet who must balance high tension simultaneously on two fronts: first with the dominant culture, which often demonstrates predisposition to a hostile response, and secondly with the faith community, which is often ambivalent at best about the requirements of faithfulness. The intensity and often attendant isolation of this role can result in a painful and bitter retreat from the prophetic task altogether.

The prophetic task, it should be noted, is carried out both individually and corporately. It is the faith community that is called to counter the prevailing culture and serve as the transformational element in a larger universal plan of redemption. In the midst of a culture some would describe as driven by the undercurrents of greed, nihilism, and exclusion, it is the faith community that stands for an alternative reality of hope, healing, and freedom from cultural and spiritual tyrannies. In this sense the faith community is subversive in every respect in its relationship with the dominant culture and is not beguiled by the culture's claims of affinity with the faith community, illustrated by the words "In God We Trust" imprinted on the coin of the realm.

Against these challenges, the prophetic function must rely on a deep sense of tradition and history. It must find its story in God's story and rehearse God's consistent faithfulness in the midst of the people's despair. In doing so it uses what Brueggemann calls "the language of hope . . . the language of amazement,"[3] which reestablishes God's radical vision of a new social reality.

The prophetic role finds expression when the faith community engages the larger culture on matters that concern the common good, when it lifts up the vision of a new social reality. It is not enough in performing the prophetic role that the faith community addresses only itself, its beliefs, and its behavior. The larger culture must also hear the word of the Lord. In his book *Doing Justice*, Dennis Jacobsen observes, "The church enters the public arena in order to be the church, in order to be true to itself, in order to be faithful to its Lord, in order to heed the summons of the Holy Spirit."[4] Engaging in public ministry means addressing the moral and social issues affecting the local, national, and global community. It means making common cause with partners who also have a vision for healing and wholeness in the larger context. It means assuming the role of public advocate, creating dialogue that is public and inclusive, and representing an alternative vision to that of the dominant culture. We are propelled into the public arena because God is there, because our faith is not compartmentalized and does not confine itself to the sanctuary.

There should be no idealistic illusions about the demands of this role. Alienation can be a high cost to pay when one carries out the prophetic role. The prophet can easily feel betrayed by the One who sent him or her. In his book *Under the Unpredictable Plant*, Eugene Petersen observes, "We repeatedly find ourselves angry with God, disappointed and quarrelsome that our procedures result in something quite different from what we had expected."[5] While it is human nature to seek validation for our work in ministry, ultimately the prophetic task is not about validating the messenger. Rather it is about justice being done, a greater vision being set forth, a new identity being forged. It is about the destiny God has for us and not the destiny we imagine for ourselves.

IMPLICATIONS FOR EVALUATION

Embracing our sense of call means we are vulnerable to the outrageous claims of faith. It means that we have a keen sense of what is of vital importance; we are connected to our passions and approach our ministry with a sense of urgency. Laid against a profound sense of calling is often an understanding of evaluation that accepts the idea that if it can't be measured it has no value; if it can't be packaged into a neat set of conclusions, then it isn't helpful. If it can't be "scored" to show a numerical result, then our questions go unanswered. We use surveys and we poll the congregation. We are tempted to focus on the "low scores" rather than focusing on issues of spiritual leadership. We work at applying empirical standards of analysis to a call-driven work without ever inquiring about the call itself. If this most vital issue is bypassed, then evaluation is reduced to measurements of relative satisfaction (or dissatisfaction) or a numerical rendering of effectiveness.

It is, of course, important to acknowledge that the clergy's sense of call and the congregation's call and mission must be open to review and challenge, that it must be tested by the faith community as a process of discernment. The clergy leader's and the congregation's sense of call and the congregation's mission can change or evolve over time and can become more faithfully aligned when subjected to careful assessment.

However, it must also be noted that there may be no more "soul-wrenching" an experience for a clergy leader than to have the faith community reject, constrain, or dilute the leader's deeply held sense of call. This experience can be the occasion for soul-searching, conflict, and even depression. ("I have become a laughingstock all day long.") It can also be the experience that precipitates the resignation, dismissal, or reassignment of the clergy leader. Likewise, however, it can be demoralizing and discouraging for a congregation to experience a clergy leader who does not take seriously the congregation's sense of call or vision and who articulates no sense of call or vision of his or her own.

It is assumed that the clergy leader is called to ministry, but rarely does anyone ask the question, "How have you lived out your call during this past year?" or "What would you say have been the constraints on your faithfully living out your call?" or "How can this congregation be more supportive of you as you attempt to live out your call?"

Of equal importance is that the congregation has the opportunity to explore similar questions regarding its own life and ministry. "How would we describe our sense of calling as a congregation?" "How faithful have we been in living out this call during the past year?" "What support do we need to more faithfully live out this call in the future?"

When evaluation is undertaken without consideration of call, self-knowledge, and the prophetic role of the clergy and the congregation, the conversation is usually an exploration of "expectations" and the degree to which these have been met by the clergy leader and the congregation. "So why is this a problem?" you might ask. As Peter Block says in his book *Stewardship*, "Given the nature of evaluations, we are as likely to be rating and paying people for compliance as we are for performance."[6] In other words, without the deeper conversations about call, self-knowledge, and the prophetic role, we may default to an evaluation process that seeks to measure the extent to which expectations have been met or the extent to which there has been "compliance" with congregational norms or with the clergy's expectations of the congregation.

Given that congregations are tradition-based organizations and that tradition-based organizations typically do not reward risk taking, a clergy leader's efforts to meet the congregation's expectations can mean conforming to the congregation's comfort level rather than advancing ministry through healthy confrontation and challenge and appropriate risk taking. Additionally, when a clergy leader's need to be liked colludes with the congregation's need for stability, the result can be not only a lack of risk taking but also a lack of faithfulness. Measuring how well expectations have been met may be little more than a measurement of how well or how successfully we have avoided conflict.

Subtle collusion in the cause of congregational peace is a short step away from a sterile and vacant faith or a faith community that lacks energy and vitality. Too often we strive to order our lives in such a way as to minimize the unexpected. We invest heavily in avoiding discomfort and inconvenience. We seek to control and orchestrate our lives, our environment, our relationships, and even our spiritual journey—to choreograph each step we take—only to discover that chaos will not be denied. In discussing the relationship between creativity and chaos, Petersen asserts, "Mess is the precondition of creativity. Creativity is not neat. It is not orderly. When we are being creative we don't know what will happen next. When we are being creative a great deal of what we are doing is wrong. When we are being creative we are not efficient."[7] Congregations and their leaders who place a high value on neatness, orderliness, efficiency, and predictability are not likely to be exploring new spiritual horizons, nor are they likely to be asking the deeper questions of calling, probing for self-knowledge, or discerning their prophetic role.

It is through the prophetic imagination that we are carried beyond our creeds, urged to storm the gates of convention, and freed for the role of co-conspirator in establishing a vision for a new social reality. It is the prophetic imagination that is the source of our creativity, that propels us to new levels of discernment and insight, and infuses us with a resilient hope for the future.

Evaluation begins at the point of our deepest longing. It is a longing for distinct identity, self-fulfillment, influence, meaning, freedom, and attachment. However, it is often the case that evaluation never touches the places of our deepest longing, never explores the constraining influences we can feel, never probes the interior dimensions of the spiritual journey. Most evaluation presumes a problem or deficiency and responds with a prescription or solution. An alternative to this approach is found in "appreciative inquiry." This process, rather than identifying and diagnosing problems and suggesting solutions, or identifying past shortcomings and suggesting remedial action, seeks to focus on the experiences that have created breakthrough energy, collaborative and synergistic thinking, and experiences that have advanced the mission of the congregation.

This approach allows the whole system to engage in a shared quest to discover and articulate who it wants to be and where it wants to go, based on where it has been. Because the process is grounded in real experience and shared history, it allows participants to affirm the very best of the past and generate the new directions it needs to take in the future.

Rather than understanding evaluation as a method of problem identification and an approach to generating solutions, appreciative inquiry seeks to focus on the best of "what is," envision "what might be," develop agreements on "what should be," and innovate "what will be."

This approach invites a different line of inquiry. Based on appreciative inquiry, the following sample questions could lead to a deeper conversation between clergy and congregational leaders. These questions are intended to set the context for evaluation by inviting dialogue regarding call, self-knowledge, and the prophetic role.

Questions of Call

1. How would you describe your sense of calling?
2. How have you honored your calling during this past year?
3. What have been the constraints to your living out your sense of call?
4. If you were to live out your call more faithfully, what would be added to your ministry; what would be deleted?
5. Describe a time when you experienced a high level of congruence between your vision of your call and your role in ministry.

Questions of Self-Knowledge

1. What are your unspoken hopes and constraining fears and what does this tell you about your leadership role?
2. Where do feedback and self-assessment converge to confirm your self-perception and where is there a disconnection?
3. What are the developmental edges for you, for the congregation?
4. In what ways do you avoid difficult issues and what is going on inside you when this happens?

Questions of the Prophetic Role

1. How do you understand your prophetic role and how does this role find expression in your work and the congregation's ministry?
2. What are the risks God may be inviting you to take now?
3. What is your vision for a new social order and how do you promote it?
4. How have you and the congregation given leadership in the larger community in the interests of the common good?

These questions are intended to set a different tone and direction for assessing the work of the clergy leader and the congregation. It is also intended to encourage mutuality in addressing the spiritual underpinnings of our ministry. By establishing conversation time and making normative the exploration of deeper questions, we enrich our learning and deepen our understanding of the journey we share. We also avoid a superficial and potentially destructive appraisal of the person as leader or of the congregation as community of faith.

Metaphorically, spiritual windsurfing requires a certain agility. It requires a willingness to get wet, to lose control, to be surprised by the shifting wind. It is a multi-disciplinary experience, combining the skills of sailing and surfing, of balance and strength. It requires sensitivity to one's environment and a willingness to test one's capacities and limits. Exploring our call, seeking self-knowledge, honoring our prophetic role, and living the mystery of this journey is to sign on for an exhilarating ride.

NOTES

1. Parker Palmer, *Leading from Within: Reflections on Spirituality and Leadership* (Washington, DC: Servant Leadership School, 1990), 7.
2. Walter Brueggemann, *The Prophetic Imagination* (Minneapolis: Fortress Press, 1978), 13.
3. Brueggemann, *The Prophetic Imagination*, 69.
4. Dennis Jacobsen, *Doing Justice: Congregations and Community Organizing* (Minneapolis: Fortress Press, 2001), 15.
5. Eugene Petersen, *Under the Unpredictable Plant: An Exploration in Vocational Holiness* (Grand Rapids, MI: Eerdmans, 1992), 161.
6. Peter Block, *Stewardship: Choosing Service over Self-Interest* (New York: Berrett-Koehler, 1993), 172.
7. Petersen, *Under the Unpredictable Plant*, 163.

BIBLIOGRAPHY

Block, Peter. *Stewardship: Choosing Service over Self-Interest*. New York: Berrett-Koehler, 1993.

Brueggemann, Walter. *The Prophetic Imagination*. Minneapolis: Fortress Press, 1978.

Friend, Howard. *Recovering the Sacred Center: Church Renewal from the Inside Out*. Valley Forge, PA: Judson Press, 1998.

Goleman, Daniel, Richard Boyatzis, and Annie McKee. *Primal Leadership: Realizing the Power of Emotional Intelligence.* Cambridge, MA: Harvard Business School Press, 2002.

Jacobsen, Dennis A. *Doing Justice: Congregations and Community Organizing.* Minneapolis: Fortress Press, 2001.

Palmer, Parker. *Let Your Life Speak: Listening for the Voice of Vocation.* San Francisco: Jossey-Bass, 2000.

Peterson, Eugene H. *Under the Unpredictable Plant: An Exploration in Vocational Holiness.* Grand Rapids, MI: Eerdmans, 1992.

Watkins, Jane Magruder, and Bernard J. Mohr. *Appreciative Inquiry: Change at the Speed of Imagination.* San Francisco: Jossey-Bass/Pfeiffer, 2001.

RESOURCES ON EVALUATION AND VOCATION FROM THE CONGREGATIONAL RESOURCE GUIDE

Block, Peter. **Stewardship: Choosing Service over Self-Interest.** San Francisco: Berrett-Koehler Publishers, 1996.

> Congregational leaders might expect a book entitled *Stewardship* to focus on fundraising and financial pledging, but this book defines "stewardship" as a choice "to preside over the orderly distribution of power" so that partnership replaces dominance and accountability replaces dependency. Grounded in the view that each of us longs to invest energy in things that matter, *Stewardship* calls us to move beyond self interest and make service the centerpiece of our corporate lives. Author Peter Block outlines key steps toward stewardship-based organizational transformation, discussing compelling challenges for church and synagogue leaders and boards as they grapple with questions of purpose, control, mission, planning, and responsibility.

Block, Peter. **The Answer to How Is Yes: Acting on What Matters.** San Francisco: Berrett-Koehler Publishers, 2001.

> This book compels us to attend to those ideals and commitments that truly matter. Peter Block points out that we often divert ourselves from our ideals by endless attention to "how" questions: "How do you do it?" "How long will it take?" "How do you measure it?" Such questions emphasize task to the exclusion of purpose and are ultimately disempowering. More appropriate questions, Block says, concern values, purpose, and context, such as "What commitment am I willing to make?" or "What's my contribution to this problem?" This book is for persons who are open to a new perspective as they reassess personal vocation and mission.

Chalan, Kathleen. **Projects That Matter: Planning and Evaluation for Religious Organizations.** Herndon, VA: Alban Institute, 2003.

> In organizational life, so much is done simply because it was done before. But Kathleen Cahalan helps readers to stop and ask, "Why are we doing this?" She also urges leaders to grasp that the necessity of posing the question rests in a particular understanding of stewardship. Alluding to Luke 6:48, she states, "As elements of Christian stewardship, planning and evaluation are ways in which Christians care for, monitor, and ensure both a strong foundation and a decent house." Readable, thorough, and immensely practical, *Projects That Matter* helps readers to recognize that time and patience are necessary for both good planning and helpful evaluation. Less organized leaders will find the step-by-step format and worksheets helpful. Other leaders will appreciate Cahalan's pragmatism and find affirmation as well as some new ideas in her work.

Friend, Howard E. **Recovering the Sacred Center: Church Renewal from the Inside Out.** Valley Forge, PA: Judson Press, 1998.

> The author draws on his experiences as a minister and founder of the Parish Empowerment Network to show how churches can meet the new ways of society. To recover the sacred center, he says, individuals and congregations must create a sacred space and must act in response to the question "What do you long for?" Churches have in the past brought disarrayed lives together; now they must risk overcoming rigidity by letting things come apart and reassemble in a new way. Suggestions for action are included.

Hudson, Jill M. **Evaluating Ministry: Principles and Processes for Clergy and Congregations.** Bethesda, MD: Alban Institute, 1992.

> Start with this slim volume if you are designing an evaluation process for clergy already in place or a contract provision for clergy soon to be called. Author Jill Hudson sees ministry as mutual and collaborative between congregation and pastorate, so she believes any evaluatioln process should be applied to *both* clergy and congregation. To evaluate the ministry *only of clergy,* she claims, is to deprive both clergy and congregation of the full opportunity for growth and development. Case studies, sample forms and processes, summaries, and references to denominational guides are included.

Hudson, Jill M. **When Better Isn't Enought: Evaluation Tools for the 21st Century Church.** Bethesda, MD: Alban Institute, 2004.

> In *When Better Isn't Enough,* Jill Hudson compellingly argues that the old ways of doing and evaluating ministry don't work anymore, and she proposes new models and processes to bring churches into alignment with the new ways of the postmodern world. Following a brief and readable sketch of the historical shifts that have led to the postmodern culture and an insightful description of its essence, Hudson presents a description of the characteristics of effective ministry in today's world and outlines an evaluation process based on these characteristics that emphasizes the mutual ministry of clergy and congregation and the discernment of the actions necessary to enhance the church's success.

Jacobsen, Dennis A. **Doing Justice: Congregations and Community Organizing.** Minneapolis: Fortress Press, 2001.

> *Doing Justice* is a primer on the theology of, and rationale for, congregation-based community organizing for urban ministry. Dennis Jacobsen, a Lutheran pastor with more than 14 years experience in this field, covers such topics as the roles of power, money, and self-interest in community organizing, and explores how to build and sustain ministries that promote justice. His book includes an index of organizations involved in congregation-based community organizing and a study guide for use by groups. The book would be helpful to congregations exploring the possibility of doing community organizing.

McMahill, David C. **Completing the Circle: Evaluating the Church's Ministries.** Bethesda, MD: Alban Institute, 2003.

> *Completing the Circle* is a short and readable book providing a spiritually grounded model for clergy performance evaluation. McMahill's approach to evaluation is based on a simple feedback and reflection process designed to elicit congregants' experience of various aspects of congregational life. As McMahill points out, part of a minister's job is to challenge church members to reach beyond what is comfortable, so the likes and dislikes of parishioners are not the best measure of a minister's performance. Instead, he argues, the basis for clergy evaluation should be the purpose and mission of the church. In McMahill's model, much of which is described

through the experiences of an invented, composite congregation, congregants are provided opportunities to describe their own experiences, to experience being heard, and to hear others describe their experiences. In this safe and honest communication environment, McMahill suggests, respectful, constructive, and helpful evaluations can occur.

Palmer, Parker. **Let Your Life Speak: Listening for the Voice of Vocation.** San Francisco: Jossey-Bass, 2000.

This exploration of vocation seeks enlightenment through self-understanding rather than aptitude testing. Palmer advocates finding one's true "calling" within rather than externally, while simultaneously stressing the role one's community can play in developing inner work. He describes the value of Quaker "clearness committees," and imparts other Quaker wisdom as well (the book's title is Quaker advice). The book also offers practical guidance, such as warning signs that one is not pursuing one's vocation (e.g., burnout and depression). An ideal resource for any groups or individuals who seek authenticity and the fulfillment of their "calling."

Peterson, Eugene. **Under the Unpredictable Plant: An Exploration in Vocational Holiness.** Grand Rapids, MI: Eerdmans, 1992.

Issuing a major challenge to clergy, author Eugene Peterson urges a paradigm shift from pastor as program director to pastor as spiritual director. He demonstrates why we should not think of pastoring in the current management terms of "efficiency," "outcomes," or "the bottom line." Drawing on both the biblical story of Jonah and his own 30-year pastoral journey, Peterson explores the urge to exert one's will rather than surrender to God's will (choosing Tarshish); the temptation to pursue a "career" (experiencing the storm); the understanding that through prayer and contemplation one may reclaim one's vocation (learning from the whale's belly); the awareness that the places and conditions to which God calls us are not incidental (finding Ninevah); and the need to avoid enslavement to "programs" so that one may discover the holiness of one's vocation (hearing God's voice under the withering plant). This book will benefit not only clergy, but also anyone involved in creating new pastoral job descriptions, shifting responsibilities among church staff, or calling a new pastor.

4

CLAIMING THE LIGHT:
APPRECIATIVE INQUIRY AND
CONGREGATIONAL TRANSFORMATION

Paul C. Chaffee

I came that they may have life, and have it abundantly.
—John 10:10.

After two years of work on a sexual harassment problem at a Fortune 500 company without producing the desired results, an organization development consultant specializing in gender issues and conflict resolution sought help from David Cooperrider, a professor at Case Western Reserve University and the originator of the methodology known as "appreciative inquiry." Reaching him by phone, the consultant told Cooperrider that, confounding her firm's best efforts—including extensive employee workshops—every chartable measure indicated accelerating harassment rather than abatement. The situation had the consultant and her colleagues stymied. They were working hard, going backwards, and asking for help.

"What is it you want to learn about and achieve?" Cooperrider asked. They wanted to "put a dent" in a "huge problem" of harassment, the consultant told him. "Is that *all* you want?" Cooperrider asked. Pressed, the consultant reached beyond the problem and replied, "We want . . . high-quality cross-gender relationships in the workplace."

In the resulting model project, employees were invited—as a first step—to write about experiences they had had involving exemplars of healthy cross-gender working relationships. Dozens of responses were anticipated and hundreds arrived, each full of stories about employees working together creatively and happily. From these stories a program evolved that transformed the corporation.[1]

Executives at Avon Mexico heard of the project's success and hired appreciative inquiry (AI) practitioner Marjorie Schiller to lead their whole corporation in an "inquiry" based on the same model. As an initial step in that process, 300 one-on-one interviews were conducted, resulting in a flood of stories about "achievement, trust building, authentic joint leadership, practices of effective conflict management, ways of dealing with sex stereotypes, stages of development, and methods of career advancement—all focused on high-quality cross-gender work relationships."[2] Eventually the company won the 1997 Catalyst Award as the best place in Mexico for women to work.

The methodology that led to these remarkable events was spawned in the early 1980s when David Cooperrider—then a student at Case Western University—was trying to figure out why the health clinic he was studying didn't have any of the problems he had been trained to "fix." What he learned from his own exploration of this question later upended the organization development profession and revitalized hundreds of different kinds of communities around the world.

Re-Grounding Relationship

Ask, and it shall given you; search, and you will find;
knock, and the door shall be opened to you.
—Matthew 7:7

As a 1980 doctoral candidate in organization development doing fieldwork at the Cleveland Clinic, Cooperrider backed into the idea of *inquiring into what people most appreciate and value* rather than into a problem to be fixed. He had been asking, "What is wrong with the human side of the Cleveland Clinic?" But he found little malaise and was impressed by the organization's flexibility, innovativeness, openness, and egalitarian spirit. So, instead of studying what didn't work, he inquired into what worked best for those at the clinic. He asked about its sources of vitality and about its highest hopes for its future. What he learned transformed the academic/professional organization development community in the United States and abroad.[3] Now more than 20 years since the Cleveland Clinic project began, thousands of appreciative projects around the world have joined the search. Whatever the corporate arena, each project begins by identifying a positive goal and its context. Then participants ask themselves—one-on-one at first—what do we most value in the given context, what works for us when we are at our best, and what are our highest hopes for the future? Following this "discovery" process, AI goes to work with what's been learned, nurtures the growing enthusiasm, and opens the way to "co-create the future." It is always collaborative work generated out of strong relationships.

Problems are not exactly ignored in an appreciative environment, but, rather than addressing them head on, appreciative practitioners help reframe core issues, however troubled and complex. AI projects with Cairo garbage collectors, Chicago revitalization, and Islamabad interfaith groups indicate that problems are not being ignored so much as reframed in ways that empower people (engaged communities) to make a difference. The reframing turns away from understanding what's wrong and shifts almost exclusively to seeking the light, moving toward the best opportunities at our disposal, however hard our circumstances.

In the case of the sexual harassment project at the Fortune 500 company mentioned earlier, the goal of putting a big dent into a huge problem was reframed as an inquiry into high-quality cross-gender leadership. Reframing instantly changes the tone and attitude around any subject, great or small, and the door opens on the most underexamined set of issues in our culture—what we most value and yearn for in life, whatever the context. A number of choices contribute to reframing:

- Regardless of the subject at hand, deficit-based language explaining what is wrong is replaced with asset-based language identifying what is right and what the individuals involved want to generate. People are asked to think beyond difficulties and their causes (e.g., a sexual harassment epidemic) to discern, study, and empower the positive values they want embodied (e.g., high-quality, cross-gender leadership teams).
- Giving *everyone's* story a place in the discussion and shifting from evaluation to valuation brings a shift in spirit, with significant increases in trust.
- In the reframing and developing dialogue, considerable attention goes to imaging and ruminating on a community's "positive core," listening to its members' highest aspirations and hopes, and empowering people to self-organize around

the issues that most matter to them. As Cooperrider has written, "Full voice, convivial community, rigorous inquiry, shared speculation and dreams, articulation of things that matter, improvisation—these are ingredients that ensure that AI praxis does not devolve into sterile happy talk."[4]

In the appreciative inquiry process, problems tend to dissolve rather than be solved, to the amazement, I confess, of someone who spent years writing about the myriad problems pastors are asked to solve in today's church. Cooperrider and company are opening the way for people within any community—even those that are deeply conflicted or subject to the harshest conditions—to learn to trust each other when the right questions are asked and answered in a safe place and then acted upon.

Most people are surprised to discover how satisfying and joyful it is to reframe issues and then to ask and respond to appreciative questions that give themselves and others the space to talk about what is most important to them. For the past five years I've watched thousands go through "appreciative interviews" (one of the first steps in most appreciative agendas), and the consensus seems unanimous—the conversations are deeply moving and often transforming.

Appreciative questions call for answers that reveal appreciation, achievement, success, and important experiences, big or small, rather than breakdown and failure. They seek the commendable and steer away from judgment. They attend to memories, feelings, and imagination as well as analysis and opinions. Appreciative interviews allow people to safely pour out their hearts about what is good in their lives, and the result is new, often unexpected relationships and a shared energy that discourages quarrels and undercuts fears of inadequacy. Because people have so much difficulty at first talking about success and achievement without a counterpoint of problems and breakdown, practitioners learn to listen with enormous patience and to keep reframing the situation, always moving away from "understanding the problem" and toward "co-creating a transformed future."

Appreciative interviews achieve these remarkable outcomes by establishing higher ground for the dialogue, a place where what is most important to us allows the irritations and arguments of life to fade into perspective or just disappear. A safe personal discussion of our most cherished values and experiences, focused on matters transcending disagreement and conflict, bonds people. This bonding may not solve disagreements, especially at first, but it definitely changes people's feelings toward one another. With this kind of interview we immediately start to see the other person as a person, not an opponent or competitor. Even in conflicted communities it is difficult to spend two hours sharing with others what one most appreciates and values without emerging from the session with a friendly, even trusting, relationship.

Observing this over and over again finally disabused me of the long-held notion that trust requires years to establish. The alchemy can happen in a few hours, and the results deserve to be called miraculous. People become aligned with each other on the basis of their shared, reanimated primary commitments. Participants quit treating issues like wrestling matches and begin collaborating on what really matters.

APPRECIATIVE INQUIRY'S POTENTIAL

The success of this approach has led to its wide use, but the scope of appreciative inquiry's application signals its potential not as a silver bullet for solving the world's ills but as a healthier, more generative framework for developing relationships that make community meaningful. AI is being applied to Suzuki violin instruction, village development in Nepal, municipal and state revitalization projects from Chicago to northeast India's Nagaland, grassroots interfaith activities on five continents, manifold educational and medical institutions, and small businesses as well as corporations like GTE (now Verizon), where 67,000 employees and managers participated in revitalizing and transforming their company.

Both Case Western Reserve University and Benedictine University offer graduate programs in AI, and hundreds of individuals each year now participate in a multitude of appreciative inquiry workshops offered through the Taos Institute. More than 80 AI excellence-in-nonprofit projects have been sponsored in 70 countries through multimillion-dollar U.S. State Department funding. More than a thousand participate in an AI Internet listserve, a daily feast of rumination about studying what is alive and vital in our relationships. A cyber-archive overseen by the listserve's moderator catalogues daily postings ranging from corporate strategic planning and acquisitions to being a good spouse or parent from an appreciative point of view.

72 WWW.CONGREGATIONALRESOURCES.ORG

Distress within America's religious sector and a weary cynicism about the panoply of "new" organizational support structures may help explain the religious community's tardy response to appreciative inquiry. Statistics published in 1996 suggest that one in three American congregations fired its last pastor.[5] In most ecosystems this would be called an epidemic. Even more disturbing, concerted hard work to overcome our ecclesial "problems" has not helped the general health of the institution much.

However, initial appreciative applications in religious communities offer considerable hope. My own first contact with this novel, epistemologically based approach to community came when circumstances in 1994 placed me in the initial planning group of what later became the United Religions Initiative (URI), a global grassroots interfaith organization. From the start, Cooperrider and Dr. Diana Whitney (a frequent project partner and one of Cooperrider's most respected AI colleagues), along with several of their doctoral students, guided the organizational design process for URI. The sudden emergence of URI represents the largest start-to-fully-developed appreciative project in the world.

During a four-year process, many thousands were involved in writing and signing a URI charter. Three years after the signing, 211 active United Religions Initiative Cooperation Circles in 48 countries had self-organized, and the number continues to increase each month. Observing AI's approach to building strong, vital relationships among different faith communities in a very short period of time has been a continuing education.

AI's remarkable ability to engender trust and enthusiasm even among distrusting people bodes particularly well as we consider revitalizing life *within* faith communities. A few years ago Loren Mead's seminal work on the "once and future church" initiated a conversation about a new world and its implications for faith communities, and spoke persuasively about the need to develop new social architecture for the church. This chapter explores how appreciative inquiry might be a beneficial contributor in that quest.

The benefits for me start at a personal level. As an interfaith-formed Christian, the discipline of being an appreciative inquirer deepens my spiritual practice, enriches me theologically, and has improved my capacity to be a good husband and father.

The issue here, though, is generating vitality, engagement, and health in communities of believers. It's been argued that AI's most congruent, comfortable context ultimately will be the faith family because congregations already encourage AI's emphasis on values, storytelling, visioning, and serving the highest good—activities easier for a church council or pastor to broach than a corporation board or its CEO. In fact, Cooperrider's father was a Lutheran pastor who struggled painfully for years before successfully integrating his congregation racially, a drama that did not go unnoticed by a son who subsequently dedicated his life to community transformation without the acid etch of protracted conflict.

As an active United Church of Christ layman, David Cooperrider used AI to bring his own congregation through a remarkably successful journey—a transformation from being a liberal, mostly Caucasian church to being a fully multicultural and multiethnic faith family. Several years later his pastor remains happy with the outcome, and still incredulous that 400 members unanimously agreed about anything, much less a complex, successful strategy to open the multiethnic door.

Diversity also characterizes AI practitioners. Contributors to the emerging AI literature come from a rainbow of religious and spiritual traditions around the world. Buddhists sharing what they treasure about their tradition are as illuminating and compelling as Christians doing the same—within the family or between traditions. Like the ubiquitous golden rule, AI offers a perspective that seeks out the goodness in *any* system of relationships and then gives participants ways to magnify and give life to that goodness. The initial jolt I experienced upon encountering AI came in the form of a stunning realization that it systematically delivered on values the Christian family holds high but often fails to embody, such as taking "the least of these my children" as seriously as everyone else in the community, and booting the debilitating judgmentalism that so often polarizes and shreds faith families.

Here a warning is in order: on first contact, most folks recognize something familiar about appreciative inquiry. I've often heard, "Oh, we already do that in our church." Indeed, wherever community gathers, even in crisis and breakdown, one can find flashes of light and goodness worth appreciating, however hidden to the casual or critical eye. Fortunate congregations—particularly vital, healthy ones—can be amazingly appreciative in all sorts of ways; I dare say they will also be among the first to embrace the developing nuance and complexity of an approach that investigates appreciation systematically. But it is important to recognize that AI is not a miracle salve, not a set of self-help exercises or a one-chapter story. Instead, it is an empowering epistemological perspective that personalizes, honors, and learns from a community's best accomplishments and most precious values. Then it opens the horizon to take us miles beyond self-interest and old expectations, all the while staying grounded in the commitment bringing us to community in the first place.

Underestimating the scope of this opportunity is a danger. The "appreciative interview" that initiates and keeps punctuating most AI projects is so simple, powerful, and popular that you can head home, immediately use it with your congregation, and think you've mastered a new, creative fad. That would keep you from exploring "provocative propositions," an equally compelling appreciative tool for nurturing organizational health and enthusiasm, along with the self-organizing, ecologically based social technology that provides traction for delivering our dreams and visions. Simply put, under-estimating this methodology kills the goose with the golden egg.

As we begin, it seems appropriate to address a question: What is it that you want to learn about and achieve? For my part, I want to learn how we can liberate the capacity of the church and its millions of followers to really do what is most important in our faith, freed from the agonies of internal conflict, focused on what we do best, and effectively translating the gospel of love to a world in pain. More specifically, I'm thrilled to have this opportunity to introduce a new treasure house for revitalizing congregations and their members.

SOME INTRODUCTORY RESOURCES

Those who are seriously interested in making use of appreciative inquiry would do well to obtain one of the new textbooks address-ing the subject systematically: *Appreciative Inquiry: Change at the Speed of Imagination*[6] by Jane Magruder Watkins and Bernard J. Mohr or *The Power of Appreciative Inquiry: A Practical Guide to Positive Change* by Diana Whitney and Amanda Trosten-Bloom. *Appreciative Inquiry: Change at the Speed of Imagination* is a mine of information, summa-rizing the emerging field of appreciative inquiry and its origins. The authors' analysis of the discipline's "DNA" of interweaving principles and processes is particularly helpful. Identifying the "positive core," reframing situations, drafting appreciative questions, and all sorts of interactive processes relating to different aspects of the discipline are included, along with ten case studies and a six-page bibliography that add to its value.

A more recent book, *The Power of Appreciative Inquiry: A Practical Guide to Positive Change,* gets my vote for best treatment to date. This book surveys the same arena found in *Appreciative Inquiry: Change at the Speed of Imagination* and other texts but goes on to chart new territory, material that will catch the attention of appreciative students and practitioners everywhere. Whitney and Trosten-Bloom's case studies come from all sorts of communities and make their book a page-turner. The weaving together of history, philosophical underpinning, and practitioner wisdom is remarkably well done.

Whitney and Trosten-Bloom's most important contribution comes in their last chapter, where they ask people richly experienced in appreciative inquiry what makes it valuable. From the answers, the authors identify and discuss six freedoms.[7] They suggest these freedoms are "unleashed" in an appreciative approach to community:

- the freedom to be known in relationship
- the freedom to be heard
- the freedom to dream in community
- the freedom to choose to contribute
- the freedom to act with support
- the freedom to be positive

This evaluation of why the process is so helpful rings true to me, and I believe the six freedoms are a wonderful introduction to the whole field. However, I would not give up *Appreciative Inquiry: Change at the Speed of Imagination* for *The Power of Appreciative Inquiry*. Having read each of these books at least twice, I'll return to both regularly.

FROM QUANTUM PHYSICS TO PASTORAL LEADERSHIP

Then God said, "Let us make humankind in our image…"
—Genesis 1:26.

Before heading to the bookstore for some appreciative inquiry texts, though, it's fair to ask *how* AI is more than a savvy gloss on "accentuating the positive," to survey AI's principles and practice, and to briefly consider how religious communities can use this gift.

Appreciative inquiry is an expression of postmodern social constructionism. As such it is preoccupied with language, learning, relationship, and generativity in living systems—and spends little time with "objective reality" or "absolutes," including ultimate truth or the "right" way to do something. As Cooperrider and Whitney state in *Appreciative Inquiry*, "Constructionism replaces the *individual* with the *relationship* as the locus of knowledge by valuing the power of language to create our sense of reality."[8]

Social constructionists pay attention to how people create meaning through dialogue. They believe that history and culture shape every expression of meaning; thus they hold that reality is never objective. Human beings are shaped and conditioned by the idiosyncrasies of history and culture. At the same time, social constructionism does not see humankind as "determined" by its past or forever subject to the vagaries of war and human failure. Rather, it references science's most recent frontiers to offer philosophic grounding for the notion that human beings have the freedom to socially construct preferred futures for ourselves. Rather than trying to prove their case, they are hard at work embodying it, and case studies are proliferating.

Social constructionists recommend nurturing a radical agnosticism about our assumptions, about whatever "meaning worlds" we live in. They suggest cultivating an ability to distinguish between what is true and our own perceptions and conclusions.[9] Recommending humility about what we "know" and the limits of our understanding is accompanied with a commensurate respect for inclusiveness and diversity, values guarding against the elitism so tempting to institutions, meaning systems, and the ego.

Both physical and social sciences have played a role in creating and understanding AI. When Cooperrider's doctoral research identified the unexpected power of focusing on positive outcomes, he and his committee chair, Professor Suresh Srivastva, asked themselves why. A multidisciplinary team including researchers in anthropology, behavioral science, medicine, psychology, and sports came on board. The team's research included examining how images help athletes compete and studying the Pygmalion phenomenon and the placebo effect. Ultimately its inquiry focused on what Cooperrider now describes as "the relationship between our images and our behavior; between what we believe to be true and what we create as truth."[10]

The principles and practice of AI summarized below grew from this research, and Cooperrider's dissertation, completed in 1986, was titled "Appreciative Inquiry: Toward a Methodology for Understanding and Enhancing Organizational Innovation." In 1987 Srivastva and Cooperrider published "Appreciative Inquiry in Organizational Life," a professional, academic paper where the term "appreciative inquiry" was used in print for the first time.[11]

Research in physics, chemistry, and the life sciences also provides new ways to understand the power and efficacy of AI. Organization development and conflict resolution consultants often mention Margaret Wheatley as one who has provided an intellectual framework for understanding and learning about community in new ways. *Leadership and the New Science: Discovering Order in a Chaotic World*, second edition, is quite accessible and a good place to start.

Wheatley's venues are Harvard and major corporations all over the world that seek her counsel. Her words are clear, spare, evocative, and, through it all, joyful. She has the remarkable ability to walk scientific neophytes like me through quantum physics, chaos theory, and the chemical, biological dynamics of open, living systems, drawing from these cosmic laboratories fascinating insights about postmodern leadership.

She suggests that the mechanical way of understanding the world described by Sir Isaac Newton in the seventeenth century is inadequate and counterproductive today, even though most of our leadership and organizational models derive from Newtonian principles and assumptions. Communities are not machines, nor the sum of the rights and rules of membership. Rather, she contends, they are alive, dynamic, vital entities, capable of being influenced and co-created for good or bad. As Cooperrider has said repeatedly to students and colleagues, "Community is not a problem to be fixed but a mystery to be embraced."

In a post-Newtonian world, power does not devolve from position in a static hierarchy but from the vitality of relationships, wherever they emerge in the community. Outcomes are not predictable, and an infinite number of potentialities await our engagement. At the beginning of *Leadership and the New Science*, Wheatley writes, "The quantum world teaches that there are no pre-fixed definitely describable destinations. There are, instead, potentials that will form into real ideas depending on who the discoverer is and what she is interested in discovering."

Later in the book Wheatley records scientists' astonishment at discovering unpredictable, beautiful, self-organizing patterns emerging from random, chaotic data when it is carefully monitored. She shares recent discoveries in chemistry and biology about how open, living systems thrive and flourish, over and over again bringing the observations back to community and leadership. And she ruminates on the implications for leadership. Near the end of the book, she suggests new kinds of leaders for a world evolving beyond Newtonian assumptions and practices:

> Here is a *very* partial list of new metaphors to describe leaders: gardeners, midwives, stewards, servants, missionaries, facilitators, conveners. Although each takes a slightly different approach, they all name a new posture for leaders, a stance that relies on new relationships with their networks of employees, stakeholders, and communities. No one can hope to lead any organization by standing outside or ignoring the web of relationships through which all work is accomplished.[12]

From quantum physics, chaos theory, and self-organizing systems, then, pastoral images emerge for leadership. From chemistry and biology come compelling insights about how quanta—and people—relate to each other in meaningful ways. My own favorite gift from these discussions is the resurrection of freedom as a significant philosophic issue, not only in understanding our lives but the Creation. Uncompromising Newtonian arguments about cause and effect, paving the dismal way to determinism and predestination, are unlocked.

This is a serious cracking of the foundation of the intellectual assumptions you and I grew up with, but this cracking and its implications are liberating rather than devastating, renewing not confusing, and joyful rather than painful to all save those so invested in their own truth as to be blind or even abusive of truth anywhere else. Appreciative inquiry sits comfortably in the post-Newtonian world, unshackled from the causes of our woes and encouraging us to freely co-create the world we pause to envision. It proposes a world where achieving peace and justice as a norm for the human family is more than a good idea or an occasional accident of history—it's a possibility we can make real day by day.

In the church we have a healthy skepticism about any new system that offers to deliver the truth, in whatever form, so it helps to know that AI is not so much a new truth as a new way of approaching the truth, whatever your culture or faith, a new way of knowing what we know and knowing each other. AI pays attention to how adaptive and imitative we are, to how we define and are drawn into the future by the images we put in front of ourselves. So, through a growing, deepening set of relationships, the dialogue focuses on the most promising, appreciated, valuable images available, whatever the context.

An appreciative attitude does not ignore the brokenness, difficulties, or tragedies in life, but seeks to reframe them in reference to the light. My father grew up in the Depression singing the deeply appreciative "Count your blessings, name them one by one..." The poet in Psalm 139 speaks of God discovering light in the darkest, toughest places as a matter of course, and AI aspires to do the same.

THE DNA OF APPRECIATIVE INQUIRY: PRINCIPLES AND PRACTICE

Finally, beloved, whatever is true, whatever is honorable, whatever is just, whatever is pure, whatever is pleasing, whatever is commendable, if there is any excellence and if there is anything worthy of praise, think about these things.
—Philippians 4:8

A principle is a "basic truth, law, or assumption," my dictionary says. According to Whitney and Trosten-Bloom, eight principles[13] represent the essential values and assumptions made in appreciative inquiry, defining notions without which AI would be mischaracterized. Like any self-respecting product of American higher education, I approached these principles analytically at first, inspired by them but having lots of questions.

Living with the principles for several years has been instructive. Each one offers a particular insight into *knowing*, individually and in relationship. In this short space the principles can only be summarized and set next to what Watkins and Mohr identify as "generic processes" characterizing appreciative projects. They devote a chapter to bringing these principles and processes together in what they call the discipline's DNA.

Appreciative Principles

- **The Constructionist Principle.** From social constructionism comes the assumption that what we know about ourselves and how we know it is fateful because it so influences how we understand and relate to God, ourselves, our personal past, and the future's potential. Being offered safe ways to relate personally to people who were strangers, for instance, is not only a pleasure—it enriches us and opens new possibilities for the future. Taking personal as well as corporate responsibility for what we know and how we know is the implicit suggestion of the constructionist principle, and doing so opens up new universes.
- **The Simultaneity Principle.** This principle suggests that inquiry and change, learning and formation, happen simultaneously. When the first question is asked in any inquiry, change begins; the nature of that initial query, its assumptions, even its tone and overtones, will significantly shape and influence the outcome. Start any organizational study with a deficit analysis, detailing how failure has spread its ugly stain, and at the end of the day you are liable to have even less trust in the room and a magnified sense of breakdown. Start the same inquiry with an asset analysis, discovering what works well even during bad times, and you are liable to get to the end of the day with a sense of blessing, renewed trust, and unexpected enrichment.
- **The Anticipatory Principle.** This principle acknowledges how much the images and notions we put forward act as self-fulfilling prophesies. The athlete visually imagines crossing the finish line in front and does. Teacher expectations of students, redundant research attests, exceed intelligence or parental support as the most important predictor of a student's success. Expectation, in other words, is yeasty, an actual creative force influencing what is to come. It should not go unexamined or underutilized. Attending to the complex relationships between the best of what was, what is, what can be, and what will be—bridging memory's treasures with high visions of the future, is inspiring and remarkably generative. And, as they say in an appreciative Nepalese rural development project involving tens of thousands of villagers, "What you look for is what you find," and "Where you think you are going is where you are going."[14]
- **The Poetic Principle.** Great poems, like people, cannot be captured by a single explanation. The poetic principle assumes that,

as a poem can be read and interpreted in multiple ways, so relationship and community can be generated and understood in endlessly valuable, authentic, freely chosen ways. The principle gives us "permission" to understand the past and influence the future in terms of our own languages and experience, our deepest passions and commitment, and to become co-creators of this many-faceted world. Collaborating with fellow travelers at this level is a measure of a life well lived.

Wrapped implicitly within the poetic principle is a spiritually grounded respect for every human being, an assumption that, given the opportunity and the context, every person is a poet and an embodied poem, capable of unique discoveries, novel syntheses, and gifts for enriching relationships with other human beings.

- **The Positive Principle.** This principle extends Cooperrider's discovery in the early eighties and should not be confused with "the power of positive thinking." The "positive core" AI practitioners ask about is the essential goodness or value in a person, relationship, community, project, or goal. In the appreciative journey from fishing for best memories to embodying best visions, the positive core is the life-giving source of energy, the container holding everything together and making it significant to us. Identifying and supporting that positive core in asset-based language, exploring it with all the epistemological tools at our disposal—personal dialogue, history, dreams, imagination, reflection, analysis, and artistic expression, lends appreciative work its passion and excitement.

Appreciative Practice

At first read, the principles above may seem unrelated, lacking symmetry or an integral logic. Theorists have begun considering such symmetry, and the spiritual implications of the discipline are inspiring discussion.[15] Perhaps a unified appreciative theory will emerge. However, in researching this chapter, it became clear that organization development consultants who have mastered AI 101 and are committed to the approach tell different stories about AI's intellectual root structure than do therapists with similar experience and commitments. The poetic principle suggests that these stories may all be true and useful, mutually inclusive in the development of a new discipline. The principles themselves remain open-ended, available for thousands of different environments and applications, though more comfortably set within Wheatley's world than Newton's.

The Power of Appreciative Inquiry by Whitney and Trosten-Bloom exemplifies this sense of an alive, still developing discipline by proposing three additional principles (listed below), all based on the authors' work as practitioners.[16]

- **The Wholeness Principle.** This principle claims that "the experience of wholeness brings out the best in people, relationships, communities, and organizations." Wholeness, related etymologically to healing, is never a "singular story" but "a compilation of multiple stories, shared and woven together by the many people involved." Rather than focusing on commonalities, we learn to enjoy our differences, which leads to "higher ground rather than common ground."
- **The Enactment Principle.** This principle observes that "acting 'as if' is self-fulfilling," pointing to visionaries like Gandhi, Martin Luther King, Jr., Martha Graham, and Franklin D. Roosevelt, whose strength came from living their dreams in their daily lives. The claim is that "transformation occurs by living in the present what we most desire in the future" or, "more simply, positive change comes about as images and visions of a more desired future are enacted in the present."
- **The Free Choice Principle.** According to this principle, "people and organizations thrive when people are free to choose the nature and extent of their contribution." Allowing people to self-select their engagement and focus on their own interests as they get involved, "liberates both personal and organizational power."

An astonishing proliferation of appreciative applications taking advantage of these eight principles grows daily, most of them utilizing one-on-one, small group, and large group activities. Group process, of course, is an industry today in the church, as elsewhere. An appreciative approach, though, offers some special tools for any group facilitator. Watkins and Mohr call them "generic processes."[17] One might call them pedagogic priorities, winners in the contest to identify what is most important to learn, to know, no matter what you are studying.

Considering these processes in terms of appreciative questions dramatizes their usefulness, especially if we set them in context.

Let us imagine, say, that at our church we've decided to do a three-day appreciative inquiry into the kind of community we'd most like to become over the next five years. Inquiries can be broad gauge or narrow, as long as the positive core is clear and the questions truly appreciative. The initial process, the "positive framing," actually precedes the inquiry, beginning with planning, and continues until the end.[18]

- **Positive Framing.** As a person of faith, what is most important to you about the Church? And what do you most value about our particular congregation? What does it do when it's at its best? What are its most important, inspiring achievements as far as you are concerned?[19]
- **Identifying Sources of Vitality.** Would you tell me a story or two about when the congregation has been most alive and effective? What was the source of the vitality, as far as you could tell? What made it compelling? Where and how is God active in this congregation? What kind of involvement has been most valuable to you—and are there ways you'd like to be engaged but haven't yet tried?
- **Discovering Themes.** As we listen to the stories in our group about how we really love and value our church, as we hear about the mountaintop experiences we each have had, what are the common threads, the themes that emerge? As we consider these themes connecting us at the heart level, and as we think about our church's next five years, what are two or three of the topics you think should be explored as we consider our future?
- **Developing Images of the Future.** If our congregation exceeds our best expectations for growth, development, and ministry over the next five years, what could it look like in 60 months? As we set our sights on the kind of congregation we would like to become, what images would you choose to convey your own best vision of our future?
- **Creating the Future.** Staying focused on our sources of vitality, remembering the themes that emerged from our stories and the issues they evoked, looking again at images that draw us in the direction we wish to go, what kind of planning does our vision ask for, and how would each of us like to address the task? What will I do, what will we do together, in these coming weeks, toward becoming the vital, effective congregation we want to become?

The linear progression of these processes is obvious, but as a formal inquiry moves forward, the processes keep getting used in different ways. Appreciative projects usually begin with one-on-one extended conversations, experiences so popular that people mistakenly assume that "appreciative interview" is the same thing as "appreciative inquiry." Indeed, the questions, answers, images, and stories from the first interviews inform and resonate through the whole process.

After the interviews, the pairs usually join in working groups of eight, tell each other's stories, and report back to the full group, which can range from a few dozen to thousands. The group then works with these stories, identifies themes, and is encouraged to dream and imagine outside of the box, with individuals being given opportunities to consider different ways to be engaged.

Following this discovery process, various funneling processes are used to take the most engaging, compelling images and "provocative propositions" and begin designing strategies for the future. The provocative propositions turn out to be as compelling and important as the initial interviews. Grounded in the values, history, and best experiences of the community, the propositions stretch and challenge the status quo, set affirmative goals on the horizon, and call for involvement from everyone in the community. At the end people are given the time to start taking the first steps in creating the future.

In learning the methodological aspects of AI it is helpful to remember that the discipline emerged from a graduate school of management preparing consultants for corporate America. Hundreds of AI practitioners are concerned with engaging CEOs adequately to wean them away from problem solving. They have designed sophisticated project models for taking advantage of the principles and processes. Almost all of this interaction involves pairs of people who develop into small, interactive working groups who eventually find themselves aligned with the whole community, energized and working on a shared vision. Many of the projects focus on appreciative strategic planning, though strategic planning is only one of many different kinds of inquiry.

The most popular AI model is called the 4-D process. It emerged in Zimbabwe from an appreciative project building relationships between nonprofits taking care of children in various parts of Africa. Typically, a full-blown 4-D appreciative inquiry takes two to five days and guides a community of learners from *discovery* to *dreaming* to *design* to *destiny*, or, as some say, *delivery*. Becoming a practitioner means mastering the group dynamics and processes attending this approach as well as other models that map the movement from appreciating to envisioning to co-constructing to sustaining.

APPRECIATIVE CULTURE

One can discern growing interest in moving beyond the methodology of discreet inquiries to exploring sustainable appreciative culture. Two characteristics of most inquiries suggest some parameters for appreciative organizations: they make inclusiveness a priority, and every participant is treated with special care.

AI is frequently called a "whole system" approach because it seeks to engage *as many players as possible*. A good practitioner working with a congregation regarding strategic planning will probably suggest that young and old, members and friends, near and far be included if possible. What about the custodian, your banker, a local neighborhood leader, and a few representatives of the AA group that uses fellowship hall? To be sure, small leadership groups initiate the planning and decision makers need early engagement. But they will be asked: Who will participate? Can we enlarge the circle? Who is being left out? This is not simply an egalitarian commitment; in practical terms, every participant left out represents important gifts lost to the community.

A second appreciative characteristic, folded implicitly into both the principles and processes, is best put in the imperative: Treat *every* participant as an important player with gifts to contribute and leadership potential, a stakeholder whose feelings, engagement, commitment, and contribution can be significant. How we see each other and are open to each other's contributions has everything to do with eventual outcomes. The appreciative interviews and small report-back groups give everyone a sense of speaking freely and being heard seriously when an inquiry is launched. Three hours into the event this usually causes a corporate buzz, an excitement and sense of solidarity, even among people who are shy or in the habit of disagreeing with each other.

So personalized treatment for everyone in the community is the groundwork for appreciative culture. This fosters a generative, creative environment where deep personal relationships are nurtured and people's gifts and commitments are identified and taken seriously. It is also *self-organizing*, which is to say that—within the boundaries of the community, its purposes and agreements—people are encouraged to gravitate to issues and work groups they find compelling and collaborate with others in that arena. Appreciative leaders are excellent listeners and inviters, encouraging people to seek their heart's desire as they get involved, a significant shift from traditional routes to leadership responsibility. The implications of this new approach to "assigning" tasks does not become clear until, in reporting back highlights of appreciative interviews, a community's excitement about who it is at its best starts to bubble.

This self-organizing tendency represents another connection to the dynamics of *living* systems Wheatley describes. Self-organization can feel strange and threatening to anyone who grew up with mechanistic models like organizational charts: the church is a pastor, a council of leaders representing various committees, a choir or two, a congregation of worshippers, and a Sunday school—familiar territory. Thinking beyond expected roles, challenged to identify what in our midst is most important yesterday, today, and tomorrow, trusting that the system needs freedom and openness more than my guidance or old models, and then encouraging people to follow their hearts in achieving a dynamic new vision . . . this is frightening territory at first, unsettling our habits and assumptions. But living in the vibrancy and enthusiasm of an environment where everyone's gifts and engagement really matter quickly becomes its own reward. Nothing valuable need be lost.

Emerging issues about appreciative culture range from enlivening our personal lives to being sustainable appreciative organizations over the long term. Diana Whitney, besides working with corporate behemoths like British Airways and Verizon, leads a workshop in appreciative living and focuses the discussion around four questions:

- Who are you at your best, when you are most alive, engaged, and committed?
- What is your positive core, the life-giving center from which your best thinking and contributions emerge?
- What are your most courageous dreams?
- What are your greatest possibilities for serving the world?

The clarity and power of these simple questions indicate Whitney's mastery of the art of writing questions and coincidentally provide an extraordinary blueprint for church dialogue groups, young or old. Equally impressive is Whitney's generous willingness to share "the good stuff" of her workshop—these questions—in promotional materials, newsletters, and this book. It exemplifies the generosity of appreciative culture.

The first book about appreciative leadership was published in late 2001. *Appreciative Leaders: In the Eye of the Beholder* was edited by Marjorie Schiller (of the Avon Mexico inquiry), Bea Mah Holland, and Deanna Riley. In a thoroughly collaborative venture, 110 AI professionals and practitioners were invited to interview individuals they would characterize as "appreciative leaders." Eventually 28 accepted the challenge and did interviews; 15 stories were selected for the book—six from business, three from medical institutions, one from a police department, two from schools, and three from distinguished students of leadership.

From this research Schiller and her colleagues developed an appreciative leadership model with characteristics categorized three ways. In terms of values, *genuine, credible,* and *respectful* best describe these leaders. Characteristics the leaders associated with worldview were *envision, inspire,* and *holistic.* In terms of practices, an appreciative leader *challenges, encourages, enables, coaches, inquires,* and *dialogues,* a list reminiscent of Wheatley's leadership metaphors. The editors go on to identify five themes shared by the leaders profiled. Though none of those profiled are religious leaders, the first theme they share is that appreciative leaders are "belief-based with an explicit spiritual orientation and practice."[20]

Five years earlier, discussing postmodern principles and practices, Diana Whitney had written, "Notions of leadership shift dramatically from the leader as authority or one responsible for vision, action, and organization, to leader who fosters public conversations among multiple stakeholders. Leadership becomes a process of ensuring relational meaning making, of ensuring that multiple, diverse voices are heard, of creating and holding space for stories to be shared and meaning to be made among globally disparate and diverse people."[21]

These pastoral overtones of AI fit with conversations on the Internet about its spiritual dimensions. As we've seen, ontological, cosmological truth claims are not raised by the discipline itself, but utilizing AI's tools, paying attention to the positive core, and taking advantage of the poetic principle delivers many of us straight into the heart of our religious faith and spiritual practice. In sum, for folk who take their congregations as seriously as their families, AI represents a revitalizing approach to community.

APPRECIATIVE INQUIRY IN THE HOUSE OF GOD

I give you a new commandment, that you love one another.
Just as I have loved you, you also should love one another.
‒John 13:34.

No one is counting yet, but dozens of AI projects are taking place in religious communities in the United States and Canada. Gregorio Banaga's doctoral dissertation addressing AI and congregational strategic planning has helped generate considerable Catholic interest.[22] The work of Robert Voyle, an Episcopal priest and psychologist, and Helen Spector, an AI master practitioner who has worked with half a dozen Christian judicatory bodies, is particularly exciting. Appreciative methodology is making inroads in Fuller Seminary's curriculum,[23] and doctoral degrees in AI from Benedictine University are seeding the work in Catholic groups across the country, as documented in Susan Star Paddock's *Appreciative Inquiry in the Catholic Church*.[24] Still, at this writing appreciative inquiry in the house of God remains largely new territory waiting to be explored.

Appreciative work in congregations, as anywhere else, begins with reflections, then questions, and then sharing the questions. What are your best images and associations with your congregation? In what ways are people engaged, clearly committed, and happy to participate? What do members most appreciate and value about their faith, this faith family, and their engagement? What kind of opportunities do people have to really share each other's stories? When people are treated really well in your community—and in its ministry—what is it like?

Another good introduction might be utilizing the five processes Mohr and Watkins identify and taking to heart the appreciative values and reframed perspective we've been discussing. Identifying and reflecting on what is most life giving and meaningful to a faith family, giving members a safe place to talk about faith and values, and learning to discover, enjoy, and gain from *everyone's* engagement is a good starting place. Both clergy and lay leaders can look to what enlivens their communities and characterizes them at their best and begin to extrapolate. "Appreciative" possibilities in the context of a faith family are endless. One that has been particularly meaningful to me relates to corporate prayer.

A few months prior to meeting David Cooperrider in 1996, I held a part-time interim pastorate in a small rural congregation that some said was in death throes and needed a dignified funeral. Instead it bounced back and is thriving today. During an 18-month interim we approached the prayers of the people in a new way. Following the Sunday sermon, I took paper and pen and walked into the middle of the congregation, barely a dozen those first few months. I invited them to reflect on the past week and share things they were thankful for and things that concerned them. People poured out their hearts. Following what were sometimes 15-minute discussions, I would lead them in prayer, mentioning all the thanksgiving and all the petitions, and together we concluded with the Lord's Prayer.

A year later the coffee-hour conversations were all about answered prayer. It didn't dawn on me until three years later, after taking an appreciative inquiry intensive, that we had developed an appreciative approach to the prayers of the people in that small church. We heard each other talk about what was important enough to be thankful for and important enough to share with God as a concern. As the year progressed, the subject of answered prayers came up again and again, to continued thanks.

Similar explorations await every aspect of congregational life. Voyle divides his time between interim ministries and appreciative training and coaching. He is full of examples about the difference AI makes in his ministries.

For years he has led clergy trainings on sexual abuse in the church—a tough, important subject full of unhappy, fearful issues. After being introduced to AI, he began similar trainings by asking people to share, one-on-one, stories of experiences in which they felt incredibly respected. What made being respected so important? And what might we learn about generating quality respect for everyone? The tough issues still must be addressed if we want congregations safe from predators and abuse. But reframed, the energy can change. We learn the joys of exemplary, gracious behavior as a context for creating safety and accountability. As a golfer noted, "Telling me *not* to hit it into the trap just about guarantees I'll hit the trap!"

So at Voyle's workshops now, the emphasis shifts away from negative expectations and images, away from "Why?!" and a judgmental attitude, moving instead toward asking, "What do we know about genuinely safe, respectful, involved relationships, particularly when some are laity and some clergy? And how can we best create these kinds of relationship in our life together?

I stumbled into an appreciative approach to prayer; more consciously all the elements of liturgy might be revisited and reinvigorated through an appreciative perspective, particularly when artists and their work are included. Rereading scripture from an appreciative viewpoint is illuminating. The familiar passages used in this chapter jump out and empower me in new ways these days.

Spiritual formation (at both personal and corporate levels), homiletics, pastoral care,[25] and congregational dynamics, including conflict resolution,[26] can all be richly rewarded using appreciative approaches and protocols.

A host of hermeneutical and theological issues await discussion. Here at the starting gate we might note that AI is a treasury of applied epistemology, and that ontology is nowhere to be found except implicitly and potentially, embodied only when an actual community makes a commitment to know itself in new ways and asks its first appreciative question. Juxtaposing *applied systems of knowing* and *implied systems of being*, thereby sidestepping any specific cosmological or ontological truth claims, may be the empowering factor in AI's success in hundreds of different kinds of environments. Put simply, AI can help all of us ask better questions, including those of us in faith families.

Religious education opportunities are a universe to themselves. AI assumes that lifelong learning and development are as important to institutions as to individuals. Much of this territory is already being explored in a variety of institutional environments. One of the 21 principles of the United Religions Initiative Charter, for instance, states, "We are committed to organizational learning and adaptation."

Ultimately, issues of mission, enrollment, and vision deserve a full appreciative exploration. First, I suspect, will come hard questions about appreciative ethics, morality, justice, and peace;[27] these tough issues may be the most illuminating and transforming of all. Perhaps in tackling them appreciatively the Armageddon scenarios tempting literalists from all sorts of traditions will fade like a bad

dream, and the joyful work of providing spiritually grounded respect and an opportunity for a good life to every person on the planet
can proceed.

We must remember that this new discipline comes from people
preoccupied with organizational dynamics, and church administration, so barren an arena in some churches, can also be revitalized
appreciatively. Clergy evaluation, for instance, is one of the toughest issues in the ecclesiastical portfolio, as attested to by books,
courses, training, and continuing bad experiences. An appreciative
approach shifts the focus toward mutual valuation exercises that foster growth and improvement and a shared sense of collaboration.[28]

Pursuing any of this systematically is impossible, however, without a transformed frame of reference.[29] Voyle says a conversion is
required, by which he means "a profound reorientation in the way
you look at the world, yourself, and God."[30] It means developing
one's perceptions and valuation to discern and pay attention to what
is most life-giving, most valuable, rather than focusing on cause
and blame when difficulties arise.

It means attending more to the abundance of God's love than to
the drama of human sinfulness, or, as Voyle says, "Did Jesus come
to stop us sinning or to make us loving?" He thinks that until love is
the actual focus of relationship, God has little room to participate.
His first sermon at a new interim post is always titled, "What in
God's Name Is Going on Here?" As long as God is part of the story,
he is interested, he says. But if it's last year's gossip, he just doesn't
have the time. Rather than exorcise demons, he seeks to create a
safe, sacred space where the community can identify and attend to
what is most important about its life now and in the future.

Helen Spector, as far as I know, is the first AI practitioner to do a
full-blown 4-D appreciative inquiry with large judicatory bodies
and denominational leadership groups. A strong-willed, controver-
sial bishop had retired, and the new bishop invited Helen to help
design a transition process and event. A large two-day gathering
was planned. First, all judicatory congregations and organizations
organized one-on-one appreciative interviews focused on their most
life-giving experiences of ministry; stories from the reports helped
shape the coming event.

Seven hundred participated, including representatives from all
judicatory congregations and organizations, 110 youth, and 30
trained as facilitators. After one-on-one interactions, small groups

self-organized around five denominational vows (with individuals selecting the group focused on the vow they found most compelling) to envision the work of the people of the diocese over the next 10 years. Later, groups were organized geographically so that people would be working with neighbors as they dreamed and made specific plans about the future of their church.

The bishop made it clear that the days of dicta from the top were over. "Tell me where your heart is leading you, the work you want to embrace," he said. "That is what we will support." Many were skeptical, but those who believed made serious commitments and went to work, and the energy and goodwill generated by the end of the second day exceeded everyone's expectations.

Spector points out that it could not have happened without the courage of the bishop "not to have the answer." She believes this willingness is the toughest appreciative issue for clergy. "From a leadership standpoint, to be able to hold the space for your people, to not give them the answer, to encourage and believe in their capacity even when they don't know they have it in them. The answer lies within them if they listen." And that, she says, is what the appreciative interview is all about. "Courage comes from leaders believing that it's in the people—that the 'story' and the capacity to be faithful is there in them—and holding the space by not telling them the answer. That is hard. There is always somebody with 'the answer.'"[31] Spector's experience is that the power of the story told and listened to by every member represents the real treasury. If handled with care and respect in an expanding circle, these storytellers, their faith journeys, and their talents represent the necessary resources to renew and transform the community and its members.

Another of Spector's projects, involving 50 leaders of a major denomination, led one executive to report, "Appreciative inquiry has enhanced our functioning, our ability to serve congregations. And our work has become energy giving instead of energy draining." Asked about her own most important learning, she said it was "the ability to frame questions appreciatively."[32]

Susan Paddock's *Appreciative Inquiry in the Catholic Church* is a short but splendid first book about Christian community and AI. Appreciative theory is clearly summarized in six quick pages. Then Paddock, a family psychotherapist and convert to Catholicism, devotes her second chapter to the congruence of AI with Catholic social teaching, Pope Paul VI's teaching on dialogue, and themes from Vatican II. Throughout the text, scripture is used to underline appreciative notions, and the final pages are an invitation to start using AI in your own community.

In this context, chapters are devoted to stories about Catholic congregations and agencies using AI for local and global community building, strategic planning and mission statements, enhancing pastoral transitions, and spiritual renewal. Considerable Episcopal interest and interfaith applications also receive a chapter. Along the way, dozen of appreciative projects are detailed, including Catholic Relief Services, a group of churches and schools in Garfield Heights, Ohio, the Diocese of Cleveland (half a dozen projects), the Archdiocese of Los Angeles, Catholic Health Association of Canada, Newman Center—Bucknell University, four religious communities, half a dozen congregations, and more. In each story, Paddock emphasizes the specific questions used in the inquiry and the results. A quick read, this book immediately demonstrates the remarkable gift appreciative inquiry represents for any community of faith and practice.

If this summary seems a bit enthusiastic it's because I'm still a beginner, hungry to discover better ways to nurture relationship and healthy collaboration, to revitalize and magnify the faith community's generative power in a world badly in need of more help from faithful folk. David Cooperrider makes a point whenever he begins a new project, whatever the context, that he is not an *expert*. But he is a fellow *inquirer* who has paid considerable attention to how we learn and what we learn.

As such he and a growing number of colleagues are happy to help create appreciative questions, to introduce the notion of positive core, to share this novel social technology of powerful relationship and trust formation. They are happy to help design a venture's learning/transformation process, focusing on what is most important to the venture's purpose and its best possible outcomes. And the church and any congregation can become the beneficiaries of these processes. The appreciative congregation, if it emerges in force, will come from faith families everywhere, with the wit and wisdom to learn how to love each other—children of God each one—in new, appreciative, and creative ways.

As an activist in interfaith relationship development, I was asked to facilitate a public discussion including a Christian seminary president, a rabbi, and two Muslim community leaders. The discussion came two months after the September 11 tragedy, and it was tempting to wade into the problem from a hundred different directions.

Instead, I began by asking each participant, "What is it that makes your faith so precious to you?" Then I asked about the gifts—the wisdom and insights—that their extraordinary traditions have to offer us about peace, about comforting the afflicted, about justice, about living when there is no justice, and about relating to the stranger. More than 150 neighborhood folks representing a dozen different faiths came together in a local city hall that night.

After the initial hour, many went to the microphone to ask questions and make their own contributions. Fascinating information was presented and hard issues were raised, *mea culpa* was heard, and the tone of the talk, fully engaged, was consistently respectful. The evening concluded as it began, with prayer and goodwill, with seeds of a plan to come together across faith divisions on a regular basis to learn from each other, and to give the local community a new kind of religious voice. Two years later, a group meets regularly, provides interfaith programs, and keeps the dialogue going.

That community evening was hardly an AI intervention, yet we enjoyed a warm, provocative appreciative culture for a few hours, and the people came out of it energized, enthusiastic, and wanting more. It is the kind of environment and experience one hopes for not only between strangers but within families, including faith families. May it be so in yours.

In benediction, let me invite you to reconsider what the author of Ephesians meant when he wrote, "Now to him who by the power at work within us is able to accomplish abundantly far more than all we can ask or imagine, to him be glory in the church and in Christ Jesus to all generations..." (Ephesians 3:20).

WHERE TO LEARN MORE

The following short sampler of available materials on appreciative inquiry represents the cream of the crop from one reader's perspective.

For reasons mentioned above, I think Whitney and Trosten-Bloom's *The Power of Appreciative Inquiry: A Practical Guide to Positive Change* is currently the most important item in the AI bibliography. And anyone who wonders whether an appreciative approach is appropriate in religious, spiritual settings needs to read

Susan Starr Paddock's *Appreciative Inquiry in the Catholic Church* and have their fears allayed.

The most recent edition of Sue Hammond's *The Thin Book* is an engaging nontechnical booklet that quickly and clearly introduces and sets the AI context for newcomers. If you need a brief introductory text—for a class or board of directors, for instance—you might want to use Cooperrider and Whitney's even shorter 40-page summary, simply titled *Appreciative Inquiry*. It's the best of many short versions.

As noted above, Watkins and Mohr's book, *Appreciative Inquiry: Change at the Speed of Imagination*, was the first thorough textbook about AI. A perfect companion volume for a college or graduate course would be the new edition of *Lessons from the Field*, a book that quickly sold out its first edition and is now back in print. *Lessons* is a collaborative collection of stories and resources, including the essays by Mac Odell and Gregorio Banaga, Jr., mentioned above. The book surveys a number of the most successful AI projects here and abroad and has the largest AI bibliography in print.

Anyone wishing to swim in deeper water can turn to *Appreciative Inquiry: Rethinking Human Organization toward a Positive Theory of Change*. This dense anthology collects 18 essays exploring theoretical aspects of the discipline—heavy slogging if you haven't been in a graduate seminar recently but important for the serious student. It includes Cooperrider and Srivastva's historic 1987 essay, "Appreciative Inquiry in Organizational Life," which challenged the tenets of traditional organization development. "Positive Image, Positive Action: The Affirmative Basis of Organizing," which may be Cooperrider's most important theoretical essay, and Gervase Bushe's provocative "Five Theories of Change Embedded in Appreciative Inquiry" are included as well.

Two more recent books are helpful for leaders who have already been introduced to the discipline: *The Appreciative Organization* is a collaborative project shared by six of AI's wisest elders. *An Encyclopedia of Positive Questions, Vol. 1* is the first in a series, it is hoped, as people everywhere learn to craft powerful appreciative questions; questions for volume two are being solicited.

AI Practitioner: The International Newsletter of AI Best Practices, a quarterly, is the first periodical to be published about the discipline and is available only on the Web by subscription.[33] Equally important, and free, is the AI listserv.[34] The first Web site devoted to AI and religious leadership is www.clergyleadership.org. Founded by Rob Voyle, it includes some valuable resources (for example, appreciative evaluation tools) that can be downloaded.

Case Western Reserve University and Benedictine University offer graduate degrees in AI. The Taos Institute[35] schedules ongoing workshops and publishes books about AI, three of which are included below. Another valuable resource is the Appreciative Inquiry Commons (online at ai.cwru.edu), a worldwide portal devoted to the fullest sharing of academic resources and practical tools on appreciative inquiry and the rapidly growing discipline of positive change.

Notes

1. Jane Magruder Watkins and Bernard J. Mohr, *Appreciative Inquiry: Change at the Speed of Imagination* (San Francisco: Jossey-Bass, 2001), 123ff.
2. David Cooperrider and Diana Whitney, *Appreciative Inquiry* (San Francisco: Berrett-Koehler, 2000), 12–13
3. Paul Chaffee, *Accountable Leadership* (San Francisco: Jossey-Bass, 1996), 4–5.
4. It has never been a solo effort, and could not be, given appreciative inquiry's dependence on relationship and collaboration. Starting with his own mentor and frequent co-author, Suresh Srivastva, Cooperrider shares credit for the growing wealth of appreciative wisdom and success with dozens of academics and practitioners creatively contributing to the field, as the bibliography demonstrates.
5. Jane Magruder Watkins and Bernard J. Mohr. *Appreciative Inquiry: Change at the Speed of Imagination* (San Francisco: Jossey-Bass, 2001), xxix.
6. Watkins and Mohr, *Appreciative Inquiry.*
7. Diana Whitney and Amanda Trosten-Bloom, *The Power of Appreciative Inquiry: A Practical Guide to Positive Change* (San Francisco: Berrett-Koehler, 2003), 238ff.
8. David L. Cooperrider and Diana Whitney, *Appreciative Inquiry* (San Francisco: Berrett-Koehler, 2000), 26–27.
9. Kenneth Gergen's work, in particular his *Toward Transformation in Social Knowledge*, 2nd Edition (Thousand Oaks, CA: Sage Publications, 1994), has had a strong influence on AI.
10. Watkins and Mohr, 29. Cooperrider's seminal essay on the role of image, published in 1990, is titled "Positive Image; Positive Action: The Affirmative Basis of Organizing."

11. This essay and the one mentioned in the previous note are both re-printed in *Appreciative Inquiry: Rethinking Human Organization toward a Positive Theory of Change* (Champaign, IL: Stipes Publishing, 2000).

12. Margaret Wheatley, *Leadership and the New Science: Discovering Order in a Chaotic World* (San Francisco: Berrett-Koehler, 2001), 165.

13. The first five of these principles, say Whitney and Trosten-Bloom on page 53 of *The Power of Appreciative Inquiry: A Practical Guide to Positive Change*, are derived directly from the early writing of Cooperrider and Srivastva (*Appreciative Management and Leadership*, 1990). The other three were added by Whitney and Trosten-Bloom themselves and are presented in their book *The Power of Appreciative Inquiry: A Practical Guide to Positive Change* (San Francisco: Berrett-Koehler, 2003).

14. Mac Odell's "Appreciative Planning and Action: Experience from the Field," a chapter in *Lessons from the Field* (see bibliography), tells the story of working in hundreds of Nepalese villages. The account is a particularly moving and instructive example of AI at work.

15. "Spirituality at Work" by Diana Whitney is an essay about taking your spirituality to work in ways that challenge and inspire your colleagues rather than make them wary. It was published in the online Appreciative Inquiry Newsletter (No. 7, November 1999). www.aradford.co.uk/Pagefiles/07newsletter.htm.

16. Diana Whitney and Amanda Trosten-Bloom, *The Power of Appreciative Inquiry: A Practical Guide to Positive Change* (San Francisco: Berrett-Koehler, 2003), 69–79.

17. Watkins and Mohr, 39. Their summary language defining "generic processes" is plain and instructive: choose the positive as the focus of inquiry; inquire into stories of life-giving forces; locate themes that appear in the stories and select topics for further inquiry; create shared images for a preferred future; find innovative ways to create that future. As they themselves say, though, using these learning categories or procedures without appreciating the principles compromises the inquiry and its power.

18. The following questions are not a protocol for a proposed interview. If they were, however, they would be preceded by several paragraphs that would set a more specific context for the interview, preparing the ground for the questions.

19. Most people have difficulty at first expressing what they appreciate without dragging in what they do not appreciate. Facilitators learn to keep setting aside the problematic by focusing on what is valuable.

20. Marjorie Schiller, Bea Mah Holland, Deanna Riley, eds., *Appreciative Leaders: In the Eye of the Beholder* (Chagrin Falls, OH: Taos Institute, 2001), 162.

21. Diana Whitney, "Postmodern Principles and Practices for Large Scale Organization Change and Global Cooperation," *Appreciative Inquiry: Rethinking Human Organization toward a Positive Theory of Change* (Champaign, IL: Stipes Publishing, 2000), 238.

22. The fruit of Gregorio Banaga's work can be found in "A Spiritual Path to Organizational Renewal" in *Lessons from the Field: Applying Appreciative Inquiry,* edited by Sue Anise Hammond and Cathy Royal (Plano, TX: Thin Book Publishing Company, 1996), 261–271.

23. Mark Lau Branson, Homer L. Goddard Associate Professor of Ministry of the Laity at Fuller Theological Seminary, recently published *Memories, Hopes, and Conversations: Appreciative Inquiry and Congregational Change* (Herndon, VA: Alban Institute, 2004).

24. Susan Starr Paddock, *Appreciative Inquiry in the Catholic Church* (Plano, TX: Thin Book Publishing Company, 2003).

25. Dozens of medical and therapeutic appreciative projects are surfacing, mentioned in AI listserve postings and publications, a number of which should interest pastors and counselors.

26. At the Interfaith Center at the Presidio in San Francisco and Pacific School of Religion, Peggy Green has developed a project titled "First Be Reconciled" for generating friendly, collaborative relationships between evangelical and gay and lesbian Christians.

27. Two weeks following the tragedies of September 11, 2001, 60 peacemakers gathered at American University in Washington, DC, for a three-day training in AI called "Positive Approaches to Peacebuilding: A Practitioners' Exploration." The majority were on-the-ground peacemakers from Bosnia, Jerusalem, West Africa, and similarly conflicted areas of the world, along with the agencies serving them.

28. Protocol for an appreciative congregational valuation process can be found at www.ClergyLeadership.com.

29. The same point pertains to the business community. AI requires a CEO to look at a corporation with new eyes. Getting that to happen is one of the toughest steps in landing an organization development contract using AI in the business community.

30. Conversation, October 15, 2001.

31. Conversation, August 21, 2001.

32. Conversation, December 12, 2001.

33. You can contact the editor, Anne Radford, at annelondon@aol.com or subscribe to the publication at www.aradford.co.uk.
34. www.ailist@business.utah.edu.
35. www.taosinstitute.org.

BIBLIOGRAPHY

Anderson, Harlene, David Cooperrider, Kenneth J. Gergen, Mary Gergen, Sheila McNamee, and Diana Whitney. *The Appreciative Organization.* Chagrin Falls, OH: Taos Institute, 2001.

Cooperrider, David, and Diana Whitney. *Appreciative Inquiry.* San Francisco: Berrett-Koehler Communications, 2000.

Cooperrider, David, Peter F. Sorensen, Jr., Diana Whitney, and Therese F. Yaeger, eds. *Appreciative Inquiry: Rethinking Human Organization toward a Positive Theory of Change.* Champaign, IL: Stipes Publishing, 2000. Originally published in *OD Journal* (Winter 1996).

Cooperrider, David, Diana Whitney, Bea Mah Kaplan, and Amanda Trosten-Bloom, eds. *An Encyclopedia of Positive Questions, Vol. 1.* Bedford Heights, OH: Lakeshore Communications, 2001.

Hammond, Sue Annis, and Cathy Royal, eds. *Lessons from the Field: Applying Appreciative Inquiry.* Plano, TX: Thin Book Publishing Company, 2001.

Hammond, Sue Annis. *The Thin Book of Appreciative Inquiry.* Plano, TX: Thin Book Publishing Company, 1996.

Paddock, Susan Star. *Appreciative Inquiry in the Catholic Church.* Plano, TX: Thin Book Publishing Company, 2003.

Schiller, Marjorie, Bea Mah Holland, and Deanna Riley, eds. *Appreciative Leaders: In the Eye of the Beholder.* Chagrin Falls, OH: Taos Institute, 2001.

Watkins, Jane Magruder, and Bernard J. Mohr. *Appreciative Inquiry: Change at the Speed of Imagination.* San Francisco: Jossey-Bass, 2001.

Wheatley, Margaret. *Leadership and the New Science: Learning about Organizations from an Orderly Universe.* San Francisco: Berrett-Koehler Communications, 1994.

Whitney, Diana, and Amanda Trosten-Bloom. *The Power of Appreciative Inquiry: A Practical Guide to Positive Change.* San Francisco: Berrett-Koehler Communications, 2003.

Resources on Appreciative Inquiry from the Congregational Resource Guide

Anderson, Harlene, Kenneth J. Gergen, Sheila McNamee, David Cooperrider, Mary Gergen, and Diana Whitney. **The Appreciative Organization.** Chagrin Falls, OH: Taos Institute, 2001.

> In this 55-page volume, the authors argue that the old hierarchical organization is no longer effective and needs to be replaced with a model based on the following premises: nothing will motivate people unless it has meaning for them; meaning is created through relationships; and appreciating others' words and actions increases value within relationships, organizations, and the world at large. The authors use examples to flesh out these concepts, contrasting the results produced by existing organizational structures, leadership approaches, evaluation methods, and communication styles with those that "appreciative organization" methods have produced in their own work.

Appreciative Inquiry Commons
ai.cwru.edu

> Hosted by Case Western Reserve University's Weatherhead School of Management, this Web site is a worldwide portal to academic resources and tools on appreciative inquiry and the discipline of positive change. Among its many offerings are tools, practical methodologies, and stories from the field; listings of upcoming workshops and conferences; listings of programs offered by consulting firms; universities and institutions with appreciative inquiry programming; annotated bibliographies of publications on appreciative inquiry, and appreciative inquiry resources available in seventeen foreign languages.

Branson, Mark Lau. **Memories, Hopes, and Conversations: Appreciative Inquiry and Congregational Change.** Herndon, VA: Alban Institute, 2004.

> Mark Lau Branson offers an account of how one Presbyterian church used appreciative inquiry to understand its history, encourage its members to discover and pursue their dreams, and call a new pastor who could help make those dreams reality. He makes clear that AI—an attitude as well as a process—broadly applies in many settings. Branson outlines a five step sequence: (1) focus on the positive; (2) inquire into stories of life-giving forces; (3) locate themes and topics for further inquiry; (4) create shared images for a preferred future; and (5) find innovative ways to create that future. He discusses the theory and provides biblical grounding for this work. He outlines the process in some detail, yet continues telling a story—how the theory played out in a real Presbyterian congregation. He proves his point by helping the reader experience it.

Clergy Leadership Institute
www.clergyleadership.com

> The mission of the Clergy Leadership Institute is to increase ministers' effectiveness by offering training that integrates theological reflection with organizational psychology. The Institute believes appreciative processes are the most effective way of enabling people to manifest their God-given talents and abilities. The Institute's Web site features detailed information about its appreciative inquiry and leadership training programs, clergy sabbatical programs, clergy search resources, coaching services for personal and professional development, and consulting for congregational development.

Cooperrider, David, Peter F. Sorensen, Jr., Diana Whitney, and Therese F. Yaeger, eds. **Appreciative Inquiry: Rethinking Human Organization toward a Positive Theory of Change.** Champaign, IL: Stipes Publishing L.L.C., 2000.

> This is a collection of articles on the change methodology known as appreciative inquiry, which focuses on what is best within an organization, defines what makes that possible, helps participants

create a vision that goes beyond those circumstances and experiences, and assists them in developing a means to transform their vision into reality. This book provides an overview of the philosophy and methodology of appreciative inquiry, its various applications, and the possibility of its universal application. Intended to serve as a source book for students of organization development, this book is written in an academic style and its content goes far beyond simple explanations and examples of appreciative inquiry, drawing from a variety of disciplines and research to illustrate the basis and power of this approach to change.

Hammond, Sue Annis, **The Thin Book of Appreciative Inquiry.** Plano, TX: Thin Book Publishing Company, 1996.

This slim volume is designed for those wishing to get a quick overview of what appreciative inquiry is and what it can do. Written by a change management consultant who has been inspired by the results she has achieved by using appreciative inquiry in her own work with client companies, this book includes easy-to-digest examples of appreciative inquiry principles, brief and inspiring case studies, sample questions, and a resource guide for those wishing to study appreciative inquiry in more depth. A quick and easy read, this is a great first book for those wishing to learn more about this methodology.

Hammond, Sue Annis, and Cathy Royal, eds. **Lessons from the Field: Applying Appreciative Inquiry,** Revised Edition. Plano, TX: Thin Book Publishing Company, 2001.

This book shares the theory and processes of appreciative inquiry through the stories of organizations and communities who have experienced the power of this change methodology. Each case study provides rich detail of the process undertaken, and the author of each of these stories shares what was done and what was learned during the appreciative inquiry process. In addition to these case studies, this book includes answers to commonly asked questions about the methodology, sample questions, graphic models of the process, and an extensive resource section. This is a book for those wishing to learn not only about the principles and practices of appreciative inquiry but also to understand the results it is capable of producing in a variety of settings.

Mead, Loren B. **The Once and Future Church: Reinventing the Congregation for a New Mission Frontier.** Bethesda, MD: Alban Institute, 1991.

> Mead asserts that the church's understanding of mission is shifting as once-familiar clergy and laity roles change and as church executives are called to provide more support with fewer resources. The result, he says, is that a new church is being born around us. While it was once assumed that a church's mission was to convert persons in far-off lands, now churches must focus on crises in their surrounding communities. And, whereas clergy were formerly assumed to be powerful guarantors of community morality, now they must help laity engage in and serve a turbulent world. While alerting us to the challenges of reinventing the new church, Mead also offers hopeful signs of the future church's emergence. Church leaders will find in this book a deeper understanding of the critical opportunities facing those who seek to renew a church that will become, in Mead's words, "a centering presence from which we may serve the new world that God is creating around us."

Paddock, Susan. **Appreciative Inquiry in the Catholic Church.** Plano, TX: Thin Book Publishing Company, 2003.

> In this short but informative book, author Susan Paddock summarizes in just six pages the theory of appreciative inquiry. She then documents the compatibility between appreciative inquiry and Catholic theology. Using case studies of organizations such as Catholic Relief Services, the Diocese of Cleveland, and a variety of Catholic schools and parishes, she explores the effective use of appreciative inquiry to build relationships and community, to do strategic planning and create mission statements, to enhance transitions, and to facilitate spiritual renewal. In her account of these case studies, Paddock emphasizes the specific appreciative inquiry questions that were posed and the results they achieved.

Ricketts, Miriam W., and James E. Willis. **Experience AI: A Practitioner's Guide to Integrating Appreciative Inquiry with Experiential Learning.** Chagrin Falls, OH: Taos Institute, 2001.

> This book outlines the transformational organization change process known as appreciative inquiry (AI), and how its results can be enhanced and accelerated with experiential learning (EL), which

involves immersing participants in structured and shared experiences that encourage risk taking followed by meaningful reflection on these experiences. In just 78 pages, the authors initiate an inquiry into the power of embedding EL exercises in the AI process to build trust and rapport, create community, enhance risk-taking, build buy-in for change, and accelerate the change process. Four client stories highlight how integrating experiential learning exercises with appreciative inquiry methods can maximize learning. Includes a glossary of terms and phrases.

Schiller, Marjorie, Bea Mah Holland, and Deanna Riley, eds. **Appreciative Leaders: In the Eye of the Beholder.** Chagrin Falls, OH: Taos Institute, 2001.

Building on the foundation of the appreciative inquiry methodology used in organizational consulting, this book examines how appreciative practices can lend power to the leadership role. This exploration takes place largely through stories of leaders who are transforming their industries or communities through appreciative ways of communicating, relating, and envisioning. Insights and inspiration can be found throughout the stories in this book, and the final chapter offers readers a model of appreciative leadership. Also included is a discussion of the characteristics, actions, attitudes, and worldviews of appreciative leaders. This is a helpful resource for anyone seeking a guide to a mode of leadership that honors the individual, brings out the best in others, and creates through vision and a desire to better the world.

The Taos Institute
www.taosinstitute.net

The Taos Institute is a nonprofit educational institution focused on social constructionist dialogues—the processes by which humans generate meaning together. Its Web site includes information about the Institute, its workshops on social construction and, more specifically, appreciative inquiry, as well as ordering information about its books: *Appreciative Leaders: In the Eye of the Beholder; The Appreciative Organization;* and *Experience AI: A Practitioner's Guide to Integrating Appreciative Inquiry and Experiential Learning.*

United Religions Initiative
www.uri.org

> The United Religions Initiative is based in daily, enduring interfaith
> cooperation. Its Web site features information about a variety of URI
> peacebuilding initiatives, press releases about recent interfaith efforts
> and accomplishments, resources and education about a variety of
> religions and spiritual traditions, a link to a URI children's Web site,
> descriptions and ordering information regarding URI publications,
> and links to other interfaith peacebuilding sites.

Watkins, Jane Magruder, and Bernard J. Mohr. **Appreciative Inquiry:
Change at the Speed of Imagination.** San Francisco: Jossey-Bass/
Pfeiffer, 2001.

> This is one of a series of books about cutting-edge developments
> and state-of-the-art practices in the field of organization develop-
> ment. This volume describes appreciative inquiry, a theory and
> practice for approaching change from a holistic framework. The
> authors define AI, outline the theory and research on which it is
> based, and describe the current state of the practice. They then
> describe in detail the five core processes of this methodology:
> focusing on the positive, inquiring into stories of life-giving forces,
> creating shared images for a preferred future, and innovating ways
> to create the preferred future. In addition to providing the ratio-
> nale for of each of these processes, the authors also provide case
> studies to show how they work. The book closes with a discussion
> of AI as a new paradigm for research and evaluation and answers
> to frequently asked questions about AI theory and technique.

Wheatley, Margaret. **Leadership and the New Science: Discovering Order
in a Chaotic World.** San Francisco: Berrett-Koehler, 1999.

> In this update of the original 1992 version of this book, author
> Margaret Wheatley relates cutting-edge scientific theories and
> principles to the issues that trouble organizations most—chaos,
> control, freedom, communication, participation, planning, and
> prediction. With up-to-date examples and stories from her own
> work as an organizational specialist, Wheatley suggests that ideas
> drawn from quantum physics, chaos theory, and molecular biology

could improve organizational performance. Though this book is more of an inspiration to creative thinking than a how-to manual, Wheatley does offer some suggestions for organizations seeking to remain healthy and to grow in this time of challenge and rapid change.

Whitney, Diana, David Cooperrider, Amanda Trosten-Bloom, and Brian S. Kaplin. **Encyclopedia of Positive Questions, Volume One: Using Appreciative Inquiry to Bring Out the Best in Your Organization.** Euclid, OH: Lakeshore Communications, 2002.

> This is a thoroughly practical guide to implementing appreciative inquiry in a congregation or judicatory. The authors begin by explaining why positive questions are important. They then offer an encyclopedia of sample positive questions, each group of which focuses around a topic. While some topics might apply more directly to corporations, others (such as "strength in diversity" and "integrity in action") apply just as directly to congregations. In addition, the authors provide guidance on how to choose your own affirmative topics—as well as how to develop positive questions and how to create a protocol for appreciative inquiry. This book is short on abstractions but full of concrete ways to begin an appreciate inquiry process in your organization.

Whitney, Diana, and Amanda Trosten-Bloom. **The Power of Appreciative Inquiry: A Practical Guide to Positive Change.** San Francisco: Berrett-Koehler, 2003.

> Has your congregation spent energy and resources on "problem solving," only to find that problems either persist or worsen? A new approach—appreciative inquiry—shows that "if you want to transform a situation, a relationship, an organization, or a community, focusing on strengths is much more effective than focusing on problems." Drawing on years of experience in applying appreciative inquiry (AI) to organizational change, Diana Whitney and Amanda Trosten-Bloom present both the principles of AI and case studies that demonstrate how AI works. Congregational leaders who have grown tired of negative approaches to problem solving will be refreshed by the theory and examples presented in this book.

5

NEGOTIATING CULTURAL BOUNDARIES: A LEADERSHIP CHALLENGE FOR CLERGY AND CONGREGATIONS

Jacqueline J. Lewis

> These I will bring to my holy mountain, and make them joyful in my
> house of prayer; their burnt offerings and their sacrifices will be accepted
> on my altar; for my house shall be a house of prayer for all peoples.
> —Isaiah 56.7

Every Sunday morning in American churches, there are bulletins, greeters, and signs on the door offering messages of welcome. Biblical images of inclusivity are abundant: Isaiah's prophecy of a time when lions will lie down with lambs; Paul's teachings on the equality of male and female, Jew and Gentile, slave and free; and John's challenge to love the neighbor whom we can see as an expression of the love of God whom we cannot see all echo the teachings of Jesus. The Beloved Community is an inclusive community, born of the love of God, neighbor, and self. From the first century, the teaching of the church has been to break down dividing walls among peoples. I agree with theologian Howard Thurman that the church is just one expression of the Spirit of the living God that calls humanity into relationships that transcend creed, race, gender, and religion.[1]

God's Spirit engenders an ethic that makes for wholeness and community. It affirms that, as children of God, we are of one family. In his book *Coming Together: The Bible's Message in an Age of Diversity*, Curtiss DeYoung develops Cain Hope Felder's argument that the Afro-Asiatic, multicultural identity of Jesus embodies the multiracial and multicultural design of Christ's church.[2] For DeYoung and his colleagues, the gospel mandates a multiracial/multicultural church. That mandate is based on the teachings of Jesus and is modeled in the narratives in Acts that trace the mission of the early church.[3]

I agree with DeYoung that, in every way, each congregation is called to manifest the gospel message of inclusion. At times, though, this mandate may be impossible to live out in all its fullness. A little church in a farming community in South Dakota may not find African American, single mothers to evangelize as might a church in urban Chicago. But whoever is "other" for each church should become "neighbor" and "friend." In other words, for me, God's saving grace, incarnate in Jesus Christ, compels the church—every church—to embrace and celebrate the difference at its doorstep and to make all who enter welcome.

In Mark's gospel, Jesus of Nazareth turns out the temple in disappointment at the activity there. For Brian Blount, professor of New Testament at Princeton Theological Seminary, Jesus did this in protest of the temple leaders who refused to allow the temple to be a house of prayer for all peoples. In *Making Room at the Table: An Invitation to Multicultural Worship,* a collection of essays edited by Blount and Lenora Tubbs Tisdale, multiple voices from diverse perspectives wrestle with issues of culture and worship in light of the biblical and theological foundations of the Christian faith and toward the goal that the church will be enabled, through its worship, to eat together as one at the table of Christ.

Among the many voices addressing the issue of inclusivity in the church, it is the voice of the Chicano living on the border of culture that Father Virgilio Elizondo represents. Elizondo, a Mexican-American Catholic priest and theologian, wrote *Galilean Journey: The Mexican American Promise* and *The Future is Mestizo: Life Where Cultures Meet.* These texts track the theological meaning of the gospel of Jesus Christ—himself sometimes at the crossroads of life and death—for Mexican American people. Elizondo suggests that Chicanos are mestizaje (from mestizo, "mixed"), a race of people who, because they are rejected by two cultures, are creating a new race from those two cultures. Jesus of Nazareth, a Galilean, multiply rejected like Mexican Americans, symbolizes the living faith that sustains the Mexican people as they share in the marginality of Christ. Other theologians have also identified their people's struggle with the struggles of Jesus. These theologies—black, womanist, feminist, liberation, and mujerista, for example—provide resources for conversations among and within different racial/ethnic communities. Some examples are James Cone's *A Black Theology of Liberation,* a seminal text in black liberation theology; Delores William's *Sisters in the Wilderness: The Challenge of Womanist God-Talk;* and Mary Eunjoo Kim's *Preaching the Presence of God: A Homiletic from an Asian American Perspective,* which addresses practical theology from an Asian American viewpoint.

Another perspective is that there is only one race, the human race. Dave Unander grew up in Chicago at a time of high racial tensions. He witnessed violence done to African Americans because of the color of their skin. He also had violence done to him for being white. A conversion experience as a young man and his studies in genetics formed questions in his mind about the validity of race from a biological perspective and what God's Word has to say about race. These questions shape his book *Shattering the Myth of Race: Genetic Realities and Biblical Truths.* Unander argues that the contemporary concept of race is a myth, and he uses insights from history, from his doctoral work in genetics, and from his evangelical Christian faith to make the case.

These resources and others enable theological conversations that deepen and widen our vision of Jesus and of God's vision for all peoples. This vision, or picture of God's preferred reality, is one that draws us to the same table.

HINDRANCES TO THE VISION

Where there is no vision, the people perish.
—Proverbs 29:18.

Being at the table together can be difficult. Even though American congregations share the call to inclusivity, studies show that over 90 percent of American Christians worship in congregations in which 90 percent or more of the people are like them.[4] Why is that the case? Some of the arguments for a homogenous church seem valid. Church growth experts argue for the successful growth of homogenous congregations; denominational leaders of all races argue for a safe haven on Sunday mornings—a place where the burden of difference is relieved, if only for an hour; and immigrant congregations sometimes have language barriers that keep them separate. Even for churches with a sincere desire to diversify there are barriers that are difficult to overcome due to location and language. For other congregations, worship style and ethos contradict the "welcome" that is extended to strangers. Thus Dr. Martin Luther King's observation that eleven o'clock on Sunday mornings is the most segregated hour in America still stands to challenge and convict each congregation to examine the difference—racial/ethnic, generational, gender, sexual orientation, and theology—in its midst, and to develop a higher capacity to deal with it, to embrace it, and to celebrate it.

Even in churches where difference is valued and celebrated, the challenge is how to honor the unique particularities of each individual even as a new culture is developed. The issue, then, is whether we choose to look at diverse communities as places where difference is ignored or undervalued or places where difference is the cornerstone of the community that is built. When we close our eyes and pretend that we are all alike we miss the opportunity to celebrate with blessed assurance the psalmist's proclamation that each of God's children is fearfully and wonderfully made (Psalm 139:14).

Since the gospel message is clear, how do we explain the difficulty the church has in living out its call to inclusivity? Howard Thurman ponders whether we are just not religious enough. I believe we are just human enough to have difficulty living out the vision that God has laid before us. The Church is called of God but is made of human beings—particular human beings who encounter difference through their own complex identity developments. Stories told to us by our culture, our parents, and our peers form our identity. In other words, as Beverly Tatum notes in her book, *Why Are All the Black Kids Sitting Together in the Cafeteria? And Other Conversations about Race,* people we encounter reflect back to us our identity, which is multidimensional and complex. According to psychology, one aspect of identity is ideology.[5] Ideology or worldview can be seen as a cognitive map that guides our intercourse with society and the physical environment. Our identity shapes the way we perceive the world and the way the world perceives us.

Sometimes our worldview makes it difficult to transcend difference and form human community. In fact, the very processes of differentiation that humans go through to become individuals are the very same processes that make it difficult for us to connect. The very gifts that make America the mosaic that it is—diversity in perspective and culture due to experience and history; varieties of gifts and values; race, ethnicity, gender, ideological, and generational differences; disparity in economics and access to education and health services—can often serve, as has been historically the case, to pull us apart more often than to bring us together. *Set Free: A Journey toward Solidarity Against Racism* is a collaborative project that brings together the combined perspectives of an African American woman, A Mexic Amerindian woman, and a white American man. Using story, analysis, and scriptural reflection, this book offers language and insight to describe all the ways that racism warps self-concept, destroys community, and cripples spiritual growth. The authors, Iris de Leon-Hartshorn, Tobin Miller Shearer, and Regina Shands Stoltzfus, focus on the identity-shaping power of racism, particularly internalized racist oppression and internalized racist superiority. They write toward the hope of building relationships of solidarity that move God's people from categories to community.

I remember seeing, as a child, a Star Trek episode in which Captain Kirk and his crew seemed to be mediating between two very diverse races of people. It turned out that they were distant relatives, one black on the left side of the face and white on the right, the other black on the right side and white on the left. They were the mirror images of each other and were filled with hatred due to their difference. I suppose it can be said that it is both alien and human to fear difference and to have difficulty negotiating the cultural boundaries difference creates.

Even in the church, the dominant story in America can mute the gospel story, yet there are clergy who relate and embody the story that calls their congregations and communities to embrace difference and to build community in the midst of it. There are lay people for whom the commitment to worshipping in churches that are racially, culturally, or ethnically diverse is not a matter of survival but one of theological and ethical conviction. I would argue that it is a countercultural story they embody. The gospel is countercultural.

How do these leaders do this? Perhaps early experiences gave them positive exposure to diverse peoples. Perhaps they are very comfortable with themselves and therefore comfortable with "others." Perhaps they have had an experience of isolation or rejection that makes them want to extend a sense of "home" to the stranger in their midst. Or maybe there was a time when they benefited from profound hospitality and have learned to offer the same to others. Whatever the capacities these leaders have, they also have the ability to see God's vision for people in right relationship with their creator and all of creation. It is a vision that is sometimes difficult to see.

Leaders Bear the Vision in a Time of Ferment

The wolf shall live with the lamb, the leopard shall lie down with the kid,
the calf and the lion and the fatling together, and a little child shall lead them.
—Isaiah 11.6

If current demographic trends continue, experts predict that almost half of the population of our nation will be non-white by the year 2050. These demographic shifts pose a crisis for some and leadership challenges to all. In addition to these demographic shifts, America has also become more religiously pluralistic. In her book *A New Religious America: How a Christian Country Has Become the World's Most Religiously Diverse Nation,* Diana Eck reports that today there are more Muslim Americans than Episcopalians, Presbyterians, or Jews. In these changing times, the culture will look more urgently to religious congregations and communities as a source of leadership on social issues. Congregational leaders must be able not only to tell and embody stories that compel their communities to live the Gospel story but to negotiate racial and cultural boundaries inside their churches and within their communities. Norman Anthony Peart's book *Separate No More: Understanding and Developing Racial Reconciliation in Your Church* uses personal experience and the biblical message to make a case for a continuum of reconciliation. After a historical analysis of race in America, particularly as it pertains to blacks and whites, Peart moves to contrast contemporary understandings of race with the biblical concept. He then lays out a strategy for reconciliation, arguing that for Christians there is no option but to reconcile, and that the task before us is difficult. Peart, who is African American, is balanced in his sense of the responsibility belonging to each group to reconcile. As I stated earlier, whether the differences we encounter are religious, gender-based, generational, theological, racial, ethnic, or cultural, whether they are about sexual orientation or worship style, the church needs to learn how to celebrate those differences. Congregations are made up of people, and people are different.

Bearing the vision for the Beloved Community is a task of leaders—and a leadership task shared by clergy and laity. As Lovett Weems notes in his book *Church Leadership: Vision, Team, Culture, and Integrity,* vision is the most significant theme in leadership studies.[6] As the larger society struggles with diversity, congregations of all types must step into the vacuum and be a public presence that is congruent both with the need of the larger community and with God's plan for humanity. How will congregations bear and interpret that vision in these times?

Truly, we are firmly located in a time of ferment and experimentation among congregations and their leaders. Indeed, preliminary research at the Alban Institute suggests that there is a "sea change in American religion." And that American congregations and the people who lead them are "simultaneously encountering great new spiritual vitality and a crisis of legitimacy of their established leadership patterns and practices."[7] Sociologist Donald E. Miller points to spiritual entrepreneurialism and civic leadership coming from local congregations and the emergence of lay pastors in various denominations as indicators of ferment and vitality.[8] On the other hand, a shortage of well-trained clergy,[9] declining quality of pastoral leadership,[10] and difficulty retaining women in ministry are indicators of the challenges facing congregations.[11] The social and cultural impact of this sea change is marked by two critical characteristics of congregations. First, congregations are ubiquitous; there is neither a small community without one nor a suburban or metropolitan area without an astounding array of expressions of religious congregations. One scholar estimated that in 1990 there were 350,000 congregations in America. Clearly the potential for the church to influence culture and individual lives is profound.

Second, there is an increasing need for congregations to negotiate cultural boundaries of difference. This is particularly true of large congregations.[12] While we are still a nation of small congregations, large congregations of more than 300 persons attending weekly religious services are increasingly prevalent across the national landscape. As reported by Mark Chaves of the University of Arizona in his analysis of the 1998 "National Congregations Study," published in 1999 in the *Journal for the Scientific Study of Religion*, 10 percent of the largest congregations account for almost 50 percent of those individuals who attend religious services. While the small congregation may be the typical congregation, the typical attendee of religious services is now attracted to a large congregation. There is evidence that larger congregations are the ones that are most likely to grow by the inclusion of people from their surrounding communities. Because they draw members from the various racial, ethnic, gender, and generational groups that exist in our communities, these

congregations need to learn how to negotiate the cultural boundaries of members in order to form a congregational community based
on shared values and beliefs. Indeed, all congregations face the challenge of building community in the face of differences that may
range from expectations in worship to deeper cultural issues. The
challenge for congregations today is to develop a language for con-
versing across cultural boundaries in order to build communities
that honor and celebrate difference.

MORE ON LEADERSHIP: A KEY ISSSUE

> The spirit of the Lord God is upon me, because the Lord has
> anointed me; he has sent me to bring good news to the oppressed, to
> bind up the brokenhearted, to proclaim liberty to the captives and
> release to the prisoners; to proclaim the year of the Lord's favor, and
> the day of vengeance of our God; to comfort all who mourn.
> —Isaiah 61:1-2

Howard Gardner, author of *Leading Minds: An Anatomy of Leadership,* describes effective leaders as those who relate and embody
stories that effectively wrestle with the stories already populating
the minds of others. I would argue that clergy who lead multiracial
and multicultural churches relate countercultural stories that rebut
the dominant story of "stick with your own kind" and inspire the
celebration of difference in the midst of community. Broadly, theo-
reticians have taken four approaches to leadership: the *great man
approach,* which focused on the personal talents or physical characteristics of men who had a significant impact on society; the
situationalist approach, which suggested that great leaders were the
product of their times; the *contingency theory approach,* which asserted
that different situations required different kinds of leadership styles;
and the *transaction approach,* in which leaders are understood as influencing and being influenced by followers.[13] The transaction approach is the one taken by Howard Gardner. For him, the
transaction—the relating of stories—takes place in the minds of leaders and in between leaders and followers. Because the work of leadership in congregations involves storytelling through education,
preaching, and liturgy, Gardner's work on narratives in leadership
is a helpful frame for us as we consider congregations.

Knowing ourselves and claiming that knowledge authentically
are essential to working with difference. Sharing and mining our

stories for values, culture, and identity is one way to know and be known. A deeper sense of difference and self-acceptance—acknowledging that not only are we "perfectly and wonderfully made," but so are all of God's people—can be one valuable outcome.

Daniel Goleman's work on emotional intelligence supports my sense that leadership starts with internal story telling and self-awareness. Ronald Heifetz' studies on leadership reflect his training as a psychiatrist and lay out the importance of the holding environment that congregational leaders create as they help people deal with the differences in their midst. Heifetz is making use of a concept from object relations psychoanalytic psychology. The holding environment or container is what parents create by putting their arms around children; in this environment, the children grow and develop. (For an example of this concept, see Donald W. Winnicott's *Playing and Reality,* London: Routledge, 1971.) In my view, that holding environment or container is shaped by building relationships, dealing openly with conflict, and by not only preaching and teaching on hospitality and acceptance but modeling it in community. A healthy leader—one who is self-aware, spiritually disciplined and anchored in faith—can significantly help her congregation adapt to what difference brings: certain stresses, some conflict, and great joy.[14]

Eric H. F. Law is a Chinese American Episcopal priest and consultant in multicultural leadership and organizational development. His book *The Wolf Shall Dwell with the Lamb: A Spirituality for Leadership in a Multicultural Community* uses theology and cultural anthropology to reflect on what it means, spiritually and practically, to be a leader in a multicultural community. For Law, a leader's spiritual resources are essential in this work. Law's follow-up book *The Bush Was Blazing but Not Consumed* picks up where the first leaves off, focusing on the power of liturgy in building multiracial communities. This conversation is ongoing in other resources like *Worship across Cultures: A Handbook* by Kathy Black. A practical help for leaders of multicultural/multiracial congregations is *Talking about Cultural Diversity in Your Church: Gifts and Challenges,* a workbook by cultural anthropologist and cultural diversity workshop leader Michael V. Angrosino. This publication provides pragmatic guidance to Christian religious professionals committed to bridging the cultural divides that can weaken the church's ability to work toward common goals. Angrosino reminds us that there is cultural diversity in even seemingly homogeneous groups, and that meeting people where they are means acknowledging that even though they seem like us, there are myriad ways in which they are not.

RESOURCES FOR THE JOURNEY

The Lord is my Shepherd, I shall not want.
—Psalm 23:1

Congregational and lay leaders need resources in order to lead in a new religious frontier. Some of what they need are models of churches in which cultural diversity is working. In *We are the Church Together: Cultural Diversity in Congregational Life,* Charles Foster and Theodore Brelsford describe a project, funded by a grant from the Lilly Endowment, that studied three Atlanta congregations during the 1992–1993 academic year. The congregations all had one thing in common: their intentional embrace of racial and cultural difference in congregational life. Foster's second book, *Embracing Diversity: Leadership in Multicultural Congregations,* grew out of the research done in Atlanta along with observations from visits to other congregations. It was written both for lay and clergy leaders of diverse congregations and for lay, clergy, and denominational leaders committed to equipping their congregants for more hospitable living in an increasingly multicultural and diverse world. In this book Foster uses stories to focus on the dynamics of leadership and the practices that support cultural diversity.

Two other excellent resources that lift up the stories of congregations living out a vision of inclusion are *A House of Prayer for All Peoples: Congregations Building Multiracial Community* by Sheryl Kujawa-Holbrook and *United by Faith: The Multiracial Congregation as an Answer to the Problem of Race* by Curtiss De Young and sociologists Michael Emerson, George Yancey, and Karen Kim. Kujawa-Holbrook, a professor of pastoral theology at Episcopal Divinity School in Cambridge, Massachusetts, is a thorough and passionate scholar; the annotated bibliography and resource list she includes in *A House of Prayer for All Peoples* are unsurpassed. *United by Faith* is an excellent study of four successful congregations. It also offers a wonderful socio-historical analysis of the early church and the first multiracial churches in America, an analysis of the arguments for monocultural churches, and a hopeful map for how multicultural/multiracial churches can be built today.

Telling stories that transform the stories of others often means preaching in a congregational context. *Preaching to Every Pew: Cross-Cultural Strategies* by James R. Nieman and Thomas G. Rogers is a compelling work that features the voices of the writers, both professors of homiletics, as well as a chorus of preachers' voices that enter the text through quotes from the authors' interviews with them. Present also are the voices of psychology, sociology, and historical analysis as the authors weave these disciplines into what reads like a wonderful sermon on a practical theology for preaching in multicultural contexts. For this study, the authors used a protocol of questions to interview, over the course of several years, scores of pastors who had served in congregations with a significant presence of Native Americans, Latinos, Asians, and people living in economic hardship. The authors believe there are already rich resources addressing African American contexts, and their conclusions here translate to those contexts as well. For Nieman and Rogers, preaching in a multicultural context is ultimately about being a good neighbor, and that is about "making serious engagement" with the particular setting in which the preacher lives and works. They conclude with insights about preaching and the knowledge of self.

How we tell the story we tell is critical. In my view, leaders build a safe container for a multiracial/multicultural church by really valuing difference rather than pretending that it does not exist. David Rhoads's book *The Challenge of Diversity: The Witness of Paul and the Gospels* grew out of lectures to leaders in the Lutheran church as they contemplated maintaining diversity in the face of a merger. Recognizing that diversity is often frightening to our nation and to our churches, Rhoads argues for a new perspective. What if we honor differences? What if we dared to make difference rather than conformity the fundamental starting point for relationships? What if we discover our unity through our diversity? Rhoads argues that diversity is the indispensable basis for mutual interdependence. Reading the New Testament and appreciating the diversity therein is one way to foster renewal for diversity in the church. Rhoads exegetes Galatians and the gospels with an eye toward the background and purpose of each text and God's vision for an inclusive humanity that lies within.

GOD'S SPIRIT: THE ULTIMATE RESOURCE FOR THE JOURNEY

The angel said to her, "The Holy Spirit will come upon you and the
power of the Most High will overshadow you; therefore the child be
born will be called holy; he will be called Son of God."
—Luke 1:35

As congregations embrace God's vision to lead God's people in the
work of negotiating cultural boundaries, they need Spirit/breath to
enable conversations that build community. God's Spirit is the breath
that enables creative speech and flows beneath the sharing of our
storied-selves. It both whispers softly, encouraging us to hear one
another, and blows like the four winds, putting new life on the dead
bones of resistance to see the other as a gift from God. The Zulu
people have a custom—The Spirit of Imbuntu, which says when
we acknowledge one another, we truly exist. When we breathe our
unique stories to the ears of the other, we both risk rejection and
enable acknowledgment as well. Hearing others, we can see them
for who they truly are. In revealing our storied selves, we see and
hear each other into existence and into community. Hearing our
own stories, we are more fully known to ourselves. What results is
a deeper sense of self, a greater self-acceptance, and greater acceptance of others around us. God's vision for right relationship and
whole community and our vision become one.

Additional resources for your bibliography might include:

- John H. Berthrong's *The Divine Deli: Religious Identity in the North American Cultural Mosaic* (Maryknoll, NY: Orbis Books, 1999)
- Joseph Brandt's *Dismantling Racism: The Continuing Challenge to White America* (Minneapolis: Augsburg Fortress, 1991)
- Katie Day's *Difficult Conversations: Taking Risks, Acting with Integrity* (Bethesda, MD: Alban Institute, 2001)
- William Chris Hobgood's *Welcoming Resistance* (Bethesda, MD: Alban Institute, 2001)
- Brian D. McLaren's *The Church on the Other Side: Doing Ministry in the Postmodern Matrix* (Grand Rapids, MI: Zondervan Publishing House, 1998)
- David Ng's *People on the Way: Asian North Americans Discovering Christ, Culture, and Community* (Valley Forge, PA: Judson Press, 1996)

- Jay Rothman's *Resolving Identity-Based Conflict in Nations, Organizations, and Communities* (San Francisco: Jossey-Bass, 1997)
- Jody Miller Shearer's *Enter the River: Healing Steps from White Privilege toward Racial Reconciliation* (New York: Herald Press, 1994).

NOTES

1. Howard Thurman, *The Luminous Darkness* (New York: Harper and Row, 1965).
2. Cain Hope Felder, "Recovering Multiculturalism in Scripture." *The Original African Heritage Study Bible* (Nashville: James C. Winston Publishing Company, 1993).
3. Curtiss De Young, *Reconciliation: Our Greatest Challenge, Our Greatest Hope* (Valley Forge, PA: Judson Press, 1995). See also Emerson and Smith, *Divided by Faith: Evangelical Religion and the Problem of Race in America* (New York: Oxford University Press, 2000).
4. Chaves, Mark, and J. D. Montgomery, "Rationality and the Framing of Religious Choices," *Journal for the Scientific Study of Religion* (Malden, MA: Blackwell Publishers, Inc., 1996), 35:128-44.
5. Erik Erikson, *Identity and Youth and Crisis* (New York; W. W. Norton & Company, 1968).
6. Lovett Weems, Jr., *Church Leadership: Vision, Team, Culture, and Integrity* (Nashville: Abingdon, 1993).
7. James P. Wind and Gilbert R. Rendle. *The Leadership Situation Facing American Congregations: An Alban Special Report.* (Bethesda, MD: Alban Institute, 2001), p. 3.
8. Ibid., 16
9. Ibid., 5
10. Ibid., 8
11. Ibid., 13
12. Military chaplains consistently negotiate cultural boundaries—racial/ethnic diversity, gender, generational, denominational/religions affiliation and class—in a context complicated on the one hand and simplified on the other by military culture (rank, hierarchy, common values and allegiances, etc.).
13. Howard Gardner, *Leading Minds: An Anatomy of Leadership* (New York: Basic Books, 1995).
14. Ronald Heifetz, *Leadership without Easy Answers* (Cambridge, MA: Belnap Press, 1994).

BIBLIOGRAPHY

Ammerman, Nancy Tatom. *Congregation and Community*. New Brunswick, NJ: Rutgers University Press, 1997.

Angrosino, Michael V. *Talking about Cultural Diversity in Your Church: Gifts and Challenges*. Walnut Creek, CA: AltaMira Press, 2001.

Black, Kathy. *Worship across Cultures: A Handbook*. Nashville: Abingdon, 1998.

Blount, Brian, and Lenora Tubbs Tisdale, eds., *Making Room at the Table: An Invitation to Multicultural Worship*. Louisville: Westminster John Knox, 2001.

Chaves, Mark. "National Congregations Study," *Journal for the Scientific Study of Religion* (August 1999).

Chaves, Mark, and J. D. Montgomery. "Rationality and the Framing of Religious Choices," *Journal for the Scientific Study of Religion* (1996).

Cone, James. *A Black Theology of Liberation*. Maryknoll, NY: Orbis Books, 1986.

De Leon-Hartshorn, Iris, Tobin Miller Shearer, and Regina Shands Stoltzfus. *Set Free: A Journey toward Solidarity Against Racism*. Scottdale, PA: Herald Press, 2001.

De Young, Curtiss. *Coming Together: The Bible's Message in an Age of Diversity*. Valley Forge, PA: Judson Press, 1995.

_____. *Reconciliation: Our Greatest Challenge, Our Greatest Hope*. Valley Forge, PA: Judson Press, 1995.

De Young, Curtiss, Michael Emerson, George Yancey, and Karen Kim. *United by Faith: The Multiracial Congregation as an Answer to the Problem of Race*. New York: Oxford University Press, 2003.

Eck, Diana L. *A New Religious America: How a Christian Country Has Become the World's Most Religiously Diverse Nation*. San Francisco: HarperSanFrancisco, 2001.

Elizondo, Virgilio. *Galilean Journey: The Mexican American Promise*. Maryknoll, NY: Orbis Books, 1983.

_____. *The Future is Mestizo: Life Where Cultures Meet*, revised edition. Boulder, CO: University of Colorado Press, 2000.

Erikson, Erik. *Identity and Youth and Crisis*. New York: W. W. Norton & Company, 1968.

Emerson, Michael O., and Christian Smith. *Divided by Faith: Evangelical Religion and the Problem of Race in America*. New York: Oxford University Press, 2000.

Felder, Cain Hope. "Recovering Multiculturalism in Scripture" in *The Original African Heritage Study Bible*. Nashville: James C. Winston Publishing Company, 1993.

Foster, Charles, and Theodore Brelsford. *We are the Church Together: Cultural Diversity in Congregational Life.* Valley Forge, PA: Trinity Press International, 1996.

Foster, Charles. *Embracing Diversity: Leadership in Multicultural Congregations.* Bethesda, MD: Alban Institute, 1997.

Gardner, Howard. *Leading Minds: An Anatomy of Leadership.* New York: Basic Books, 2001.

Goleman, Daniel. *Emotional Intelligence: Why It Can Matter More than IQ.* London: Bloomsbury, 1996.

Goleman, Daniel, Richard Boyatzis, and Annie McKee, *The New Leaders: Transforming the Art of Leadership into the Science of Results.* New York: Little, Brown, and Company, 2002.

Heifetz, Ronald. *Leadership without Easy Answers.* Cambridge, MA: Belnap Press, 1994.

Kim, Mary Eunjoo. *Preaching the Presence of God: A Homiletic from an Asian American Perspective.* Valley Forge, PA: Judson Press, 1999.

Kujawa-Holbrook, Sheryl. *A House of Prayer for All Peoples: Congregations Building Multiracial Community.* Bethesda, MD: Alban Institute, 2002.

Law, Eric H. F. *The Wolf Shall Dwell with the Lamb: A Spirituality for Leadership in a Multicultural Community.* St. Louis: Chalice Press, 1993.

_____. *The Bush Was Blazing But Not Consumed: Developing a Multicultural Community Through Dialogue and Liturgy.* St. Louis: Chalice Press, 1996.

Nieman, James R., and Thomas G. Rogers. *Preaching to Every Pew: Cross-Cultural Strategies.* Minneapolis: Augsburg Fortress, 2001.

Peart, Norman Anthony. *Separate No More: Understanding and Developing Racial Reconciliation in Your Church.* Grand Rapids, MI: Baker Books, 2000.

Rhoads, David. *The Challenge of Diversity: The Witness of Paul and the Gospels.* Minneapolis: Fortress Press, 1996.

Rothman, Jay. *Resolving Identity-Based Conflict in Nations, Organizations, and Communities.* San Francisco: Jossey-Bass, 1997.

Tatum, Beverly. *Why Are All the Black Kids Sitting Together in the Cafeteria? And Other Conversations about Race.* New York: Basic Books, 1997.

Thurman, Howard. *The Luminous Darkness.* New York: Harper and Row, 1965.

Unander, Dave. *Shattering the Myth of Race: Genetic Realities and Biblical Truths.* Valley Forge, PA: Judson Press, 2000.

Weems, Jr., Lovett. *Church Leadership: Vision, Team, Culture, and Integrity.* Nashville: Abingdon, 1993.

William, Delores. *Sisters in the Wilderness: The Challenge of Womanist God-Talk.* Maryknoll, NY: Orbis Press, 1993.

Wind, James P., and Gilbert R. Rendle. *The Leadership Situation Facing American Congregations: An Alban Special Report.* Bethesda, MD: Alban Institute, 2001.

Winnicott, Donald W. *Playing and Reality.* London: Routledge, 1971

RESOURCES ON NEGOTIATING CULTURAL BOUNDARIES FROM THE CONGREGATIONAL RESOURCE GUIDE

Angrosino, Michael V. **Talking about Cultural Diversity in Your Church: Gifts and Challenges.** Walnut Creek, CA: AltaMira Press, 2001.

This workbook is a practical help for leaders of multicultural/ multiracial congregations. Written by cultural anthropologist and cultural diversity workshop leader Michael V. Angrosino, this publication provides pragmatic guidance to Christian religious professionals committed to bridging the cultural divides that can weaken the church's ability to work toward common goals. Angrosino reminds his readers that there is cultural diversity in even seemingly homogeneous groups, and meeting people where they are means acknowledging that even though they seem like us, there are myriad ways in which they are not.

Barndt, Joseph. **Dismantling Racism: The Continuing Challenge to White America.** Minneapolis: Augsburg Fortress, 1991.

Defining racism as "prejudice plus power," Joseph Barndt asserts that efforts against racism have often been incorrectly focused on minority populations rather than the majority. "The cause of racism is in the white society. The effects are felt in the communities of color," he writes. Rather than attempting to soften the effects, we need to attack the cause, he says. The book examines individual, institutional, and cultural racism, and includes a section on racism and the church. Barndt asks congregations to incorporate multicultural aspects in their worship *before* they become multicultural and to work to achieve a pluralistic witness to the world.

Berthrong, John H. **The Divine Deli: Religious Identity in the North American Cultural Mosaic.** Maryknoll, NY: Orbis Books, 1999.

> This book is a timely theological and philosophical examination of the reality of religious pluralism in the U.S. and the world and a challenge to Christian doctrine that views such a reality as evil or even impossible. This book, which relies as much on personal experience as scholarship, is a provocative inquiry into such thought-provoking questions as: *Is deli-style religion really religion at all? Is this trend merely a youthful rebellion or does it represent religion's new form? What does it mean to assert that there is only one God and that God is the creator of all that is? If God is the God of all creation, does that not include all people and all religions?* This is an important book for anyone who has ever grappled with these or similar questions in the practice of his or her faith.

Blount, Brian K., and Leonora Tubbs Tisdale, Editors. **Making Room at the Table: An Invitation to Multicultural Worship.** Louisville: Westminster John Knox Press, 2001.

> This collection of 12 essays from professors at Princeton Theological Seminary explores how to make worship more inclusive of youth, ethnic minorities, and other persons who are frequently marginalized. The book includes several essays on biblical and theological themes that ground this agenda in scripture and traditional Christian thought.

Day, Katie. **Difficult Conversations: Taking Risks, Acting with Integrity.** Bethesda, MD: Alban Institute, 2001.

> In *Difficult Conversations* Day urges congregations to move beyond superficiality and to have difficult conversations, out of which they can grow in understanding and faith. The author helps congregations understand what issues they have been avoiding (violence, race relations, abortion, homosexuality, leadership standards) and why. She discusses models of cultivating difficult conversations and how ongoing difficult conversations can lead to spiritual growth and action. This book will be useful to small group leaders and adult educators in congregations willing to engage in difficult conversations.

De Young, Curtiss Paul. **Coming Together: The Bible's Message in an Age of Diversity.** Valley Forge, PA: Judson Press, 1995.

Author Curtiss De Young addresses the growing need for multicultural expression of Christian truths, giving examples of the need to learn about each other's cultures if we are to reach a "oneness of humanity." De Young notes that all too often the church and its white Westernized people have used the Bible and its message as an instrument of oppression rather than liberation. The combination of biblical references, real-life examples of failure and success in valuing cultural and racial differences, and the discussion questions in each chapter make this book a resource for group discussion as well as a guide for broadening the member base of churches.

De Young, Curtiss Paul, Michael O. Emerson, George Yancey, and Karen Chai Kim. **United by Faith: The Multiracial Congregation as an Answer to the Problem of Race.** New York: Oxford University Press, 2003.

A team of sociologists and a Church of God minister draw upon interviews, questionnaires, and on-site studies to present a well-argued appeal for multiracial congregations. *United by Faith* presents a rich review of the diversity in early Church gatherings, the attempts at racial integration in American congregational history, and the factors at work in multiracial congregations today. Asserting that churches can and should preserve the distinct cultures of all groups, the authors respond to arguments that favor more uniracial congregations. The book concludes with a vision of churches as models of reconciliation.

Elizondo, Virgilio. **The Future is Mestizo: Life Where Cultures Meet, Revised Edition.** Boulder, CO: University Press of Colorado, 2000.

The Future is Mestizo discusses the prophetic mission of Mexican Americans, *chicanos,* who have one foot in each of two cultures. Virgilio Elizondo asserts that this mission is to serve as bridge-builders, translators, and visionaries on the border of a new *mestizaje,* a new culture and people formed from two ethnically disparate cultures and peoples. Envisioning an ultimate religious *mestizaje,* the author asks: did not Jesus—who was born in Galilee and whose parents migrated to Bethlehem, then to Egypt, and later back to Galilee—introduce such radicality into his own Jewishness, proclaiming the reign of God, where all are welcomed and accepted?

Emerson, Michael O., and Christian Smith. **Divided by Faith: Evangelical Religion and the Problem of Race in America.** New York: Oxford University Press, 2000.

Based on their extensive research, sociologists Michael Emerson and Christian Smith discuss racial division and the theological world view of evangelical Christians. They contend that this world view inadvertently helps to perpetuate racism by emphasizing individualistic, personal responses to social inequality and minimizing racism's systemic, structural roots. The authors also note that the evangelical movement's immersion in its own subculture tends to isolate it from larger societal issues. As a result, some evangelicals deny even the presence of discrimination. Congregational leaders seeking to explore the connection between theological world views and racist realities will find this resource invaluable.

Foster, Charles. **Embracing Diversity: Leadership in Multicultural Congregations.** Bethesda, MD: Alban Institute, 1997.

Charles Foster explores the impact of cultural and racial diversity in U.S. and Canadian society on the identity and mission of congregations. He examines leadership dynamics in congregations that embrace racial and cultural diversity, and he invites readers to explore the dynamics of "difference" at work in their own congregations' leadership since the notion of a single model for multicultural congregations contradicts the very notion of diversity. This book has been written for leaders of racially and culturally diverse congregations, but it will also appeal to denominational officers and seminary students committed to equipping the congregations they serve for living hospitably in a racially and culturally diverse world.

Hawn, C. Michael. **One Bread, One Body: Exploring Cultural Diversity in Worship.** Bethesda, MD: Alban Institute, 2003.

Michael Hawn seeks to bridge the gap between the human tendency to prefer cultural homogeneity in worship and the church's mandate to offer a more diverse and inclusive experience. The author and his seminary colleagues studied four United Methodist congregations that are grappling with cross-cultural ministry. Their case studies illustrate the pain and the possibilities encountered in capturing the Spirit of Pentecost in worship. Hawn offers a practical theological framework as well as numerous strategies and an extensive bibliography for implementing "culturally conscious worship." This book will benefit congregations that want to undertake the hard work of cross-cultural worship.

Hobgood, William C. **Welcoming Resistance: A Path to Faithful Ministry.** Bethesda, MD: Alban Institute, 2001.

Exploring the types, bases, and processes of change, *Welcoming Resistance* encourages readers to understand resistance in a congregation's mission-focused work. Author William Hobgood describes *kinds* of resistance (ranging from emotional to rational), the *interests* undergirding resistance (ranging from self to congregation), and the *levels of leadership initiative/intervention* (ranging from maintenance to transformation) that call forth corresponding levels of resistance. Crucially, Hobgood turns to the leader's task of responding to resistance or reactivity. The book concludes by providing leaders with a template for assessing resistance in their own congregations, and listing some "rules" for managing congregational initiatives and resistance.

Kujawa-Holbrook, Sheryl A. **A House of Prayer for All Peoples: Congregations Building Multiracial Community.** Bethesda, MD: Alban Institute, 2002.

While unflinchingly acknowledging the problem of racism in North America and the consequent dearth of multiracial congregations on the continent, author Sheryl Kujawa-Holbrook offers readers hope for change in this compelling book. That hope comes in the form of six diverse congregations working in their communities to realize the prophet Isaiah's vision for a "house of prayer for all peoples." Though their stories reflect the struggle and pain of confronting the racism in their midst, they are also stories of reward, promise, and the courage of commitment. Combined with Kujawa-Holbrook's thoughtful observations, analysis, and recommendations, this book offers inspiration, encouragement, and a place to begin for all

clergy and parishioners seeking to create a welcoming home for all
the world's peoples in their own congregations. The book is capped
with an annotated list of over 300 resources for those wishing to
explore the topic further.

Law, Eric H. F. **The Wolf Shall Dwell with the Lamb: A Spirituality for
Leadership in a Multicultural Community.** St. Louis: Chalice Press,
1993.

The author has observed that when people from diverse backgrounds engage in conversation, whites of Northern European
origin tend to dominate, alienating those of other origins. He
analyzes the reasons why this happens and offers ideas for creating
more equality. One such idea is "mutual invitation," where one
person invites another to speak, who then invites another, until all
have had an opportunity. This is a valuable book for those who
have been disappointed by the quality of interaction among
multicultural groups.

Miller, Donald E. **Reinventing American Protestantism: Christianity in
the New Millennium.** Berkeley: University of California Press, 1997.

This scholarly and sympathetic study of three of the newest Christian movements in the United States (Calvary Chapel, Hope
Chapel, and the Vineyard Churches)presents a portrait of new
paradigm congregations in a post-Christian society. The author
argues that in the experience of the Calvary, Vineyard, and Hope
Chapel groups is the outline of a new Christian reformation. In
their decentralized and entrepreneurial modes of founding congregations is to be seen the replacement for the bureaucratic structures
of mainline religion.

National Congregations Study
saint-denis.library.arizona.edu/natcong/

The **National Congregations Study,** based on a 1998 survey of
1,236 randomly selected congregations, offers valuable information
about the worship, programs, social composition, norms, and
organizational structures in American religious life. The study's
focus is on congregations as the local communities through which
people participate in religious practice. Clergy, lay leaders, and

researchers will find a reliable source of demographic information in this study, and visitors to the study's Web site may create frequency and cross tabulation tables from the survey's many variables.

Nieman, James R., and Thomas G. Rogers. **Preaching to Every Pew: Cross-Cultural Strategies.** Minneapolis: Fortress Press, 2001.

> *Preaching to Every Pew* presents the findings of interviews the authors conducted with scores of pastors who had served in congregations with a significant presence of Native Americans, Latinos, Asians, and people living in economic hardship. For the authors, preaching in a multicultural context is ultimately about being a good neighbor, and that is about "making serious engagement" with the particular setting in which the preacher lives and works. This compelling book features not only the voices of the authors, both professors of homiletics, but also the voices of the dozens of preachers interviewed. Present also are the voices of psychology, sociology, and historical analysis as the authors weave these disciplines into what reads like a wonderful sermon on a practical theology for preaching in multicultural contexts.

Peart, Norman Anthony. **Separate No More: Understanding and Developing Racial Reconciliation in Your Church.** Grand Rapids, MI: Baker Books, 2000.

> In this book, author Norman Anthony Peart uses personal experience and the biblical message to make a case for a continuum of reconciliation. After presenting a historical analysis of race in America, particularly as it pertains to blacks and whites, Peart contrasts contemporary understandings of race with the biblical concept. He then lays out a strategy for reconciliation, arguing that there is no option for Christians but to reconcile, and that the task before us is difficult. Peart presents a balanced view of the responsibility belonging to each group to reconcile.

Yancey, George. **One Body, One Spirit: Principles of Successful Multiracial Churches.** Downers Grove, IL: InterVarsity Press, 2003.

> Defining a multiracial church as one where "no more than 80 percent of the attendees in at least one major worship service are

from one racial group," George Yancey explains the barriers against—and principles for—creating and maintaining multiracial churches. Yancey emphasizes that building multiracial churches requires effort; "just being nice" to people of other races won't work. Consequently, less than eight percent of American churches are multiracial. But for those who are willing to act on the belief that multiracial churches "show a powerful witness to a divided society," this book presents important principles and tools for welcoming and inclusion.

6

LAY MINISTRY

Jean Morris Trumbauer

Lay ministry is a reality as old as the early church and the epistles of our scriptures, yet it is also a fresh reality and a considerable challenge for today's church and the emerging church of tomorrow.

"Gifts" and "call" are inseparable in ministry. Both are entrusted to us by the Creator. Every person is called to ministry—children and adults, men and women, the ordained and non-ordained alike. God calls us and invites us to respond to that call using our many unique gifts. A review of Paul's words in Romans and Corinthians quickly reminds us of the considerable emphasis on the gifts of the laity in the early church. Few passages speak so clearly about the need for us to share our complementary gifts for ministry as 1 Corinthians 12:14; 17-19.

> The body does not consist of one member but of many....If the whole body were an eye, where would be the hearing? If the whole body were an ear, where would be the sense of smell? But as it is, God arranged the organs in the body, each one of them, as God chose. If all were a single organ, where would the body be?

Each of us is a member of the community and contributes unique gifts to the community. We are necessary to our specific community of faith, to the universal church, and to all of God's creation. If we aren't ministering with our gifts, the body is incomplete.

We are reminded in the words of the writer of 1 Peter 4:10 (TEV) that "each one, as a good manager of God's different gifts, must use for the good of others the special gifts he [or she] has received from God." Laity have both the right and the responsibility to use their gifts in ministry.

131

And yet, for those who grew up in the first half of the 20th century, "lay ministry" was simply off the radar of most congregations as both the ordained clergy and church members assumed and expected that the clergy (alone or with a few paid ministerial assistants) would provide all the ministry needed for the faith community—worship, leadership, preaching, pastoral care, education, youth ministry, and evangelism—as well as most of the serious decision making for the congregation. As we enter the 21st century, lay ministry and its attendant concerns are the subjects of new energy and hope in the church as well as deep resistance, floundering experiments, turf struggles, and considerable confusion about how to proceed.

The recognition of God's call to everyone to share their gifts for the work of the reign of God in the world is at the heart of the shifting paradigm of ministry the church encounters today. This shift toward greater valuation of lay ministry by the church and of laity claiming their gifts for ministry stems from many sources. The proclamations of Vatican II in the Roman Catholic tradition led to involving laity in parish councils, liturgy planning, adult and children's education, and pastoral care and social justice work. Sometimes this Vatican II perspective alone was sufficient to propel Catholic parishes toward lay ministry systems; in other parish settings, it was the awareness of the rapidly growing shortage of Catholic clergy that did so.

In the Protestant traditions, there has been a steady stream of laity leaving mainline churches for more evangelical and fundamentalist churches, which often emphasize the equipping of the laity for discipleship. This movement in evangelical churches was promoted by leaders such as Bruce Bugbee, developer of the *Network Series*; Bill Easum, church consultant and author of *Sacred Cows Make Gourmet Burgers*; and the work of Sue Mallory, Brad Smith, Sarah Rehnborg, and others from Leadership Training Network. Their work has also influenced many mainline churches.

Meanwhile, publications and seminars by several others from mainline traditions—such as Loren Mead of the Alban Institute, Marlene Wilson of Volunteer Management Consultants in Boulder, Colorado, and Jean Morris Trumbauer of Trumbauer Consulting in Minneapolis, Minnesota—have provided ready resources for local church leaders in revisioning the church and empowering lay leadership.

Finally, one ought not to discount the influences and resources that professionals in secular volunteer management positions have brought to the church. Many such professionals—usually women— were also active members of congregations and encouraged their own churches to strengthen the engagement of the laity in the ministry of the church and began to provide their congregations with valuable knowledge and resources to undergird this effort.

At the same time, as secular nonprofit and public agencies were developing sophisticated volunteer management systems, members of congregations served as volunteers in these agencies and began to notice the difference in how volunteers were treated there as compared to their experiences in their own congregations. Their influence also was brought to bear on local congregations. The language of "volunteering" in the church and synagogue became widespread and by the turn of the century the terms "lay ministry," "shared ministry," "discipleship," "equipping the laity," and "gifts-based ministry" had also become mainstream.

Today, congregations seek out resources for lay ministry for any number of reasons. Some of them have increasingly experienced diminishing numbers of members who are willing to participate as volunteers or lay ministers in implementing and maintaining the congregation's established programs. Moreover, the most involved members are often evidencing significant burnout. Other congregations have never had much lay involvement but have steadfastly remained clergy- and staff-dependent. Both types of congregations begin to reach out for assistance when they arrive at the point of panic or when their alarm reaches at least a moderate level. The greatest danger in these environments, however, is that leaders and staff will seek a quick fix rather than commit themselves to the long-term effort of building a lay ministry system that will last.

Still other faith communities express more interest in lay ministry development as they become more mission-driven congregations. Their studies of scripture and theology and their learnings from various nationally known religious leaders kindle a new excitement about the possibilities of redirection and renewal in congregations. Leaders of such faith communities are not so much obsessing about lack of lay involvement or with filling program slots as they are about renewing their experience of church and their unique calls to mission in this time and place. These congregations are those that tend to commit their human and financial resources to a long-range effort—a transformative endeavor that represents a significant paradigm shift in ministry.

Finally, some new efforts at lay formation and participation rise from a congregation experiencing new models and approaches in some other arenas of church ministry. In more wholistic approaches to stewardship, both money and people's personal gifts are valued. In new congregational commitments to evangelism and discipleship, the major focus is the role and engagement of the laity. And in such lay pastoral care programs as BeFriender Ministry and Stephen Ministry, lay persons receive many hours of training to prepare them to serve others experiencing grief, illness, isolation, and crisis. Once matched with someone in need within the church or community, they have the ongoing benefits of supervision and support as they meet regularly in peer groups.

ORGANIZING FOR LAY MINISTRY

Much of congregational interest in lay ministry today focuses on developing new emphases on gifts-based ministry, including materials for gifts discovery as well as the development of ministry team approaches rather than the structure and practices of traditional committees and boards. In a parallel fashion, congregations today often attempt to strengthen their infrastructure for lay ministry in order to build more wholistic shared ministry systems that move beyond obsessions with recruiting sufficient volunteer ministers. In support of such new initiatives, congregations form lay ministry committees or teams and hire part-time or full-time directors of lay ministry or gifts ministry coordinators.

For some 26 years my own work focused primarily on encouraging and providing resources for systemic change in congregations rather than short-term fixes. In one judicatory, for example, over a six-year period I completed two-year contracts with nearly 40 local congregations. I used a four-part process: assessing, doing leadership training, facilitating long-range planning, and providing resources for implementation of shared ministry and gifts-based ministry systems. While I discovered that a single workshop or two-hour consultation might plant seeds that would later lead to a congregation investing in long-term change, many of these congregations who held a single training session never went on to engage in the leadership development and strategic planning necessary for strong lay ministry systems to emerge. I quickly found that the best use of my gifts and time were spent in working in longer term contracts with congregations who were willing to commit the time, money, and leadership resources to bring about paradigmatic change.

The Emerging Shared Ministry System

A major challenge for congregational leaders today is how to engage in the practical steps that represent living out our emerging images of church and of the ministry of the laity, both within the congregation and in daily life. All too commonly, congregational leaders still talk about "volunteers" and identify "volunteer ministry" with two leadership functions, namely recruitment and recognition. Each of these functions is often still framed in an old paradigm: *Recruitment* equals "who we can get to make our programs run" and *recognition* means "whether or when we will sponsor our annual Volunteer Celebration."

Becoming familiar with a shared ministry systems approach allows congregational leaders to step back and get the big picture. I've described *shared ministry* this way:

> Shared ministry lives out the affirmation that God calls all people to ministry. As members of faith communities, we are invited to serve together in a spirit of mutuality as partners. Working collaboratively, we strive to discover, develop, engage, and support the gifts of each person and, as responsible stewards, to participate in God's ongoing creative and restorative activity in our communities and the world.[1]

Often it is only when we start to design the practical steps to implement this approach to lay ministry that we begin to grasp the depth of a new vision and find hidden energy as well as hidden resistances.

Changing the Focus from Tasks to Gifts

A systems model for shared ministry has as its focal point the gifts of the faith community rather than completion of program tasks. It recognizes that each faith community has a unique composition of gifts that is more than the sum of the members' gifts. These gifts typically await discovery, release, and connection with specific opportunities that allow both individuals and the congregation to respond in unique ways to the call to serve as co-creators and healers with God. Many of these opportunities will be within the institutional church as members minister to the ill and the suffering, teach children and adults, and assist in worship by providing music, reading scripture, welcoming, and so forth. But the major engagement of our gifts for ministry will always be beyond the congregation. In this larger arena of our daily lives we share our God-given gifts for ministry in marriage and parenting, schools, friendships, the workplace, the organized outreach work of the church and in neighborhood service groups, and as local and global citizens. Shared ministry means empowering and preparing all members to steward their gifts in every arena of their lives.

Today's congregational leaders are asked to reverse their traditional approaches of twisting arms, filling slots, and fretting over the specifics of recognition parties in the spring. As a community of leaders they share in a series of processes that aid members to connect their gifts with ministry opportunities in their lives. These include the following:

- Planning
- Discovering gifts
- Designing
- Recruiting
- Interviewing
- Matching
- Training
- Supervising
- Supporting
- Evaluating
- Managing data

Each of these processes presents opportunities to assist members to grow in understanding themselves as stewards of their gifts and ministers in daily life.

INTERRELATING LEADERSHIP PROCESSES

In many churches, it is not uncommon for the planning and recruitment functions to be given far more attention than others. The shared ministry systems approach is meant to demonstrate the interrelationship of the eleven leadership processes. Careful attention to designing ministries, discovering gifts, and establishing quality training and support systems leads to more successful invitations during the recruitment process. In turn, a respectful, honest, and gifts-based recruitment that does not measure success merely by the number of people who sign up to participate establishes relationships of trust between leaders and members, which in turn leads to deeper relationships, learning, and quality ministry in the congregation and beyond. And all these processes provide rich opportunities that can expand people's awareness of their gifts and call.

This model also helps leaders define their own roles as ministry. Whereas congregational leaders often view their responsibilities as burdens, they begin to see that planning, designing, discovering gifts, recruiting, supporting, and evaluating are, indeed, ways of ministering to others. Through these actions of leaders, members learn and grow and even experience healing, and the church becomes a resource for daily living rather than just a program machine.

A shared ministry system is both dynamic and synergistic. Neither its practical processes nor its underlying assumptions are static. They are always deepening and changing as leaders and members learn from their relationships in sharing the ministry and reflect upon their experiences. A healthy functioning shared ministry system is itself a form of ministry, one that enriches our experiences of both congregational ministry and the ministry of our daily lives.

USING THE MODEL

As congregations begin to engage this model, a common question is which of the eleven leadership processes "comes first." My own preference is for leaders to understand the main system components and theological assumptions and then do some planning. In the first two years choose two to four leadership processes for special attention. Incorporate new methods of doing them and seek new understandings of their impact. As the plan is extended in future years, other processes will naturally receive greater leadership attention and creativity.

A majority of the congregations with whom I have worked focused their first plan on some combination of designing, discovering gifts, recruiting, and matching, but the emphases chosen will depend on the individual congregation's needs, strengths, and weaknesses, as well as upon which system components the leaders envision as particularly energizing (very frequently, discovering gifts).

For those congregations who choose to begin with the gifts discovery process, here are some things to keep in mind:

- **Gifts include more than talents!** We are more than our skills and strengths. Our gifts include our life journey, interests, knowledge, preferences, relationships, and spiritual heritage. I call these *traditional gifts* because they are often easily acknowledged. We also have *gifts of style*—motivational styles, learning styles, and personality types, among others. And we often discount or reject aspects of our uniqueness that I call *gifts of vulnerability*. The culture and the church often do not acknowledge the importance of these gifts, which include our bodies and senses, emotions, values, passions and dreams, and weaknesses and wounds. These are among the most treasured gifts of all.

- **All our gifts are spiritual gifts.** Our unique design is provided by the Creator and intended for a spiritual purpose—to allow us to work as partners in God's ongoing creative and restoring work in the world. All members of the human family are designed by the same spiritual source and called to return their gifts in service to the community of creation as God intended.

- **Every arena of our lives engages our gifts.** We share our gifts in the programmatic ministry of the congregation; stewardship involves more. We minister within our families and friendships, in workplaces and schools, and in local communities and the world.

- **Gifts are discovered through a variety of processes.** "What is the best gifts inventory you can recommend?" leaders ask. Yet no inventory is best for all congregations and inventories used alone do not provide fundamental solutions to the challenges of gifts-based shared ministry. Solo methods tend to miss the realities of congregational diversity. We are of differing genders and generations. We represent varied learning styles and different economical, educational, and ethnic backgrounds. Our theological viewpoints, awareness of our gifts, and amount of time we are willing to devote to discernment vary. All these factors affect which forms of gifts discernment will best serve each member. I suggest a kind of menu approach that offers a variety of gifts discovery approaches over a period of months or years—educational events, inventories, small groups, interviews, mentors, coaching, videos, reading, music, and so forth.

- **Gifts discernment is not a separate "program."** While special planning and catalyst teams are usually essential to initiating gifts-based ministry, a broader partnership is ultimately required. Gifts discernment needs to be a central ongoing mission of today's church. Each member—from the small child to the terminally ill elderly person—needs to receive assistance and support in discerning and stewarding their gifts and call in every life arena. For this to happen, gifts discernment must be built into all the major arenas of church life and ministry from formation to pastoral care, from evangelism to social outreach.

REFRAMING LEADERSHIP

Like gifts discovery, the notion of leadership may need to be reframed to support the emergence of a shared ministry system. New visions of church call forth new positions and configurations of leadership. During the past 20 years, among the most important of these new leadership positions have been staff and lay leader groups who serve as catalysts for envisioning, designing, implementing, and evaluating ministry systems.

Typically, dozens of leaders are involved in completing an assessment tool based on the shared ministry systems model. They then attend an all-day training session addressing the theological foundations of gifts-based ministry in an emerging paradigm of church and introducing practical how-to tools. A shared ministry task force then writes a two- to three-year plan, which is commented upon by other leadership groups. Then, step by step, the shared ministry team, working in close collaboration with other lay leaders and staff, begins implementation. This sort of preparation helps congregational leaders avoid years of discussion that does not lead to action or endless initiatives that lead to dead ends.

A growing number of professional ministry associations are being formed to provide support for this special work. In the metropolitan area of St. Paul and Minneapolis, Minnesota, for example, the Directors of Church Volunteer Ministries has existed for 16 years and now numbers over 90 professionals representing most mainline Protestant and Roman Catholic congregations. In South Central

Ohio, a professional group called D.O.V.E. (Directors of Volunteer Experiences) was formed in the latter part of the 1980s and numbers more than 15 participating members. This group is also ecumenical. Such professional associations (which sometimes include members of shared ministry teams as well as the director) meet regularly to share new processes they have developed, provide training, mentor new people in the field, and provide ongoing mutual support to one another.

Shared ministry is not a "quick fix" for a shortage of volunteer ministers nor does it represent just another passing fad. It is an exciting adventure. It enlivens our vision and experience of church. It calls us to reframe our leadership efforts as real opportunities to affect members' lives. It leads us to claim our gifts and ministry in every arena of our lives. It requires that we let go of many of the ways we have "always done things," relinquish some of the control of our program turf in order to better serve the common good, and work as partners rather than lone rangers.

Imagine a congregation where these things are happening—one in which everyone from small children to the ill elderly are able to name their gifts, appreciate themselves as a unique creation of God, and participate with others in the creative and redeeming work of God in the world! Now imagine your own community of congregational leaders working as partners in shared ministry to make this dream come true.

Resources on Lay Ministry

A multitude of resources are available to leaders of lay ministry systems development, including theoretical works as well as comprehensive material that presents conceptual models and practical tools for implementing these models. Recent years have also seen an explosion of resources and materials to use for gifts-discovery processes in the church. Moreover, since the mid-nineties, comprehensive systems approaches have emerged for organizing and leading lay ministry efforts.

Three major schools of materials and resource consultants are available today for lay ministry development. One group of work comes from the more evangelical community, another from mainline Protestant and Roman Catholic viewpoints, and a third from secular volunteer management professionals. Some congregations choose one or another; other congregations pick and choose from models and literature from all three points of view.

Representative of materials frequently used by mainline Protestant and Roman Catholic resources is *How to Mobilize Church Volunteers* by Marlene Wilson, a small volume published in 1983 as an extension of Wilson's work as the key volunteer management trainer and consultant in the United States at that time. Wilson provides brief overviews of theology and practical tools and tips for beginning to strengthen lay ministry. Several practical appendices, including an assessment form, are particularly helpful. Wilson's two-part video by the same name presents related training.

A much more comprehensive expression by Wilson is her secular volume *The Effective Management of Volunteer Programs*, which continues to be one of the foundational works in volunteer management, providing excellent sections on motivation, interviewing, designing jobs, and awareness of organizational climate.

More comprehensive works directly related to congregational life and mission were created in the mid-1990s. Sarah Rehnborg, together with Sue Mallory and Brad Smith, developed a manual entitled *The Starter Kit for Mobilizing Ministry.* (Published by the Leadership Training Network, this manual was recently significantly revised and published as *The Equipping Church Guidebook* by Mallory, Smith, Rehnborg, and Wilson. This newly published version accompanies Mallory's book *The Equipping Church: Serving Together to Transform Lives.*) Just a few months after *The Starter Kit* appeared on the scene, my own comprehensive volume, *Sharing the Ministry: a Practical Guide to Transforming Volunteers into Ministry*, was published by Augsburg Fortress Publishers.

In *The Equipping Church* Mallory describes in great detail her journey leading Brentwood Presbyterian Church in its commitment to become a congregation that equipped its members for effective lay ministry in the church and the world. Mallory's honest detailing of the opportunities and joys, the challenges and resistances the congregation encountered as it changed its paradigm of ministry will be valuable and delightful reading for all directors of lay ministry in any denomination. Moreover, the stories of other equipping congregations will provide additional models that illustrate the principles and practices of equipping congregations.

The Equipping Church Guidebook by Mallory, Smith, Rehnborg, and Wilson is a detailed resource and companion volume to *The Equipping*

Church. It provides a wealth of information for leaders of congregations as well as facilitators and trainers who wish to initiate or further the practice of equipping laity and engaging them in service. In graphics, sidebars, and sample forms it leads the reader through the steps resulting in an equipping form of ministry. Assessment and process charts, samples from model congregations, discussion questions, ministry descriptions, and some interview helps are included. A few of the resources are reproducible without special permission. While primarily a large-church model, the wisdom and experiences of the congregations that illustrate the guidebook are translatable to smaller ministry contexts. Other special strengths of the guidebook include the authors' understandings of congregational culture and the change process.

My own volume, *Sharing the Ministry: A Practical Guide for Transforming Volunteers into Ministers,* outlines a systems understanding of what I call "shared ministry," which includes planning, discovering gifts, designing, recruiting, interviewing, matching, supporting, supervising, evaluating, managing data, and planning. At the end of each chapter describing these parts of the process there are reflection exercises, sample forms, letters, and other resources designed to assist directors of lay ministry, clergy, and other congregational leaders in planning, implementing, and continuing to develop a wholistic lay ministry system The strengths of this material—provided in a three-ring binder format—are its organization, practical illustrations, an extensive annotated resource section, and over 50 reprintable sample pages.

Its companion manual, *Created and Called: Discovering Our Gifts for Abundant Living* (Augsburg Fortress, 1998), takes the foundation of *Sharing the Ministry*—namely the gifts of the people and discovering gifts—and expands them into a 250-page manual with over 75 reprintable pages. An extensive theology of gifts is included, along with background material, teaching helps, reflection guides, and numerous supplementary activities to help congregational members discover traditional gifts (life experience, talents, interests and preferences, spiritual heritage), gifts of style (personality, motivational, and learning styles), and gifts of vulnerability (body and senses, values, emotions, passions and dreams, and weaknesses and wounds). Administrative helps, a gifts inventory, and extensive congregational examples and planning resources are also included.

These remain the most comprehensive materials, each done in manual style and each representing somewhat differing theological perspectives. Mallory's Leadership Training Network materials are written from a more evangelical position and Jean Morris Trumbauer's *Sharing the Ministry* and *Created and Called* reflect mainline Protestant and Roman Catholic outlooks. Even though the Mallory and Trumbauer materials and their accompanying training resources represent different theological traditions and styles, their practical materials and suggestions are generally consistent with each other, though presented in different layouts and style. Many congregational leaders find that each set of resources is a good supplementary resource to the other.

Where to Begin

Several of the following strategies will be helpful to those seeking resources for lay ministry and gifts identification. Congregations who are beginning these efforts will find it helpful to engage in several of the following actions:

- Identify three or four local congregations known for their lay ministry development. Send representatives to visit with leaders and staff at these congregations or, alternatively, invite the director of lay ministry or a member of the lay ministry leadership team from each of these congregations to participate in a meeting of your board, council, or lay ministry team. Try to schedule conversations with members of congregations that have different approaches.
- Start with comprehensive manuals such as *Sharing the Ministry* and *Created and Called* by Jean Morris Trumbauer and *The Equipping Church* and *The Equipping Church Guidebook* by Sue Mallory, Brad Smith, Sarah Jane Rehnborg, and Neil Wilson. These resources, in combination, provide theological background from both mainline and evangelical viewpoints, information about church culture and change, practical hands-on tools and samples, and stories of congregations engaged in gifts-based shared ministry. In addition, these materials will help leaders develop plans for gifts-based shared ministry systems as well as help leaders identify and deal with common obstacles and resistances that occur during the initiation phases of these efforts.

- Read and discuss some of the Mallory or Trumbauer materials as in-service resources for staff meetings, boards, or task forces over several months. Slimmer volumes—such as Easum's *Sacred Cows Make Gourmet Burgers*, Lloyd Edward's *Discovering Your Spiritual Gifts*, or Loren Mead's *Transforming Congregations for the Future* and *Five Challenges for the Once and Future Church*—are also useful introductions to a new paradigm of ministry.
- Send a congregational team to a reputable workshop on lay ministry or gifts-based ministry systems. The attendance of a team will provide both a theological and practical overview of contemporary gifts-based shared ministry/lay ministry, thus making the planning of your next steps much easier and creating more ownership at the beginning of your new lay ministry efforts. Moreover, participation in such seminars alerts participants to the experiences of other congregations, raises awareness of potential resistances, and provides strategies for moving through the change process. Trumbauer Consulting and Coaching from Minneapolis, Minnesota (Jean Morris Trumbauer and Associate Judy Urban) and the Leadership Training Network (Sue Mallory and Associates) are among the most well-known and comprehensive of such learning opportunities and each provides consulting services as well. A number of the other companies listed earlier in this essay, such as LifeKeys and the Catherine of Siena Institute, provide specific gifts-identification training.
- Determine whether or not a professional network or association of directors of lay ministry exists in your local community or in the surrounding region. Members of these associations are usually eager to share information and experiences about lay ministry systems with your congregation. (The professional group named Directors of Church Volunteer Ministries in Minnesota— online at www.dcvm.org—is a primary example.)
- Select a core library of basic gifts-based shared ministry resources. Several of the resources described earlier will make good choices. Others are listed in the following section.

Gifts-Discovery Resources

In addition to the Trumbauer and Mallory resources for gifts-based ministry, several other authors provide gifts-discovery materials.

Episcopal priest Lloyd Edward's *Discovering Your Spiritual Gifts* presents a small set of well-balanced learning activities to assist people with gifts discovery. This small volume, published by Cowley, is especially helpful in assisting readers to see weaknesses and wounds as gifts for ministry.

Another well-known set of materials are the LifeKeys resources. *LifeKeys* is a book assisting people in discovering their traditional spiritual gifts as well as passions, values, and personality. Authors David Stark, Jane Kise, and Sandra Krebs Hirsch were among the first writers and trainers to approach gifts for ministry in a more wholistic way that extended beyond traditional spiritual gifts and the gifts of talents. I have especially valued their work on the gift of values. This volume includes inventories, self-tests, and other exercises. A companion work written by these authors and also published by Bethany is the *LifeKeys Discovery Notebook*, which features a number of gift exercises and is a help to trainers. A related work of assistance to teens is *Find Your Fit* by Jane Kise and Kevin Johnson.

Representing more traditional gifts identification based on lists in Paul's Epistles are *Rediscovering Our Spiritual Gifts* by Charles V. Bryant and the companion workbook by John I. Penn; *Discover Your Gifts and Learn How to Use Them* by Alvin J. Vander Griend; and the *Network* series by Bruce Bugbee, Don Cousins, and Bill Hybel.

Discerning Charisms: A Workbook for Navigating the Discernment Process was written by Sherry Anne Weddell and Eryn Huntington for the Catherine of Siena Institute, now located in Colorado Springs, Colorado. This resource was developed primarily for Catholics interested in a spiritual gifts approach based on Paul's letters. The *Catholic Spiritual Gifts Inventory* and a workshop audiotape of their *Called and Gifted* workshops are also available from the Institute. These materials and the Institute's training provide a solid biblical basis for discerning gifts and call to ministry.

Two short volumes that are other favorite discernment books of mine are Pierre Wolff's *Discernment: The Art of Choosing Well* and, from the *Listening Hearts* series, *Listening Hearts: Discerning Call in Community* and *Grounded in God: Listening Hearts Discernment for Group Deliberations*. The Wolff volume presents an easy-to-understand presentation of an Ignation approach to discernment, and the *Listening Hearts* books address both individual and communal decision making.

Two other short books are helpful reading for both individuals and gift group facilitators. In *How to Find Your Mission in Life* Richard Bolles delineates in lively fashion three levels of vocation and calling, and in *Discovering Our Gifts*—an excellent resource for gifts leadership teams—author Thomas D. DeVries includes brief prayers, teaching materials, and activities.

In our contemporary setting, one would be remiss to omit resources that address risk management processes related to lay ministry systems. I included a basic chapter outlining basic risk management functions and strategies in a shared ministry system in my book *Sharing the Ministry*. Many congregations also turn for advice on this subject to the Church Law and Tax resources from Christian Ministry Resources, where Richard R. Hammar, Steven W. Klipowicz, and James F. Cobble have developed a whole kit on the subject. Entitled *Reducing the Risk of Child Sexual Abuse in Your Church*, this kit includes a small booklet, a training manual, additional material, and audio- and videotapes. I have found these to be excellent resources for introducing the need for risk management policies and procedures in congregations. Another very helpful overview volume produced by the Minnesota Office of Citizenship and Volunteer Services is *Planning it Safe: How to Control Liability and Risk in Volunteer Programs*.

Among influential philosophical and theological volumes that have helped to form my own views of lay ministry development are two volumes by Protestant authors and three by Catholic writers.

Many people are familiar with William Easum's provocative volume *Sacred Cows Make Gourmet Burgers: Ministry Anytime, Anywhere, by Anybody*. Even if one does not agree with all of Easum's assertions, this is a must read—a good volume to provide one perspective on a new paradigm of ministry in our age and a vivid picture of "permission giving leadership."

Another early 1990s volume addressing a new paradigm of ministry is *The Equipping Pastor: A Systems Approach to Congregational Leadership* by R. Paul Stevens and Phil Collins. The authors here address clergy roles in the liberation of the laity and introduce a systemic understanding of the congregation and its ministry.

The most influential theological volumes for me were *Emerging Laity: Returning Leadership to the Community of Faith* (now out of print); *Community of Faith: Crafting Christian Communities Today*, and *Seasons of Strength: New Visions of Adult Christian Maturing*, written by the pastoral theologian and religious historian James D. Whitehead and his wife, developmental psychologist Evelyn Eaton Whitehead. Each of these books provides powerful analysis, metaphors, and encouragement for a new paradigm of ministry that stresses the gifts, call, and vocation of the laity. Although these publications were written primarily for Catholic audiences, the Whiteheads are familiar authors for many Protestant leaders. If any writers are a sign of hope for and recognition of the reality that every member of the body of Christ is called and gifted for ministry, it is the Whiteheads. As a lay professional leader in lay ministry development, the reading of these volumes has brought me to tears, to escalating enthusiasm and new hope, and has lent me incredible sustenance for the journey.

Useful Secular Resources

Some of the most valuable of the secular resources that directors of lay ministry will want in their libraries are the following:

- Marlene Wilson's *The Effective Management of Volunteer Programs.* Wilson addresses in some depth several basic elements of a volunteer management system. For many years this volume was the basic text in organizing secular volunteer management.
- Sue Vineyard's *Beyond Banquets, Plaques and Pins: Creative Ways to Recognize Volunteers and Staff; Secrets of Motivation: How to Get and Keep Volunteers and Staff; The Great Trainer's Guide: How to Train (Almost) Anyone to Do (Almost) Anything;* and *How to Take Care of You...So You Can Take Care of Others.* Vineyard is another of the pioneers in volunteer management. Her books are often written in an easy-to-read list format. They provide very helpful information and tools for the practitioner.
- Helen Little's *Volunteers: How to Get Them, How to Keep Them.* The author of this volume identifies 12 basic needs of volunteers and strategies for meeting each need.

Data Management Software

Ten to 15 years ago the innovative congregations developing more organized programs for shared ministry often designed their own software to track the participation of their lay volunteer ministers.

Today, a number of software companies that specialize in membership and financial software for congregations are also strengthening the volunteer tracking component of their programs. Parish Data Systems, Church Management Systems, and others now have an increased capacity in this regard. Shelby's newly developed *Servant* module, in particular, allows some tracking of member gifts and some helps in matching those gifts with opportunities to serve.

What has often been lacking, however, is evidence that software developers really have a depth of experience in the more advanced systems of gifts-based shared ministry and the attendant needs for advanced software that will adequately serve these programs. However, today we see more software that is initiated organically in these settings. I especially value the software products of the BusNet Company in Eden Prairie, Minnesota (*Shared Ministry Info/System*) and *Members to Action* software from DataWiz Solutions in McLean, Virginia. Each of these two software systems can import basic membership information from a number of popular church management software products. Both are reasonably priced. Each of the developers worked in depth with practitioners in the gifts-based shared ministry fields and with lay ministry consultants. Their software products effectively track members' gifts and help connect those gifts with opportunities for ministry. They each have excellent search functions, helpful screens and reports, and instruction manuals. Many other functions are provided to assist with the management of today's lay ministry programs.

The BusNet product is provided as a single-user or multi-user program and is compatible with most PC networks. It has two major aspects—discovery of gifts and ministry sign up. Some support services are provided. Call 1-800-318-3607 or e-mail jlatta@busnet-inc.com for more information.

Members to Action, from DataWiz Solutions, is available for both Windows and Macintosh and a 90-day version is available at DataWiz's Web site, www.memberstoaction.com (or call 1-877-328-2949). Small congregations receive a considerable price reduction. Annual support contracts are also available.

Web Sites

A number of Web sites provide information, resource products, training schedules, and networking links for congregational leaders seeking resources for lay ministry systems. These seven are among my favorites:

- www.avaintl.org (secular), Association for Volunteer Administration
- www.dcvm.org (religious), Directors of Church Volunteer Ministries in Minnesota
- www.connextion.org (religious), Sue Mallory resources and training
- www.mavanetwork.org (network group), Minnesota Association for Volunteer Administration
- members.aol.com/Trumbauer (religious), Trumbauer Consulting and Coaching Associates
- www.pointsoflight.org (secular), Points of Light Foundation
- www.volunteermanagement.com (both secular and religious), Volunteer Management Associates

EMERGING QUESTIONS

More and more practical models and resources for lay and gifts-based ministry are being developed in local congregations across the country. Many of these resources are shared among members of professional groups of lay ministry directors as part of regional consulting projects or through denominational offices. New gifts-discovery materials are also emerging from the ministries of local congregations; some of these are being published and more need to be. One of the most urgent needs at this time is for gifts-discovery materials and lay ministry opportunities designed for children and teens. In addition, there are virtually no helpful videos available to help develop lay ministry systems and plans except for the training videos from Marlene Wilson mentioned earlier.

A growing number of congregations are now seeking to integrate the ways in which lay ministry and gifts discovery continue to serve the local congregation itself but reach beyond to the outreach ministries of the congregation and even further to what is often called "ministry of daily life" or "ministry in the marketplace." Gifts-based lay ministry that is true to its theological origins will surely need to do more than ensure the maintenance of internal congregational programs. Congregational models for a broader approach to lay ministry need to be developed and shared in the larger church community.

I believe that the next wave of published resources for gifts-based shared ministry is likely to emerge from local faith communities or clusters of congregations as they experiment and develop their own materials. Every effort needs to be made to encourage the sharing of these locally developed resources within local communities, within judicatories, and across denominational and geographic borders.

The field of lay ministry has lacked sufficient empirical research to test the long-term effects of the various models that have been tried in the last decade. Among several issues that will benefit from research-based studies are the following:

- an examination of the barriers to and supports for congregations developing lay ministry and gifts-based systems and models
- an exploration of the emerging roles, professional relationships, and effectiveness of directors of lay ministry and gifts-based ministry coordinators and the shared ministry or gifts teams with whom they work as partners in local congregations (Faith communities would also benefit from study of the professional groups formed by directors of lay ministry across the country.)
- an evaluation of the relative effectiveness of traditional congregational structures (councils, boards, committees, commissions) initiating lay ministry and gifts discovery efforts as compared with the initiation of such lay ministry efforts organized by self-forming ministry teams and other new program structures or governance systems
- a deeper analysis of the structures and processes of gifts-based shared ministry systems that will best address the ministry contexts of small congregations

Lay ministry has evolved to the point that it provides a rich environment for carefully designed research studies as well as the ongoing development of models and resource materials. One need will be the provision of grants to those interested and competent in engaging in such research.

Conclusion

I believe that most faith communities on this continent—Protestant, Catholic, Jewish, and others—would be genuinely surprised at the depth and breadth of lay ministry resources available today. A rapidly growing number of congregations now focus strongly on lay ministry development —its theological foundation, its new structures and processes, its impact on congregational life and participation, and its increasing capacity to strengthen each person's "stewardship of self" in every arena of life. I have highlighted just a few of the resources on a burgeoning bookcase of materials.

In my own research and practice, I use and adapt approaches and materials from mainline Protestant, Catholic, evangelical, and secular sources. Whether or not the particular theological concepts and language match one's own, there are things to learn from all these sources as one initiates and strengthens lay ministry models, organizational systems, and processes, and develops and adapts materials for gifts discovery.

The opportunities and challenges of the next stage in lay ministry development are many. Leaders of faith communities who wish to initiate new efforts in gifts-based shared ministry will no longer face a scarcity of resources but rather an abundance of them from which to choose. It is my hope that congregations in both the early stages of new lay ministry systems as well as those more advanced in such efforts will share their models, materials, and learnings with other congregations across denominational lines.

I look forward to the day when congregations of all traditions enthusiastically embrace the belief that the heart of the ministry of each faith community is assisting people to discover the unique gifts and callings embedded in them by the Creator—gifts that allow them to respond to God's call to serve as partners in living out the dream of the Reign of God in the world.

NOTE

1. Jean Morris Trumbauer, *Sharing the Ministry: A Practical Guide for Transforming Volunteers into Ministers* (Minneapolis: Augsburg Fortress, 1995, 1999), 50.

BIBLIOGRAPHY

Bolles, Richard. *How to Find Your Mission in Life.* Berkeley, CA: Ten Speed Press, 1991.

Bryant, Charles V. *Rediscovering Our Spiritual Gifts: Building Up the Body of Christ through the Gifts of the Spirit*, with companion workbook by John I. Penn. Nashville: Upper Room Books, 1991.

Bugbee, Bruce, Don Cousins, and Bill Hybels. *Network: The Right People . . . In the Right Places . . . For the Right Reasons* (videos/manuals). Grand Rapids, MI: Zondervan Publishing House, 1994.

DeVries, Thomas. *Discovering Our Gifts.* Mahwah, NJ: Paulist Press, 1990.

Easum, William M. *Sacred Cows Make Gourmet Burgers: Ministry Anytime Anywhere by Anyone.* Nashville: Abingdon Press, 1995.

Edward, Lloyd. *Discovering Your Spiritual Gifts.* Boston: Cowley Publications, 1988.

Farnham, Suzanne, Joseph P. Gill, R. Taylor McLean, and Susan M. Ward. *Listening Hearts: Discerning Call in Community.* Harrisburg, PA: Morehouse Publishing, 1991.

Farnham, Suzanne, Stephanie Hull, and R. Taylor McLean. *Grounded in God: Listening Hearts Discernment for Group Deliberations.* Harrisburg, PA: Morehouse Publishing, 1996.

Hammar, Richard R., Steven W. Klipowicz, and James F. Cobble. *Reducing the Risk of Child Sexual Abuse in Your Church.* Matthews, NC: Christian Ministry Resources, 1993.

Huntington, Eryn, and Sherry Anne Weddell. *Catholic Spiritual Gifts Inventory.* Seattle: Catherine of Siena Institute, 1998.

Kise, Jane A. G., and Kevin Walter Johnson. *Find Your Fit: Dare to Act on God's Design for You.* Minneapolis: Bethany House Publishers, 1998.

Kise, Jane A.G., David Stark, and Sandra Krebs Hirsh. *LifeKeys.* Minneapolis: Bethany House Publishers, 1996.

Little, Helen. *Volunteers: How to Get Them, How to Keep Them.* Naperville, IL: Panacea Press, 1999.

Mallory, Sue, Brad Smith, Sarah Jane Rehnborg, and Neil Wilson. *The Equipping Church Guidebook.* Grand Rapids, MI: Zondervan Publishing House, 2001.

Mallory, Sue. *The Equipping Church: Serving Together to Transform Lives.* Grand Rapids, MI: Zondervan Publishing House, 2001.

Mead, Loren. *Transforming Congregations for the Future.* Bethesda, MD: Alban Institute, 1994.

———. *Five Challenges for the Once and Future Church.* Bethesda, MD: Alban Institute, 1996

Planning it Safe: How to Control Liability and Risk in Volunteer Programs. St. Paul, MN: Minnesota Office of Citizenship and Volunteer Services, 1998.

Rehnborg, Sarah. *The Starter Kit for Mobilizing Ministry.* Tyler, TX: Leadership Training Network, 1994.

Stark, David Sandra Krebs Hirsch, and Jane Kise. *LifeKeys Discovery Notebook: Discovering Who You Are, Why You're Here, What You Do Best.* Minneapolis: Bethany House Publishers, 1998.

Stevens, R. Paul, and Phil Collins. *The Equipping Pastor: A Systems Approach to Congregational Leadership*. Bethesda, MD: Alban Institute, 1993.

Trumbauer, Jean Morris. *Created and Called: Discovering Our Gifts for Abundant Living*. Minneapolis: Augsburg Fortress, 1998.

———. *Sharing the Ministry: A Practical Guide for Transforming Volunteers into Ministers*. Minneapolis: Augsburg Fortress, 1995, 1999.

Vander Griend, Alvin J. *Discover Your Gifts: And Learn How to Use Them*. Grand Rapids, MI: CRC Publications, 1996.

Vineyard, Sue. *Beyond Banquets, Plaques and Pins: Creative Ways to Recognize Volunteers and Staff*. Downers Grove, IL: Heritage Arts, 1989.

———. *The Great Trainer's Guide: How to Train (Almost) Anyone to Do (Almost) Anything*. Downers Grove, IL: Heritage Arts, 1990.

———. *Secrets of Motivation: How to Get and Keep Volunteers and Staff*. Downers Grove, IL: Heritage Arts, 1991.

Vineyard, Sue, and Hirenda Nath Mukerhjee. *How to Take Care of You...So You Can Take Care of Others*. Grand Rapids, MI: CRC Publications, 1996.

Weddell, Sherry Anne, and Eryn Huntington. *Discerning Charisms: A Workbook for Navigating the Discernment Process*. Seattle: Catherine of Siena Institute, 2000.

Whitehead, Evelyn Eaton, and James D. Whitehead. *Community of Faith: Crafting Christian Communities Today*. Lincoln, NE: Backinprint.com, 1992.

———. *Seasons of Strength: New Visions of Adult Christian Maturing*. Winona, MN: St. Mary's Press, 1995.

Whitehead, James D., and Evelyn Eaton Whitehead. *Emerging Laity: Returning Leadership to the Community of Faith*. New York: Doubleday, 1986.

Wilson, Marlene. *Effective Management of Volunteer Programs*. Boulder, CO: Volunteer Management Associates, 1996.

———. *How to Mobilize Church Volunteers*. Minneapolis: Augsburg Fortress Publishers, 1990.

Wolff, Pierre. *Discernment: The Art of Choosing Well*. Liguori, MO: Liguori Publications, 2003.

Resources on Lay Ministry
from the Congregational Resource Guide

Bugbee, Bruce, Don Cousins, and Bill Hybels. **Network: The Right People...In the Right Places...For the Right Reasons** (videos/manuals). Grand Rapids, MI: Zondervan Publishing House, 1994.

> Replacing antiquated, ineffective "time and talent" surveys, the Network system offers a step-by-step process involving small groups and one-on-one interactions with trained in-house volunteers to help members of congregations discern their gifts, find their passions, and gain insights into personal style. The system also clearly identifies and provides instruction for the various jobs needed to make it all work. While the system is presented in a conservative-to-moderate Christian "voice" with an evangelical bent, it will be useful for a variety of congregations and denominations. The complete kit includes two videos and a set of manuals for each of the system's roles.

Centered Life
www.centeredlife.org
Center for Lifelong Learning, Luther Seminary
2481 Como Avenue
St. Paul, MN 55108
(651) 641-3353, Fax: (651) 641-3351

> Asserting that humanity's task is "to care for God's creation and share the gospel of Christ," Centered Life helps individuals and congregations discern and live their callings. ("Callings" refers to all of the ways you spend your time—in your family, community, workplace, and church.) Congregations that join Centered Life complete a seven-phase process to help them equip and support their members with doing God's work. They are supplied with an assessment tool, the assistance of Centered Life staff, and other

resources tailored to their particular strengths and needs. Additional resources, such as the "Discover Your Strengths" workshop, are described on the Web site.

Cobb, John B., Jr. **Reclaiming the Church: Where the Mainline Church Went Wrong and What to Do About It.** Louisville: Westminster John Knox Press, 1997.

> Most churches, particularly those in "mainline" denominations, are facing the problems of declining attendance and increasing marginalization. John Cobb believes the remedy is more foundational than programmatic. It lies with the church (1) rediscovering its passion for the conviction that the Christian faith is of supreme importance to individual church members, the body of the church, and the world and (2) engaging in serious theological reflection about our shared faith. This book avoids giving easy, formulaic answers and calls for the whole church to engage in the theological endeavor. It will greatly benefit congregational leaders who want to call their churches to a deeper Christian understanding.

Countryman, L. William. **Living on the Border of the Holy: Renewing the Priesthood of All.** Harrisburg, PA: Morehouse Group, 1999.

> William Countryman claims that all people minister as priests and receive priestly ministrations from one another. In so doing, they give and receive a new understanding of the world. Each priest's vocation, whether fundamental or ordained, is "discerned through honest assessment of our individual gifts and longings and in conversation with one another." Countryman suggests ways the fundamental priesthood of all can be facilitated in the functioning of a congregation. He advocates envisioning "team ministries so that they are not merely extensions of the rector or chief pastor." He also advocates forming cluster groups of congregations with shared leadership to support ministries that no one congregation could accomplish singly.

Dickhart, Judith McWilliams. **Church-going Insider or Gospel-carrying Outsider?: A Different View of Congregations.** Chicago: ELCA Division for Ministry, 2002.

While congregational leaders say they want members to carry the gospel into their daily lives, they encourage members to focus instead on sustaining internal church ministries. Judith McWilliams Dickhart challenges lay and ordained leaders to move beyond thinking of their mission as simply perpetuating worship attendance in the same building at the same time each week. She believes we must equip Christians with resources for living their faith in the world. The author supplies narratives that illustrate how some people are finding fruitful ways to integrate faith and life. This book is a resource of the ELCA's Division for Ministry program, "SPLASH! The Ripples of the Baptized."

Droel, William. **Full-Time Christians: The Real Challenge from Vatican II.** Mystic, CT: Twenty-Third Publications, 2002.

For Father William Droel, the real challenge of Vatican II lies not in the adoption of new liturgical language or changes in Roman Catholic customs but in the spirituality of our everyday lives. He believes that our spirituality is most revealed in our daily interactions with those we encounter at work, at home, and in our communities. While Droel acknowledges the enormous contribution of lay people as pastoral counselors and catechists within the church, he also challenges lay people to embrace a life globally centered on the gospel and focused on more fully living the good news of God's universal love and salvation through Jesus.

Friend, Howard E. **Recovering the Sacred Center: Church Renewal from the Inside Out.** Valley Forge, PA: Judson Press, 1998.

Using metaphor, story, and reflection, Howard Friend develops a theological and practical guide to congregational renewal. He begins by exploring the concept of "sacred center"—something that is both akin to a true "self" and closely connected to the divine. Next, he reframes four subjects theologically, taking the "sacred center" into consideration: scripture, sacred space, personhood, and transformation. Friend applies this theology to the life of congregations from several different angles. Finally, he shares stories from his ministry experience to highlight the transforming power of recovering the "sacred center." This book will serve as valuable guide for congregations in search of renewed vitality.

Goetz, David L., Editor. **Building Church Leaders: Your Complete Guide to Leadership Training.** Matthews, NC: Leadership Journal, 1998.

This loose-leaf collection contains reproducible handouts useful for leadership training and discussion on 12 crucial areas of congregational life: assessing church needs; character of a leader; reaching people; church health; spiritual care; handling conflict; recruiting and staffing; finances; motivating leaders; worship; vision; and building a team. Selected by the editors of *Leadership Journal*, the material comes from leaders such as John Maxwell, Marlene Wilson, Bill Hybels, and others.

The Gospel and Our Culture Network
www.gocn.org
101 E. 13th Street
Holland, MI 49423-3622
(616) 392-8555, Fax: (616) 392-7717

The Gospel and Our Culture Network (GOCN) operates to "provide useful research regarding the encounter between the gospel and our culture" and to "encourage local action for transformation in the life and witness of the church." Its founders believe that such a network is necessary because shifts in Western society have resulted in the marginalization of the church and the popularization of values (consumerism, individualism) at odds with the gospel. As a network, it fosters intra- and cross-denominational connections between lay persons and clergy, between educators and pastors, and between denominational executives and congregational leaders. Its Web site features online discussion groups, a newsletter, and a book series.

Guder, Darrell L. **The Continuing Conversion of the Church.** Grand Rapids, MI: Eerdmans Publishing, 2000.

Observing that "we are constantly tempted to assert that our way of understanding the Christian faith is a final version of Christian truth," Darrell Guder argues for redeveloping the theology and practice of mission. The author cites the historical influence of individualism and reductionism on evangelism and discusses present-day challenges to evangelical ministries. He also explores the meaning of "continual conversion" and explains the importance of acting to change church institutional structures and practices. Seminary students and teachers, lay and ordained congregational leaders, and others involved in mission work will find this resource invaluable.

Johnson, Abigail. **Reflecting with God: Connecting Faith and Daily Life in Small Groups.** Herndon, VA: Alban Institute, 2004.

Here is a step-by-step guide for leading theological reflection groups. After explaining why it is important to ponder theological topics, Abigail Johnson moves into the nuts and bolts of setting up theological reflection groups. She then leads the reader through each step of group facilitation, touching on important elements of the process. She also examines the "ripple effect" of reflection groups on a community, recognizing that the conclusion of a group does not mean the end of thinking, examining, and questioning. A reflection group such as the one described by the author helps to develop Christians who are dedicated to taking scripture, theological concepts, and the church seriously.

Mallory, Sue. **The Equipping Church, Serving Together to Transform Lives.** Grand Rapids, MI: Zondervan Publishing House, 2001.

Beginning with the injunction that pastors are to "equip the saints for the work of the ministry," *The Equipping Church* passionately relays the process that lay minister Sue Mallory and her team followed in developing a culture and system in the church for supporting lay ministry. Not a "quick fix" program, this book identifies processes that must be tailored to each church's culture and vision. Mallory's discussion of difficult issues, and her identification of resources, make this book highly practical. Congregational, educational, and denominational leaders seeking to implement a vision for a vibrant church—with members equipped to fulfill their callings—will benefit from implementing its ideas.

Mallory, Sue, Brad Smith, Sarah Jane Rehnborg, and Neil Wilson. **The Equipping Church Guidebook.** Grand Rapids, MI: Zondervan Publishing House, 2001.

This guidebook accompanies Sue Mallory's book, *The Equipping Church*, and provides extensive detail on both developing a church culture and implementing a system for lay ministry in the local church and community. Part 1 describes how to develop a church vision and culture ripe for implementing lay ministry. Part 2 provides the steps for building an equipping ministry system— preparing, connecting, and equipping people for service. Within the text are lists of ideas, tables, and charts for teaching tools as well as forms and job descriptions to adapt. This book would be useful for church staff, lay leaders, seminarians, and teachers of lay ministry.

Moots, Paul. **Becoming Barnabas: The Ministry of Encouragement.** Herndon, VA: Alban Institute, 2004.

Becoming Barnabas takes a fairly obscure character in Scripture and crafts around his actions an entire way to do ministry. Paul Moots particularly looks at Barnabas's generosity, his willingness to partner with others, and his ability to forgive as essential to the work of the church. Written for lay and ordained congregational leaders, this book encourages opening leadership opportunities to the entire congregation. The author understands and responds to the difficulties and fears that arise when leadership responsibilities expand beyond usual channels, persons, or committees. While giving up control is not easy, Moots explores the possibilities that can emerge when we are willing to share control with others.

Ogden, Greg. **Discipleship Essentials: A Guide to Building Your Life in Christ.** Downers Grove, IL: InterVarsity Press, 1998

Discipleship Essentials is designed to be used in weekly sessions as a small-group (three or four people) curriculum or for individual study. Drawing on the principles and patterns presented in this workbook, groups learn to model their lives after the example Jesus set for his disciples. Three important values drive "disciple-making": a desire to know the truth of God's Word, a willingness to live in caring and ongoing relationships with one another, and a commitment to mutual accountability for our actions and agreements. Lessons for the weekly sessions are thematically arranged and feature "core truths," Bible studies, and additional readings.

Ogden, Greg. **Unfinished Business: Returning the Ministry to the People of God.** Grand Rapids, MI: Zondervan, 2003.

> Greg Ogden asserts that the unfinished work of the Reformation is to expand responsibility for ministry to all people, not just clergy. Describing the church as an "organism" rather than an "institution," Ogden also expands the venue for ministry to include the church, the world, and all aspects of life. He explores the roles of the church, the pastor, and leadership in the New Reformation and emphasizes the church as an equipping entity. He includes examples and models to support his ideas, making this an in-depth resource on empowering people for ministry. This book is an updated version of a classic text, *The New Reformation: Returning the Ministry to the People of God.*

Schwab, A. Wayne. **When the Members Are the Missionaries: An Extraordinary Calling for Ordinary People.** Essex, NY: Member Mission Press, 2002.

> For Wayne Schwab, the work of the church is supporting members as they discover their callings in the "mission fields" of daily life: home, work, the local community, the wider world, and the faith community. Schwab provides the theological foundations of his vision, examples of individual missions, materials to discern and support missionaries, a process for congregational transformation, and models for judicatory and national church restructuring. This book will be helpful to any congregation—large or small—seeking to reclaim the promise and responsibility offered through baptism. Readers may visit a Web site (www.membermissionpress.org) to learn how congregations are using the book.

Stevens, R. Paul, and Phil Collins. **The Equipping Pastor: A Systems Approach to Congregational Leadership.** Bethesda, MD: Alban Institute, 1993.

> Drawing on systems theory, covenant relationships, and Biblical references, the authors present a model through which clergy can move congregations from focusing on self-preservation to fulfilling their ministry as Christian ambassadors. Shifting the focus from equipping individuals to equipping the whole church, they affirm the importance of interdependence among church members and

explore various dysfunctional relationships that work against interdependence. Visionary servant leaders must recognize that their authority ultimately rests in God and that they can only effectively fulfill their calling through a life of prayer. Leaders must also affirm that ministry is not what we do with "extra time" but what we do with all of life.

Trumbauer, Jean M. **Created and Called: Discovering Our Gifts for Abundant Living.** Minneapolis: Augsburg Fortress Press, 1998.

True to its title, *Created and Called* emphasizes that we are co-creators with God and that each person is gifted and called to ministry. Unlike manuals with similar themes, *Created and Called* explains how our gifts are more than our most visible talents and skills: they include our interests, motivations, styles, values, hopes, and vulnerabilities. Jean Trumbauer helps us to recognize and integrate our gifts and apply them to needs in both the church and the larger community. With reflection guides, exercises, samples, and resources in each chapter, *Created and Called* is an excellent tool for small groups, adult education classes, and leadership programs.

Trumbauer, Jean M. **Sharing the Ministry: A Practical Guide for Transforming Volunteers into Ministers.** Minneapolis: Augsburg Fortress Press, 1999.

The author presents a new paradigm of volunteer ministry based on the assumptions that each person is uniquely gifted for ministry, that church ministry is shared, and that staff and lay leaders are to help identify, develop, use, and support the gifts of all members. After explaining the shared ministry systems model, Trumbauer explores in detail its many processes: planning, discovering gifts, designing, recruiting, interviewing, matching, training, supervising, supporting, evaluating, and managing data. Includes reflection exercises, sample models, and suggestions for further resources in each chapter. Readers may also purchase a set of "personal reflection guides" that will facilitate gifts discernment.

Vineyard, Sue, and Hirenda Nath Mukerhjee. **How to Take Care of You . . . So You Can Take Care of Others.** Downers Grove, IL: Heritage Arts Publishing, 1989.

The authors believe that human service workers and volunteers in a variety of venues are at especially high risk of physical, emotional, mental, and spiritual depletion. Their own self-care is often sacrificed while they endeavor to meet the needs of others. Interweaving illustrative stories with simple self reflection tools and practical suggestions, they explore change, grief and stress, dimensions of both depletion and wellness, and methods of gaining balance in our lives. The book will be of interest not only for people who seek greater self-care but also for leaders who wish to build healthier and more respectful systems for volunteers and caregivers.

Wilson, Marlene. **How to Mobilize Church Volunteers.** Minneapolis: Augsburg Books, 1983.

Marlene Wilson asserts that church leaders who plan projects and programs should not focus on filling empty volunteer slots; instead they should identify church members' gifts, leadership styles, and needs. Using her management background, Wilson suggests guidelines for understanding personality types and improving a church's attitudes toward volunteering, planning methods, and mission goals. She then lists exercises that church leaders can use in motivating lay members to offer their talents in the church and community. The sample job descriptions, creativity checklist, personal action plan, and evaluation forms provide concrete ways for church members to develop a vibrant model of service.

Wilson, Marlene. **Creating a Volunteer-Friendly Church Culture.** Loveland, CO: Group Publishing, 2004.

Creating a Volunteer-Friendly Church Culture is the first in Marlene Wilson's latest "volunteer leadership" series. This volume focuses on those most-needed elements for voluntarism to thrive in congregations. Wilson's many years of experience as a volunteer management educator and consultant richly inform this series, which also includes these books: *How to Energize Your Volunteer Ministry; Volunteer Job Descriptions and Action Plans; Volunteer Recruitment, Interviewing, and Placement; Volunteer Orientation and Training;* and *Volunteer Encouragement, Evaluations, and Accountability.* Volumes may be purchased individually or as a set.

7

Understanding Congregational Anxiety

Thomas F. Fischer

"How can they do that?"

"Are they out of their minds?"

"Can't they see how they are destroying each other?"

"When will they finally realize what they're doing?"

Virtually every congregational leader has had thoughts like these upon encountering congregational conflict. Often even more troubling than the conflict itself is a recognition that the parties to the conflict seem unaware of the consequences of their actions. What may help congregational leaders cope with and help heal such conflict is an understanding of the nature of anxiety. Key in this understanding is a recognition that groups tend to demonstrate the same patterns of behavior as individuals during times of high anxiety, and that these patterns are often so ingrained in a congregation's way of life that they may, to a large extent, be predictable.

Are Individual Responses to Anxiety *Predictable*?

Typically, individuals deal with their anxiety in whatever way they believe they have dealt successfully with it previously. When anxiety strikes, some people find that denial is effective in minimizing their anxiety. Others may respond to anxiety by becoming aggressive. Anxiety may cause still others to withdraw or become passive. It can also trigger passive-aggressive tendencies or the use of indirect communication patterns, such as triangling. There are also those who get a "rush" from anxiety; when there is no reason to feel anxious they create one to experience the rush.

Whatever method or approach one uses to address anxiety, several things are certain. The first is that when an anxious situation is presented, many people prefer to react to the anxious situation than address its cause with a solution. For example, when a congregation experiences a financial shortfall, the anxiety produced may cause people to react by undermining the leadership. If they wished to address the cause of the anxiety, they would respond by developing constructive steps for resolving the shortfall in the short and long term.

Even more certain is that whatever methods or patterns have been used to manage anxiety in the past will, by default, continue to be used over and over again. Because these anxiety management approaches "work" for the individual, they are repeated. To the extent that they are repeated, they may become habitual and, by inference, almost predictable.

One pastor, in an attempt to enliven a sense of vision in his unhealthy congregation, shared a vision for ministry much like one that was realized in his previous church. His previous church saw the vision as an opportunity and a challenge to direct congregational renewal. The present church, however, became anxious. Within three months, the ruling board demanded the pastor's resignation. The pastor knew that his predecessor was also forced out. After further investigation, he discovered why; the congregation experienced vision as a trigger for anxiety. Their "predictable" way of managing it was to remove the cause of anxiety—in this case the pastor.

Like individuals, congregations demonstrate a certain, almost predictable, "sameness" in their responses to anxiety. These responses, as in individuals, can be recognized as recurring patterns throughout the life cycle of a congregation. If, as Freud said, "the child is the father of the man," the recurrent patterns by which a congregation will manage anxiety will be fairly well established during its childhood. For many congregations, this begins to take a definite, recognizable form somewhere around their fourth or fifth year of existence. By the tenth year of existence these patterns of managing anxiety can be strongly entrenched. Perhaps this helps explain why church planters have recognized that new churches that stop growing or fail to grow after their eighth year have only a miniscule chance of becoming vibrant, growing congregations.

There are also relationships between individual and congregational patterns of dealing with anxiety. In particular, there is often a direct relationship between the way dominant individuals in the congregation manage anxiety and the way the congregation as a whole responds to anxiety. For example, in one healthy congregation with which I have worked, key leaders are forward-minded, flexible, and supportive of healthy vision. This is due in large part to the personal style of the main patriarch of the congregation. Because he is forward-minded, flexible, and supportive in his private life, his influence has become the dominant mindset of the congregation. As a result, the introduction of change, vision, or anything that would transform the organization is by default considered from the perspective of a forward-minded, flexible mindset. Because of this healthy approach to anxiety, the congregation continues to prosper with an ever-enlarged sense of vision, growth, and vitality in its mission.

In one unhealthy congregation I have observed, reactivity and verbal abusiveness by one or two dominant individuals has become the congregation's "preferred" dominant pattern for dealing with anxiety. During a major congregational conflict, one such member publicly attacked the pastor with anger and abusive language. The pastor was devastated. He couldn't understand what he had done to deserve such treatment . . . until the next morning when he visited the hospital after learning that the spouse of the abusive individual had had a heart attack the evening before. As the pastor entered the cardiac intensive care unit he was shocked to find the parishioner who had attacked him shouting at her husband's physician, revealing a pattern in her response to anxiety—abusiveness.

SELF-DIFFERENTIATION: A KEY TO HEALTHY LEADERSHIP

This experience helped the pastor understand that people are fairly consistent in their responses to anxiety. As the saying goes, "As the people go, so goes the church." It also helped the pastor to relieve himself of much unwarranted guilt. As the pastor reflected on this experience, he was—perhaps for the first time—able to let go of his feelings of guilt and recognize that the situation had not been his fault. This awareness is a foundation for healthy leadership. Murray Bowen,[1] Edwin Friedman,[2] Peter Steinke,[3] and others refer to this awareness as an important part of "self-differentiated leadership." Leaders who have the capacities for self-differentiated leadership are able to stay calm and stay the, especially in anxious times.

Congregational leaders desiring to transform anxious congregational patterns have found that teaching self-differentiation to the church's leadership teams can be one of the most effective ways to begin transforming unhealthy congregational responses to anxiety. Under the direction of Richard Blackburn, the Lombard Mennonite Peace Center of Lombard, Illinois is one of the most prestigious organizations teaching this approach throughout the world. Its workshops and seminars provide a remarkable foundation for healthier, self-differentiated leadership.

Even as self-differentiated leadership is directed to the management of healthy emotions, Daniel Goleman, Richard Boyatzis, and Annie McKee describe in their book *Primal Leadership: Realizing The Power of Emotional Intelligence* how leadership is more about *emotion* than it is about strategy.

> If a leader resonates energy and enthusiasm, an organization thrives;
> if a leaders spread negativity and dissonance, it flounders. This break
> through concept charges leaders with driving emotions in the right
> direction to have a positive impact [in their organization].[4]

One of the most important keys to leadership, then, is the ability to not become emotionally entangled in a congregation's anxious responses. This means leaders must understand the dramatic effect of emotionality and anxiety in organizational systems. This also requires that leaders be able to overcome their own anxious reactivity and stay the course even among the most highly anxious churches. Obviously, this is much easier said than done. Even the best leaders may find this difficult in the most anxious congregations, even over the short term.

EQUILIBRIUM AND PREDICTABLE BEHAVIORS

To the extent that organizations maintain the status quo, they demonstrate the natural tendency toward equilibrium. Just as physics shows that "an object at rest tends to stay at rest," so organizations of all kinds will tend to continue to demonstrate a sameness or predictability. This does not mean, however, that these organizations are necessarily healthy. By the same token, such patterns are not necessarily unhealthy either. Many healthy churches enjoy the stability of a ministry characterized by cycles of discerning vision, stretching toward attainment of that vision, successfully dealing with opposition and other barriers, and enjoying the fruits of their labors. To a significant degree, such healthy patterns are as predictable as unhealthy ones. There are, however, limits to that predictability. While leaders can anticipate that they will likely experience the same dynamics in their ministry as those experienced by the pastors who preceded them, each minister's experience will be akin to a different verse of the same song since each new pastor is different from his or her predecessors, and new people and personalities may have entered the congregation.

Can Change Happen?

To paraphrase a common cliché, churches, like people, can change—but not very much. This means most changes will be met with various levels of resistance. The larger the change, the greater the potential for resistance. Congregations seeking to break the so-called "150 barrier" in weekend worship attendance, for example, will almost predictably resist the relational, programmatic, and organizational shifts required to attain and sustain long-term worship attendance of 150 people. Likewise, congregations that had their origins in congregational splits will tend to split again and again...and again. In one schismatic congregation, not only were the splits predictable, but the timing of when they would reoccur was also predictable. In this congregation, each of four successive pastors spent his or her first three years overcoming the antagonism that existed in the congregation. In each pastor's fourth and fifth years, the church grew dramatically. At the beginning of the sixth year, the growth came to a screeching halt, and during the seventh year each of the pastors was sabotaged by congregational anxiety. This repeated cycle seemed to center around congregational anxiety triggered by the following issues:

1. **Finances:** The congregation, which had no long-term debt, was wary of taking any risks that might require even small, short-term loans.
2. **Growth:** Many long-time members of the congregation were threatened when they realized that twenty-five percent of the congregation had joined in the last two years. Such growth meant they would lose their influence. Most important, it would

threaten their patterns of dealing with anxiety. Indeed, the new families, simply by virtue of managing anxiety differently, would create greater anxiety among the longer-term members.

3. **Trust:** One of the key indicators of congregational anxiety can be the inability to trust others, especially leaders, during anxious times. As leadership was distrusted, accusations of embezzlement, false teaching, and incompetence permeated the organization, though there was no truth to any of the charges.

4. **Poor Anxiety Management:** One of the underlying and most significant triggers for the group's anxiety was the inability of the dominant forces of the congregation to manage their individual anxiety in a healthy manner. When anxiety runs amuck, so do people. It was this out-of-control anxiety—and not the presented (and unsubstantiated) issues of conflict—that really caused members to leave. They left the church because they were afraid of, or were unwilling to deal with, anxiety.

This "seven-year itch" pattern was repeated five times in this congregation's first forty years of existence. At this writing this church is in its third year with its current pastor. Guess what? The congregation is starting to grow! What will happen next? One can *hope* that history will not repeat itself, but it's hard not to be pessimistic given the congregation's history.

These seemingly predictable patterns of behavior can be very challenging for church leaders. Leaders who have been in situations similar to the "seven-year itch" congregation described above will understand the agony of such an experience and the gutwrenching soul-searching they engender. All of the pastors who served that congregation wondered at one time or another what they had done to deserve such treatment, and the pain of seeing God's people attacking each other, leaving the congregation, or standing by and doing nothing was overwhelming. A sense of being helpless to intervene to prevent further damage only added to their sense of failure and loss. Much of this pain could have been avoided, however, had they only understood the historical patterns of the congregation. Understanding the predictability of such patterns is an important first step toward gaining insight as to how to intervene in anxious congregations.

UNDERSTANDING ANXIETY

Congregational anxiety is a real and growing phenomenon in the church. When asked what he thought of the new seminary applicants, one psychologist who administers psychological tests for a major seminary responded, "They are getting dumber and crazier."

Ministry and leadership are certainly not easy tasks. Conrad Weiser's remarkable book *Healers Harmed and Harmful*[5] describes the emotional pain that often accompanies congregational leadership. Every leader, regardless of his or her personality structure and values, is vulnerable. Upon reading this in-depth work, many readers will no doubt find Weiser's comments closer to reality than they would care to admit. Recognizing these vulnerabilities, however, is the first step toward a healthier self and a healthier leadership style.

Systems Theory Vs. Psychology

Leaders must not only understand how *individuals* respond to anxiety but also how systems—composed of a dynamic interrelationship of individuals within a group—respond to anxiety. The literature on this subject is diverse and there appears to be an ongoing tension between systems practitioners (who focus on the system's functioning) and psychologists (who focus on the individual's functioning). Psychologists say the reasons for behaviors reside in the individual psyche, so they place the responsibility for anxiety on the individual. Heinz Kohut's theory of psychodynamic psychology is dominant in this vein. Abraham Maslow's emphasis on individual "self-actualization" and Erik Erikson's "Hierarchy of Needs" are but some of the many psychological theories that focus on individual cognition and other psychological dimensions of behavior.

Systems practitioners, on the other hand, believe individual behavior is largely determined by the systems in which they live. Some systems theorists downplay—or even deny—the role of *individual* anxiety, claiming that anxious individual behaviors are solely due to the system's response to anxiety.

The Systems Approach

According to systems theory, if one can change the system, individuals in the system will change their behavior. Murray Bowen has greatly influenced systems theory and its application to family therapy. For him, systems theory provided ways to describe how—and why—families behave as they do. Bowen suggests his family systems theory offers a "way of thinking that may help bridge the compartmentalization of knowledge that presently exists."[6]

> Bowen deviated from the mainstream of psychiatric thinking of the 1940s and 1950s in two important ways: First, his theory was developed on the assumption that an understanding of man's emotional functioning must extend beyond psychological constructs to recognize the human's relatedness to all life, and second, his theory assumed that an adequate understanding of human behavior must rest on a foundation that went beyond the study of the individual to include the relationship system. In essence, Bowen proposed that the family operated in ways that were consistent with its being a system and that the system's principles of operation were rooted in nature.[7]

Which theoretical perspective—the psychological or systems view—is correct? There appears to be truth in both. The most important task for leaders may be to discern what truths psychology and systems theory apply to dealing with congregational anxiety.

Five Roles in Systems

It is this balance between a systems approach and an individual psychological approach that is necessary to best understand congregational anxiety. This balance recognizes that individuals can and do determine their own behaviors. At the same time, however, individuals will be affected by an ongoing interrelatedness with the system in which they live and function. This interrelatedness between the individual and the system occurs at innumerable levels, both seen and unseen.

An examination of how families maintain equilibrium provides one example of how individual behavior and the influence of systems interrelate. Typical families assign a role to each of their members. The most commonly identified five roles are "scapegoat," "mascot," "hero," "spiritual leader," and "lost child." Families that are able to perpetuate each of these roles as desired by the family will be considered "successful" insofar as they are able to maintain their equilibrium. Whether this equilibrium is healthy or unhealthy is not the family's primary concern. Instead, its *overriding* concern is to perpetuate the status quo by maintaining and perpetuating these roles. For this reason, even unhealthy families will tend to perpetuate their unhealthy, dysfunctional existence, and healthy families will tend to perpetuate their healthy function. Thus, as each family member plays out his or her assigned role in the expected manner, each family member contributes to the maintenance and perpetuation of the family equilibrium...for better or worse.

Churches are like families in that they utilize these same roles for the same purpose: *to maintain equilibrium.* This can be seen in healthy churches that are remarkably charitable, forgiving, supportive, and excited about their leaders. It can also be seen in churches that repeatedly force out their pastors.

In churches with a pattern of removing their pastors, the five roles mentioned above are assigned in a way that essentially guarantees that each new pastor will ultimately be forced out. For instance, the system might assign the pastor the role of scapegoat and the role of hero to the head antagonist. The role of the lost child might then be assigned to those who might otherwise intervene, rendering them powerless. As the system determines, such individuals will be reduced to simply praying and watching helplessly on the sidelines as the scapegoated pastor is attacked and discarded.

The system may also repeatedly assign the role of spiritual leader to a congregational patriarch or matriarch. Whether leading, participating in, or enabling the dismissal, the spiritual leader will struggle to keep faith alive within the congregation. Sooner or later, this individual may also emerge to encourage healing and promote peace through Bible studies, worship, or other activities. Individuals who assume the mascot role will attempt to provide relief from tension through humor, fun, or spontaneity.

What is important to notice in this example is that each of these roles complements and is interconnected with all the others. The resulting effect is simple. Equilibrium is maintained and the same healthy—or unhealthy—dynamics are perpetuated.

These roles are present in virtually *all* human relationship systems. This specifically includes families *and* churches. Though largely unseen or unnoticed, the degree to which each of these roles is operative—and who fills these roles (or combination of roles)—has an enormous bearing on the family (or congregational) system's nature, identity, behavior, and function.

Internationally known consultant Lyle Schaller confirms that these roles are in the church. In his book *The Middle-Sized Church: Problems and Prescriptions*, Schaller describes six congregational roles. In *Looking in the Mirror: Self-Appraisal in the Local Church*, he adds that one can expect to find these roles in the church in broadly similar proportions to those found in the general population.

When individuals begin to understand the interaction of roles within family or congregational systems, they start to gain important insights into the wide range of emotional responses that occur in organizations and individuals. As reads one bumper sticker, "The more dysfunctional they are, the crazier they get."

Anxiety in Community

Certainly the church is not the *only* anxious community in our society. Instead, it is one of the many anxious communities that make up what may be a largely anxious society. Yet every congregational leader must deal with anxiety in individuals and in relationship systems. In *Looking in the Mirror*, Lyle Schaller notes that demographic data suggest that one can expect about three percent of the individuals in any organization to be extremely dysfunctional, a statistic I've learned to use as a coping mechanism. Simply by saying "three per hundred" I remind myself to maintain a healthily differentiated perspective when encountering these anxiety-driven behaviors in the church.

Separation Anxiety

If, as Weiser indicates, unresolved separation anxiety is an undeniable basis of psychological trauma, one can expect that much of the anxiety of the church is centered around separation anxiety. Interestingly enough, both systems practitioners and many psychologists agree with this diagnosis. Rabbi Edwin Friedman is the author of the highly acclaimed application of family systems theory to congregational life, *Generation to Generation: Family Process in Church and Synagogue*. Echoing Bowen's research in family systems theory, Friedman claims that all conflict is the result of imbalanced and unmet expectations of closeness (fusion) and separateness (distance). In other words, conflict is the result of people's anxiety of either being too close and too controlled or too distant and abandoned.

Closeness and Separateness

The struggle between closeness and separateness is played out in the church—and in *every* relational interaction—on a daily basis. According to Friedman, every interpersonal interaction can be defined, discussed, and analyzed in terms of closeness and distance and how closeness and distance are used to manage relationships. This relational proximity, then, is of pivotal importance for everyone in highly relational communities, including churches, synagogues, and other religious organizations.

The following comments are some expressions of the dynamics of separation (closeness and distance) by parishioners toward their pastors.

- The pastor is too controlling (or not controlling enough).
- Why won't the pastor visit me? (or visit me more often?)
- The pastor doesn't like me. That's why the pastor is always so critical!
- After all I've done I don't deserve to have the pastor treat me that way!
- How dare the pastor ignore me, challenge me, or doubt me!
- If I don't do what the pastor asks of me, maybe she won't like me anymore.

Note that the separation issue is not played out only by the parishioner in relationship to the pastor, but also by the pastor in relationship to the parishioner. Pastors, then, must be aware of their own separation issues. Depending on how deeply entrenched—and evident—the pastor's separation issues are, all of the above issues can be seen in pastors, too.

The following comments are examples of some expressions of the dynamics of separation by pastors toward parishioners.

- Why are the leaders so controlling?
- Why doesn't anybody respect me or listen to me?
- Don't the people care for me?

- I don't deserve to be treated this way. Maybe if I change they'll love me.
- How can members ignore me?
- I hope I do everything right so that people don't get mad at me and leave the church!

Naturally, there are times when some of these responses might be healthy, the important point to remember is that it is in the *responses* of individuals that one can see anxiety at work. When dealing with anxiety, an important rule of thumb is this: the more reactive the response, the greater the anxiety that is at work. When anxiety is present, all relationship interaction between individuals in the system becomes distorted. This distortion can transform otherwise healthy relationships into unhealthy, anxiety-dominated relationships. As anxiety increases, unhealthy behaviors, ranging from compulsivity to narcissism and despondent passivity, may also appear.

Anxiety and Relationships

Sharon Wegscheider Cruse, Janet Woititz, Judith Viorst, Melody Beattie, Steven Carter, Julia Sokol, John and Linda Friel, and Henry Cloud are best known for their insights on anxiety and relationships. Their insights on codependency, boundaries, shame, control, and adult children of alcoholics greatly help us understand the roots of anxiety and its effect on relationships.

Melody Beattie's book *Talk, Trust, and Feel*[8] describes how individuals troubled by separation anxieties go through various cycles, behaviors, and thought processes indicative of these anxieties. This results in unhealthy relationships. Such relationships may be abusive, codependent, addictive, or unhealthy in other ways. The people in these unhealthy relationships are afraid either to be alone or to be too close to others, and they thus are not able to enjoy healthy relational intimacy with others.

Healthy relational intimacy is based on the ability to learn how to develop trust in the unhindered verbalizing and sharing of feelings in relationships. As Beattie noted, when individuals are not able to "talk, trust, and feel" with others, anxiety increases. In response, defense mechanisms arise. If the anxiety is not released by talking, trusting, and feeling, anxious individuals will develop patterns of acting out their anxiety in behaviors. The maxim, "What is not *talked* out is *acted* out" describes this phenomenon.

Acting out often disrupts, upsets, and destroys relationships in families and churches. If uninterrupted, individuals may also begin acting out in defiance in their relationship with God. This "acting out" is one major cause for unusual and seemingly inexplicable behaviors ranging from uncontrolled rage to verbal and physical abuse. Unfortunately, this acting out may also be evidenced in misconduct by pastors, leaders, and parishioners who choose not to engage in healthy talking, trusting, and feeling with their spouses and, instead, engage in inappropriate relationships.

Giving a "Voice" to Relieve Anxiety

In their best-selling book *Getting to Yes: Negotiating Agreement Without Giving In*, Roger Fisher and William Ury apply the principles of the Harvard Negotiation Project to relationships and organizations. One of Fisher and Ury's most important urgings to leaders is to give people a "voice" to express their feelings as a means of reducing anxiety. In relational terms, giving people a voice is really inviting them to healthy relationships in which they can talk, trust, and feel.

Unfortunately, not everyone has the capacity to express his or her "voice," much less use it appropriately. In some cases, giving voice to individuals enmeshed in addictive emotional processes may make as much sense as allowing an abusive, intoxicated person a public forum by which to attack others with impunity. The more he or she talks, the more absurd the situation may become. This increasing absurdity will almost certainly result in greater anxiety for all present.

Anxiety: The Addictive Connection

Facing separation anxiety is one of most painful experiences of grief and brokenness. Consequently, many people avoid experiencing the feelings associated with their separation fears. In order to cover the "black hole" of emptiness caused by abandonment and separation, individuals turn to a virtually unlimited number of addictive substances and compulsive behaviors.

Several years ago, while immersed in numerous readings about alcoholics and the effects of addiction on their families, I consulted with a 150-year-old congregation nestled in a beautiful resort community on the Great Lakes. The pastor called me and asked for a consultation. He explained how the congregation was beset with uncontrollable anxiety and conflict. Overwhelmed by the congregational anxieties, he had submitted his resignation as pastor, effective in 90 days. As consultant, my role was to calm things down and enable him to have a "healthy" exit.

The consultation began with a MinistryHealth.net seminar entitled "Understanding Anxiety: Emotional Process in the Congregation." As we discussed anxiety, I shared how much of what happens in highly anxious congregations is very similar to what happens in alcoholic families.

A "Eureka" Moment: We're Addicted!

In one of the most memorable "eureka" moments of my consultation ministry, six congregation leaders (of 25 in attendance) came up during the break and asked, "Tom, do you do alcoholic counseling? My spouse is an alcoholic." These individuals came forward because they began to recognize that the anxiety their congregation was experiencing had dynamics nearly identical to those of their alcoholic families. Apparently, these anxious leaders brought their family anxieties to bear in the congregation's relationship system. As they did, their anxious patterns of behavior permeated the church at virtually *every* level of its functioning.

After the seminar, the congregational chairperson described how she had been married to an alcoholic and was currently married to a husband who was rabidly anti-alcohol in any form whatsoever. "What happened? I don't understand it," she said. I responded, "When you changed spouses, you didn't escape addictions. You simply *changed* addictions. As your first husband was addicted to alcohol, your current husband is addicted to being anti-alcohol. Each extreme will bear the same addictive dynamics."

At the end of our discussion she, like others who came forward, realized they had brought an anxiety-based pattern of behavior into the church. As these dynamics were identified and discussed, the leaders began to develop a consensus on how to change themselves…and the church.[9]

The next finding that emerged from our interaction was that the highly anxious dynamics of distance and closeness played out in this church. Locked into relationship patterns common to alcoholics and other addiction-prone individuals, the leaders of this church were unable to talk, trust, and feel. Thus, they acted out their anxieties in ways that resulted in serial pastoral force-outs, a continued inability to develop healthy ministry vision, and the development of leaders who were not able to maintain a healthy sense of boundaries and self-differentiation. Having infiltrated the highest levels of this church, the patterns of anxious, addiction-driven behavior became, in themselves, addictive. One might even say that the membership became intoxicated by the emotional dynamics of the anxiety. Sadly, they nearly brought this 150-year-old community of faith to an end.

Fortunately, through subsequent consultations, this congregation was able to begin to unravel its anxiety, retain its pastor, and begin creating a healthy "talk, trust, and feel" congregation. A key to renewal for this church was that its members were able to withstand the anxiety necessary to change from an unhealthy, anxious-based system to a healthier level of functioning.

The greatest joy for those in this congregation was that once they began the path of recovery, they realized that the pain they experienced was really a gift of God. The unhealthy addictive dynamics they so painfully experienced led them to a sense of spiritual brokenness, and it was this brokenness that led them to develop healthy, healing connections with the community. They invited an Alcoholics Anonymous group to meet in the church, they started support groups for grief and depression, and they made dramatic inroads in providing for the homeless in the region.

Three years later this congregation appears to be healthily focused on its mission, is supportive of its pastor (who retracted his resignation), and is making significant progress in helping individuals in the community deal with anxiety in healthier ways.

Churches that "act out" are not uncommon. Those who are willing to painfully work through the process of introspection and growth, however, are not nearly so common. But when such growth occurs, congregations can begin to sow the seeds of long-term renewal and anxiety reduction.

Is the Church *Really* Addicted?

It would be easy to overstate the presence of addictive dynamics on many levels in organizations and churches. Yet addictive dynamics are quite entrenched in civilized Western society. Abraham Twerski and Craig Nakken's book *Addictive Thinking and the Addictive*

Personality: Understanding the Addictive Process, Compulsive Behavior, and Self-Deception[10] is perhaps the one book that affirms the prevalence of addictive behavior patterns in organizations. The relational dynamics of addiction Twerski and Nakken describe in organizations are virtually identical to those found in John and Linda Friel's *Adult Children: The Secrets of Dysfunctional Families*, Robert J. Ackerman's *Perfect Daughters: Adult Daughters of Alcoholics*, and several books on codependency. Melody Beattie's *Codependent No More: How to Stop Controlling Others and Start Caring for Yourself* provides further agreement and insight on addictive behaviors. My own article, "Ten Commandments of Dysfunctional Families," at MinistryHealth.net, further describes these dynamics, which are seen in pastors and parishioners alike.

It's undeniable: unhealthy, anxious congregations behave like addictive individuals and families. Interestingly enough, it is specifically anxious, addictive dynamics that Rabbi Edwin Friedman attributed as a factor contributing to the "failure of nerve" in contemporary Western society.

Needed: Ecclesiastical Sobriety?

One unexpected but remarkable resource for understanding and intervening with addictive behaviors—and the unhealthy, addiction-driven, anxiety-ridden individuals who are in them—is Toby Rice Drew's four-volume series, *Getting Them Sober*. Recommended by the likes of "Dear Abby" and Melody Beattie, each volume contains approximately 40 to 50 one- or two-page chapters. These short gems, which were originally written for family members of alcoholics to assist them in responding in healthy ways to their addictive relatives, provide many insights into antagonistic and controlling behaviors. These extremely helpful and easy-to-read resources are remarkably appropriate for congregational leaders in addictive-prone organizations.

Developing an understanding of the dynamics of addictive emotional processes is an important way to maintain a healthy self and healthy leadership. Toby Rice Drew underscores the importance of intervention in addictive relationship systems in volume 3 in his *Getting Them Sober* series. As he says in that volume, "If you live with insanity long enough you will (a) feel insane, and (b) act insane."[11]

Anxious churches may be addicted. Those that are have a choice: to heal or not to heal. If you are the leader, you have a choice. You can either go insane or apply strategies to establish a sense of sanity.

ADDICTION AND ANXIETY

One of the interesting aspects of the relationship between addiction and anxiety is that anxiety can contribute to addiction. Addiction can mask pain for a while, but sooner or later, as Nakken notes, addiction starts to create pain, the very thing the person is trying to avoid. In creating pain, the process also creates a need for the continuation of the addictive relationship. The addict seeks refuge from the pain of addiction by moving further into the addictive process.[12]

This dynamic is seen in highly anxious congregations that have unhealthy reactive patterns of conflict. After discovering that fusing with those who are willing to take control of their anxiety eases their own anxiety, clusters of these anxious individuals join together in unhealthy anxiety-based relationship groups. As anxious individuals participate in these groups, they feel that their anxieties are lessened. But they are not. They are merely masked under a heightened level of addiction-based and anxious "Band-Aid"™ relationships.

Those to whom anxious individuals give their control are also anxious. Instead of directing their energies inward to develop healthy ways to deal with their own anxiety, these anxious individuals often direct their energies outward by manipulating and controlling others and their environment.

What is the result? *Both* groups get what they want—namely, a mechanism by which they can have their anxiety controlled, even if by unhealthy means. Frequently, anxious individuals use fusing with others as a defense mechanism against their fear. In other words, they avoid the fear of things going out of control by fusing with those who are more than willing to take control and responsibility for them. This is one of the roots of codependency. By allowing others to fuse with them, those in control also gain a powerful defense mechanism. By exerting power, they keep individuals distanced from them. The greater their need for control, the more they will seek emotional isolation from others.

This dynamic describes *numerous* congregational dynamics. It describes, for instance, how—and why—so-called antagonists often express such extreme needs for power and control. Those needs

are rooted in their fear. It also describes why trying to shift the unhealthy equilibrium away from a historically entrenched antagonist is such a precarious proposition. When one threatens, withholds,
or destroys a person's unhealthy defense mechanisms, that individual will likely react in very intense, visible ways.

When an antagonist steeped in anxious, addictive behaviors is
confronted, a multitude of other events may also be triggered. One
thing that is likely to happen is that anxiety will be triggered in both
the antagonist *and* those who are fused to the antagonist. That's why
confronting an antagonist seldom is a one-on-one venture. When an
antagonist is disturbed, all those who depend on that person to ease
their anxieties are also disturbed, and the hornets' nest that results
can be overwhelming.

In some cases, this anxiety-based fusion may also describe how
some pastors are able to draw crowds and grow congregations. This
fusion may be expressed as a type of charisma, preacher worship,
blind allegiance, or out-and-out brainwashing and mind control. For
this reason, family systems theory may suggest the reality that church
growth and health are not faith issues *per se*. Instead, they are issues
of interpersonal bonding between two parties. If they ease each
other's anxieties by filling their needs for anxiety management, a
bond is formed, charisma is born…and emotional loyalty ensues.

Healthy Churches/Healthy Faith

Insofar as churches and their leaders are effective in applying healthy
principles of faith to their lives and interrelationships as God's
people, the church will be more effective in realizing God's mission.

Perhaps the most important principle for anxiety management is
a proper understanding of the grace of God. "For it is by grace you
have been saved, through faith—and this not from yourselves, it is
the gift of God—not by works, so that no one can boast" (Ephesians
2:8-9 NIV). Grace, in the Christian tradition, is how we are saved.
But one of the key hallmarks of grace is also the promise that God
will never, ever abandon the faithful. His promise of grace is simply
the promise of unconditional non-abandonment. When individuals
know and trust that God will always be there, their anxiety of abandonment begins to subside.

When congregational leaders recognize that the fear of abandonment is at the root of anxiety, they recognize that the preaching of

grace is the greatest single way to relieve anxiety. God's promise is that he will be with us always to the end of the world (Matthew 28:18-19). To the extent that individuals trust this, they will find their anxiety is relieved. To the degree to which the church is able to effectively proclaim and help individuals internalize grace in all its doings and help individuals affirm that God is surely with them—always, everywhere, every day—anxiety will be reduced and church health will increase.

Like (Addictive) Family, Like (Addictive) Church?

By more than coincidence, the fusion and enmeshment that happens in anxious congregational systems between anxious individuals mimics what happens in addictive family units.

For example, an abusive, alcoholic husband may be in abusive control of his family. In spite of all the pain, fear, hurt, and abuse, the wife stays with the husband. The children are told to keep quiet. Fearing the father's wrath, they stay in the family. They refuse to rebel. They do not follow common sense and do what is right to deal with this addictive, abusive father. Why? Because they believe that even though it is frightening to be in the family, it is even more frightening to *go out alone* from the family. This is the power of separation anxiety. When people believe their survival is at stake, they will do anything—as irrational as it appears—to survive. Unfortunately, much "survival" behavior in anxious systems can encourage self-sabotage. Janet Geringer Woititz describes how this self-sabotage takes hold in such individuals in her book *The Self-Sabotage Syndrome*. Those leaders affected by self-sabotage can experience a wide variety of manifestations of pain ranging from workaholism, indecision, entrapping perfectionism, burnout, poor management of employees, and, among other things, inept or inadequate responses to crises.

In churches where an anxious "survival" dynamic is dominant, turning it around is extremely difficult and often hazardous. Adding to the difficulty is trying to avoid triggering any tendencies toward self-sabotage that may exist. Some anxious congregations may heal and experience increased health and renewed vitality. However, most congregational systems will almost always tend to feel threatened by any intervention. When high levels of anxiety are triggered, so are the unhealthy organizational system's mechanisms designed to return it to its original unhealthy, anxious equilibrium.

Vision-Proof Churches

For this reason highly anxious churches may be considered "vision-proof." Like individuals caught in what Nakken calls "the negative reinforcement of an addictive personality,"[13] vision-proof churches often get caught up in repetitive patterns characteristic of alcoholics or other addicts:

- I don't really need people.
- I don't have to face anything I don't want to.
- I'm afraid to face life and my problems.
- Objects and events are more important than people.
- I can do anything I want, whenever I want, no matter whom it hurts.

Some "maintenance" churches are anything *but* healthy. Some are outright addicted—in a big way! Their attitudes reflect those demonstrated by alcoholics. Note the similarities!

- We don't need people!
- If we don't need people, we certainly don't need *more* people!
- So what if we've got problems? We don't have to face anything we don't want to.
- We don't care who gets hurt as long as we get our way and keep on getting what we want and doing what we've always done.
- We can do anything we want to and no one—not even God—is going to stop us.

Could "We've never done it that way before" be indicative of anxious congregations dominated by addictive emotional processes? Note that what is common to all these anxious responses is an inability to manage anxiety. A key capacity for anxiety management, as mentioned above, is the ability to talk, trust, and feel.

Whenever there is a breakdown of communication and the honest and forthright sharing of feelings and support, anxiety increases. The increased anxiety results in an emergent pattern of distrust. Without healthy trust, the decline of the church inevitably follows. Congregational health, like individual health, is rooted in healthy capacities to talk, trust, and feel. This must occur within oneself, in one's relationship system, and, especially, with one's God.

Ministry to Addictive Churches

Perhaps some of the most difficult experiences of pastoral ministry occur in churches dominated by addictive emotional processes. Totally unaware of the situation, passionate, gifted, and well-intended men and women of God (clergy and lay) go into such churches to "save" them. They naïvely believe that by simply providing quality ministry, leadership, and their own remarkable skills, the churches will move from anxiety to health. Certainly the people will understand simple logic, they think. Certainly they'll understand God's Word, right?

No, they won't understand it, perhaps not at all!

The prophetic tradition in the Christian scriptures records numerous times when great spiritual leaders were sabotaged or ineffective at ministering to the people of God. "Repent!" was often their message. A violent, reactive, and vehement "No, thanks!" was often the response. Whether one considers Moses, Abraham, Paul, or Jesus, the words of Isaiah apply: "Ever seeing but not perceiving, Ever hearing but never comprehending" (Isaiah 69 NIV).

Dealing with Congregational Addiction Today

Like prophets, pastors and other church leaders should expect that they, too, may have difficulty being heard by anxious crowds. After all, the ministry bears the mantel of the early prophetic tradition in our day. Unfortunately, the pattern that often plays out goes something like this:

1. A naïve but energetic and remarkably competent individual becomes the pastor of an addictive church.
2. The pastor believes that if everything is done perfectly, people will respond positively and love/respect/accept the pastor's ministry.
3. When the congregation doesn't respond as expected, the pastor simply tries harder and harder to please others through ministry accomplishments. As the pastor exerts greater efforts, he or she becomes unintentionally absorbed and involved in the addictive emotional process.
4. The congregation rejects the pastor and anything he or she has done to bring growth.

5. The pastor, broken and devastated, goes into a deep depressive cycle with a loss of self-respect, self-confidence, self-control, self-importance, and self-love. Without intervention, the pastor may leave the ministry by active choice or by "acting out anxiety" via professional misconduct.
6. The unhealthy addictive congregation gets another pastor.
7. See step #1.

Pastoral Acting Out

Addictive emotional processes affect everyone within their influence. Congregations are not the only ones susceptible to addictive emotional processes. Pastors are also vulnerable. This vulnerability may lead to pastoral misconduct, including sexual misconduct.

Patrick Carnes is one of the most respected pioneers in the area of sexual misconduct. In *Contrary to Love: Helping the Sexual Addict*, Carnes provides remarkable insights regarding the progression of addiction in general and sexual addiction in particular. His books make the anxiety-addiction connection undeniable. Perhaps one of Carnes' most important premises, echoed by the writings of many others, is that addictions seldom appear as a *single* addiction. Instead, they nearly always come in multiples. For congregations, this means that consultants, pastors, leaders, and members will have to find ways to untangle the web of intertwined, overlapping, and confused—but interrelated—foci of the addictive process. The key for untangling the web is to address the root cause: uncontrolled and improperly managed anxiety.

For pastors, this means that when misconduct occurs, it is not just *one* issue—the sexual misconduct—that must be dealt with. Instead, the misconduct may involve acting out an entire complex of multiple addictions, unhealthy coping mechanisms, and out-of-control childhood issues within the context of an anxious congregational setting. The higher the levels of organizational anxiety—covert or overt, acute or chronic—the higher the likelihood that pastoral anxiety will increase. Tragically, with increased anxiety one can expect a corresponding increase in misconduct.

Pastors entangled in the whirlwind of congregational anxiety often find themselves overwhelmed with myriad unidentifiable sources of anxiety. Ironically, the harder those who don't understand the anxieties try to identify and work through them, the more anxious they become. As anxiety triggers a sense of being out of control, anxious pastors begin acting out their anxiety in a variety of unhealthy out-of-control ways. This may include everything from sexual misconduct, leaving the ministry, becoming overly rigid or overly flexible, expecting perfection from those around them, or becoming apathetic.

Whatever the nature of the acting out, pastors, their families, and churches experience great pain. As in the case of Humpty-Dumpty, picking up the pieces after the great fall is often extremely difficult and painful. Sometimes it can seem impossible. Successful recovery requires several years and removal from unhealthy environments.

When acting out occurs, the answer is not merely to discipline the individual. Simply being judgmental and removing the pastor is not really helping the hurt, nor is it directing the pastor to healing. Often, simplistic solutions such as "just get rid of the pastor" or "you're gone" are not only naïve, they may also be rooted in the anxiety of those who throw the first stone. Too afraid to risk dealing with the offender, too anxious to face the possibility of extending forgiveness and trust, and lacking the capacity to talk, trust, and feel, these individuals may simply cast hurting pastors aside, often toward greater pain and hurt.

Without compromising God's will in these matters, healthy intervention is necessary for both the pastor and the congregational system in which ministry was conducted. Both parties are affected. Both must deal with the intense multiplicity of anxious interactions that propelled the acting-out behavior. If possible, intervention should guide the individual—and congregation—through intense brokenness, forgiveness, renewal, and restoration to an appropriate place within the Kingdom of God and the experience of grace.

The Function of Addictive Patterns

Another interesting similarity that addictive organizations and individuals share is that the addiction can take on several different patterns. Peter Steinglass, general editor of *The Alcoholic Family*, notes that there are several types of addictive patterns. These patterns serve various functions. The first and most important is self-preservation. Whether real or imagined, perceived danger or threat to one's fragile, anxious world will trigger addictive reactions.

A second and related function of addictive response patterns is to manage internal anxiety levels. Highly irrational and reactive behaviors can be demonstrations of the release of addictive anxiety. Often this anxiety is targeted—usually unfairly—at specific persons.

Highly intense reactivity, abruptly ended communication, and other otherwise inexplicable relationship breakdowns can often be attributed to reactive responses characteristic of addictive types of anxiety. A very tragic consequence of these reactive episodes is self-sabotage. Individuals with addictive anxiety not only hurt those around them, but they also hurt—or destroy—themselves. Their highly anxious state prevents them from being able to regulate their negative behavior, frequently with negative results.

A third function of addictive responses is to maintain a façade of calmness; projecting a false sense of security gives the appearance of being in control. As soon as this façade is threatened, addictive individuals fear that others will discover their painful secret—that they really are fragile, vulnerable, fearful, and very anxious. Their addictive response enables them to maintain the façade without having to face their truth. Their addictive response also keeps them from learning how to have healthy relationships. This task consists of being able to learn three key elements of healthy relationships: the capacity to talk and share oneself; the capability to trust in oneself and others; and the ability to learn, share, and accept one's true feelings.

Types of Addictive Patterns

Like alcoholics, some anxious churches demonstrate their anxiety in "binges." This happens when suddenly, out of the calm, the church becomes consumed by anxiety. These binges, or anxiety eruptions, often occur at regular intervals. In these churches, it seems that there is a natural inclination to demonstrate addiction-based behaviors (like jettisoning a pastor) on an almost predictable timetable. This was the case with the church described earlier, which was on a seven-year cycle; every seven years the congregation would experience an anxious "binge" resulting in the ouster of its pastor.

Other churches, like chronic alcoholics, cannot go through a single day without being anxious. They need to maintain an unhealthy addictive equilibrium by satisfying their urges every day. No matter what day you arrive, they're sick—and often not willing to recover. In these churches, manifestations of chronic anxiety can be observed, the most obvious being intense emotional closeness or intense emotional distance.

Those responding with intense emotional closeness often demonstrate a type of gang-like enmeshment. In this scenario, both the extremely strong leader and the enmeshed followers are driven by anxiety typical of addictive individuals. When anxiety erupts, the response is usually instant warfare. Large groups of individuals are almost instantly energized with more than necessary force to remove the source of the threat. Many conflicts, especially more extreme ones, are of this nature.[14]

Those whose anxious response is characterized by emotional distance tend to avoid interaction with the source(s) of anxiety at all costs. On the surface they may appear friendly, but this friendliness often masks an inability to appropriately confront wrong, hold others accountable, and otherwise engage in healthy relationships. These congregations offer unhealthy excesses of "trust." This false trust results either in (1) minimal or virtually nonexistent procedures, guidelines, and policies for appropriate organizational accountability, or (2) excessive development and enforcement of policies and guidelines. Either extreme mitigates against healthy flexibility, reinforces unhealthy control, and provides a framework to ensure that certain predictable patterns will continue to reoccur *ad nauseum.*

These churches are doomed to remain vision-less, ineffective, and passive. Their only hope is that they, like the enmeshed group above, learn healthy relationship skills. In addition to learning how to talk, trust, and feel, they need to learn anxiety management, boundaries, and how to maintain a healthy sense of self (so-called "self-differentiation") in groups.

Pastoral Intervention in Anxious Organizations

Pastoring an anxious church steeped in addictive emotional processes can be like leading a recovery support group. In fact, anxious churches may have a number of the same characteristics as people in addiction recovery groups, including:[15]

1. High leader expectations
2. Participant passivity

3. Resistance to extending beyond themselves
4. Shallow sacrifice
5. Entitlement mentality
6. "Poor me" focus
7. Projection of guilt
8. Inappropriate anger directed at leader
9. Unmanaged high anxiety and frustrations at inability to control it
10. Inability to recognize options
11. Egocentric focus on their own needs
12. Unwillingness to change
13. Overall ineffectiveness of empathy
14. Selfish focus on their own needs at others' expense
15. Grouping together based on similar pain to justify and perpetuate their pain
16. Tendency to become inconsistent in their faith walk
17. Lack of healthy boundaries
18. Pain-driven behavior
19. Immediate gratification orientation
20. Low self-esteem
21. Controlling behaviors
22. Undermining of leadership
23. Defensive behaviors

These are just *some* of the many forms of anxious congregational behaviors. As leaders learn to understand that congregations function and respond as systems, they begin to see the complex interaction of groups and their respective ways of managing anxieties. As leaders recognize, understand, and respect these dynamics, they begin to see that church leadership is not just a matter of leading or motivating individuals. It's also a matter of shaping, influencing, and leading systems away from crippling anxiety to greater health and vigor and more effective realization of the congregation's mission.

Speed Leas and George Parsons's *Understanding Your Congregation as a System: The Manual* and the accompanying *Congregational Systems Inventory* provide an excellent way to learn about and introduce the concepts of systems theory in a congregation.

A Spiritual Perspective

Unhealthy intimacy patterns in which people act out—and do not talk out—are also of spiritual concern. Those who cannot "talk, trust, and feel" God cannot love God with "all their heart, mind, and soul." Healthy spirituality requires capacities for healthy intimacy with God in one's entire being. As Paul wrote in Ephesians 5:

> In this same way, husbands ought to love their wives as their own bodies. He who loves his wife loves himself. After all, no one ever hated his own body, but he feeds and cares for it, just as Christ does the church—for we are members of his body (Ephesians 5:28-29 NIV).

As this text demonstrates, in order to love one's spouse one must learn to love oneself first. This love requires a capacity for healthy "talk, trust, and feel" intimacy.

The prime directive of spiritual organizations such as churches—and specifically the Christian church—is to teach love. "God is love," "God so loved the world," and other scriptures speak of God's nature. In so doing they call individuals to love God. When people are called into discipleship, the scriptures often require that they separate from their material and relational connections in the world:

- Once the hand is put to the plow one cannot look back.
- Once you start fleeing you can't turn around or you'll become a pillar of salt.
- If you're going to be a disciple you can't bury your father.
- If you're a rich young man you can't follow Jesus if you're still tied to possessions.
- If you want to be like Elijah, butcher your oxen, burn the yoke, and move on.
- If you're a fisherman you must leave your nets and boats behind.
- If you follow Jesus your family will be divided mother against daughter.
- If you want to live in God's promises you'll have to move out of Haran...even if you're 75 years old. And when, 25 years later, God finally gives you a son he'll test your discipleship by seeing if you're able to separate yourself from your son by offering him as a sacrifice.

This is how God tests love: by causing us to have to undergo separation from earthly loves. As Job discovered, he gives so that when he takes away we will love him and exclaim, "The Lord gave, and the Lord has taken away; blessed be the name of the Lord" (Job 1:21). If separation anxiety is a root cause for unhealthy individuals and organizations, then the number one task is to provide a spirituality that recognizes, accepts, assists, and celebrates the process of separation, brokenness, and spiritual renewal.

Perhaps it is not coincidental that many in this so-called "postmodern" age are seeking this sort of authentic and genuine spirituality apart from the institutional church. In unhealthy, anxiety-based, addictive congregations, such authentic spirituality cannot exist. The addictive process overwhelms it.

Grace and Trust Overcome All

The first key for confronting and transforming anxious and addictive emotional processes is grace. Grace, as understood in the Christian tradition, is defined by Paul in Ephesians 2:8–9: "By grace you have been saved through faith, and this is not your own doing; it is a gift of God—not the result of works, so that no one may boast."

This traditional understanding sometimes obscures an important aspect of grace, which is God's unconditional promise not to abandon us. Grace is God's guarantee that no matter what happens, he's always there. No matter how great or painful the loss, God will never leave. Old Testament Jews and others also shared this same view of God. Indeed, it is characteristic of most spiritual systems.

The second key is trust. To trust God does not merely mean to have faith in him. Rather, we can think of trust in this way: trusting God means to let God have his way no matter what the pain, the inconvenience, the cost, the sacrifice—even if it means death—and to say, "It's OK."

Highly anxious churches plagued with separation anxieties do not evidence the elements of healthy churches: vision, relational warmth, the ability to sacrifice, and the capacity to experience joy. Why? Because they are held hostage to their fear of being separated from the things and people they depend on in the material world. And what kind of emotions do hostages show? Those who have given up become cynical, depressed, despondent, unresponsive, blaming, introspective, bitter, and cold. Congregations held hostage by their fears demonstrate these and other symptoms of anxiety.

A FAITH ISSUE?

Put in this perspective, congregations overcome with addictive emotional patterns have a serious *spiritual* problem. Like the church of Ephesus, they have not only lost their first love, they are dangerously close to losing faith altogether! Why? Because they are not willing to leave what is comfortable to follow God's call to them. They fear separation because they really aren't sure if God's grace-based promise not to abandon them is really true. If they cannot be sure, then they cannot trust God's leading and let God have his way...and say "It's OK."

Pushing the Envelope of Grace and Trust

In this context, perhaps one of the most important tasks for those who would seek to transform anxious organizations is to continually keep the people of God on the cutting edge of grace and trust. There are numerous ways to do this: sermons, liturgical rites, assimilation programs, and stewardship campaigns are all necessary. Tithing is also an important strategy for challenging members to trust. "Test me in this," God told Israel through Malachi. "See if I will not bless you."

Big Hairy Audacious Goals

Like Martin Luther King, Jr., who was compelled to proclaim, "I have a dream," all God's servants have compelling reasons to have "God-possible dreams." Such dreams are those visions that can only be accomplished by God. Secular writers call these seemingly impossible dreams BHAGs.[16]

BHAG is an acronym for "big, hairy, audacious goal" (although some church folks call them big, holy, audacious goals). "No BHAG, No Growth," I wrote in my article "Get A BHAG" in MinistryHealth.net.[17] One might also say, "No BHAG, No *Faith*." Scripture is a voluminous collection of BHAGs—creation, miracles, resurrection, grace; who would have ever believed it was possible? It's just one BHAG after another. Apparently God must love BHAGs; he's done so many of them.

Examples of BHAG

How can you stretch a congregation's faith? How can the leadership get people into a lifestyle of grace and trust? What is one of the greatest tools for teaching congregations how to manage anxiety? Get a BHAG! Here are some examples BHAGs for congregations:

- Experiencing the spiritual renewal of a congregation that had been mired in anxiety, conflict, antagonism, and self-centered ministry.
- Moving the church to a new location.
- Totally shutting down a declining church, restructuring its worship and ministry, changing its name, and restarting it in the confidence of God's blessing.
- Setting a faith budget well beyond the reasonable expectation of anyone and achieving it.
- In faith, adding staff to promote and extend the ministry of Jesus Christ from your church.
- Adopting extraordinary mission goals that your church has never even imagined it could meet.
- Planting a new church with the assistance and sponsorship of your congregation or a cluster of congregations.
- Personally surviving a congregational split. Overcoming temptations to commit suicide, surrender to mental illness, or resign is no mean accomplishment. It's nothing short of miraculous. Indeed, if God were not there for us in the conflict, who could stand?
- Following the BHAG when God calls and beckons you and the congregation to stretch toward his vision.

As long as there's a possibility for a BHAG, the church has possibility for growth. If BHAGs continue to be rejected there is a strong possibility that unhealthy, anxious emotional processes will begin— or have already begun—taking control of the organization.

CONCLUSION: ADDRESSING ANXIETY

The more one sees how anxious responses imitate behaviors found in addictions, the greater the likelihood one can understand the often incomprehensible anxious responses seen in congregations.

When leaders see that the real issue in the church is the anxiety that underlies the surface responses, they can begin to develop a more effective presence in the congregation.

Daniel Goleman, Richard Boyatzis, and Annie McKee's book *Primal Leadership: Realizing the Power of Emotional Intelligence,* mentioned earlier, offers remarkable insight for leadership. Applying insights offered by theories of emotional intelligence, Goleman et al. provide scientific support for the idea that organizations that encourage leadership styles that enable such things as flexibility, tolerance for ambiguity, risk-taking, and innovation are organizations that develop healthy anxiety management.

As leaders model a less anxious style of leadership, they will discover that the principle of biblical grace is the key theological tool for addressing congregational anxiety. As grace is proclaimed, God uses it to bring individuals—and eventually the whole congregational system—to recovery. As congregations are led to understand grace, God calls the entire congregational system to greater anxiety management.

Perhaps the ultimate test of the system's ability to manage anxiety is to take a BHAG step of faith. Can you lead your congregation to that goal for the glory of God? Understanding the role of your own—and your congregation's—anxiety is an important first step. Don't be afraid to take it . . . today!

NOTES

1. Murray Bowen and Michael Kerr, *Family Evaluation* (New York: Norton Publications, 1988).
2. Edwin Friedman, *Generation to Generation: Family Process in Church and Synagogue* (New York: Guilford Press, 1985).
3. Peter Steinke, *How Your Church Family Works* (Bethesda, MD: Alban Institute, 1993).
4. Daniel Goleman, Richard Boyatzis, and Annie McKee, *Primal Leadership: Realizing The Power of Emotional Intelligence* (Boston: Harvard Press, 2002).
5. Conrad W. Weiser, *Healers: Harmed and Harmful* (Minneapolis: Augsburg Fortress, 1994).
6. Bowen and Kerr, *Family Evaluation* (New York: Norton Publications, 1988), 28.
7. Bowen and Kerr, *Family Evaluation,* 24–25, italics added.

8. Melody Beattie, *Talk, Trust and Feel* (New York: Hazelden/Ballantine, 1991).

9. See Fischer's "Ten Commandments of Dysfunctional Families," article no. 64, online at ministryhealth.net.

10. See also Craig Nakken, *The Addictive Personality: Understanding the Addictive Process and Compulsive Behavior* (Center City, MN: Hazelden, 1996).

11. Tony Rice Drew, *Getting Them Sober,* vol. 3 (Baltimore: Recovery Publications, 1994), 73.

12. Nakken, 29.

13. Nakken, 28.

14. Cf. Speed Leas's Level IV and Level V Conflict.

15. Thomas F. Fischer, "Support Groups: Paradigm for Transformational Ministry," article no. 349, online at ministryhealth.net.

16. James C. Collins and Jerry I. Porras, *Built to Last: Successful Habits of Visionary Companies* (New York: HarperBusiness, 1994).

17. Thomas F. Fischer, "Get a BHAG," article no. 169, online at ministryhealth.net.

BIBLIOGRAPHY

Anderson, Neil, and Charles Mylander. *Setting Your Church Free.* Ventura, CA: Regal Books, 1994.

Beattie, Melody. *Talk, Trust and Feel.* New York: Hazelden/Ballantine, 1991.

Carnes, Patrick. *Contrary to Love: Helping the Sexual Addict.* Center City, MN: Hazelden, 1989.

Collins, James C., and Jerry I. Porras. *Built to Last: Successful Habits of Visionary Companies.* New York: Harper Business, 1994.

Cosgrove, Charles H., and Dennis D. Hatfield. *Church Conflict: The Hidden System behind the Fights.* Nashville: Abingdon Press, 1994.

Drew, Tony Rice. *Getting Them Sober.* Baltimore: Recovery Publications, 1994. Available from www.gettingthemsober.com.

Farber-Robertson, Anita. *Learning while Leading.* Bethesda, MD: Alban Institute, 2000.

Fisher, Roger, and William Ury. *Getting to Yes: Negotiating Agreement without Giving In.* New York: Penguin, 1981, 1991.

Friedman, Edwin H. *Generation to Generation: Family Process in Church and Synagogue.* New York: Guilford Press, 1985.

Gabbard, Glen O. *Psychodynamic Psychiatry in Clinical Practice,* 3rd ed. Washington, DC: American Psychiatric Press, 2000.

Daniel Goleman, Richard Boyatzis, and Annie McKee. *Primal Leadership: Realizing the Power of Emotional Intelligence*. Boston: Harvard University Press, 2002.

Fischer, Thomas. "Healthier Congregations" and "Understanding Anxiety: Emotional Process in the Congregation." Available online at ministryhealth.net.

Johnson, David, and Jeff VanVonderen. *The Subtle Power of Spiritual Abuse*. Minneapolis: Bethany House, 1991.

Mains, David. *Healing the Dysfunctional Church Family*. Wheaton, IL: Victor Books, 1992.

Parsons, George, and Speed Leas. *Understanding Your Congregation as a System: The Manual*. Bethesda, MD: Alban Institute, 1993.

Schaller, Lyle. *Looking in the Mirror: Self-Appraisal in the Local Church*. Nashville: Abingdon Press, 1984.

———. *The Middle-Sized Church: Problems and Prescriptions*. Nashville: Abingdon Press, 1985.

Shawchuck, Norman, and Roger Heuser. *Managing the Congregation: Building Effective Systems to Serve People*. Nashville: Abingdon Press, 1996.

Steinglass, Peter L., et al. *The Alcoholic Family*. New York: Basic Books, 1993.

Steinke, Peter L. *Healthy Congregations*. Bethesda, MD: Alban Institute, 1996.

———. *How Your Church Family Works*. Bethesda, MD: Alban Institute, 1993.

Susek, Ron, and D. James Kennedy. *Firestorm: Preventing and Overcoming Church Conflicts*. Grand Rapids, MI: Baker Books, 1999.

Weiser, Conrad W. *Healers: Harmed & Harmful*. Minneapolis: Fortress Press, 1994.

Woititz, Janet Geringer. *The Self-Sabotage Syndrome*. Deerfield Beach, FL: Health Communications, 1989.

RESOURCES ON CONGREGATIONAL ANXIETY
FROM THE CONGREGATIONAL RESOURCE GUIDE

Collins, James C., and Jerry I. Porras. **Built to Last: Successful Habits of Visionary Companies.** New York: HarperCollins, 1994.

Jim Collins and Jerry Porras assert that companies "need to change in response to a changing world, while simultaneously preserving their core values and purpose." Such an assertion might apply to congregations as well. The authors compared 18 visionary companies with the same number of control companies to determine what factors create visionary companies "built to last." One key principle among visionary organizations: "clock building, not time telling." While "time-telling" organizations last as long as a great idea or charismatic leader, "clock-building" organizations last beyond the tenure of a particular project or leader. Another key principle: "Try a lot of stuff and keep what works." Many organizations stumble on major success through trial and error, experimentation, and risk taking. Similarly, congregations that are not afraid to use their gifts, and to let God reveal what works, will generate new vitality. This book provides valuable insights for congregations seeking to build an enduring purpose. The paperback version is highly recommended because the introduction explains how these principles apply to nonprofit organizations such as congregations.

Cosgrove, Charles H., and Dennis D. Hatfield. **Church Conflict: The Hidden Systems behind the Fights.** Nashville: Abingdon Press, 1994.

Applying family systems theory to the local church, *Church Conflict* helps conflict-ridden congregations to heal and mature by changing the way they understand themselves as God's family. Using family systems theory, authors Charles Cosgrove and Dennis Hatfield help

196

church leaders to discover the problems, issues, and unhealthy behaviors in the wider church family that are often behind individual problems, issues, and misbehavior. Since the way a church handles conflict can make or break its ministry, this resource is a valuable aid to church leaders for resolving conflicts in the congregation and training church members to handle conflict in a healthy way.

Farber-Robertson, Anita, with Meredith Brook Handspicker and David Whiman. **Learning while Leading: Increasing Your Effectiveness in Ministry.** Bethesda, MD: Alban Institute, 2000.

This book is based on the assumptions that effective leadership requires honest self-examination and that this is a difficult task because we have blind spots concerning the impact of our behavior and the thinking underlying it. As a result, our actions are often inconsistent with our most dearly held values and we are either unaware of this inconsistency or plagued with feelings of shame about it. The aim of *Learning while Leading* is to provide tools for identifying inconsistencies between our values and our actions, and for discovering and correcting the erroneous thinking that has made these inconsistencies possible. The ultimate goal of this endeavor is to enable us to become more fully aligned with our deepest values and beliefs, reclaiming the true source of religious authority. This is an important book for anyone interested in real change and growth both in themselves and in the communities or institutions they serve.

Fisher, Roger, William Ury, and Bruce Patton. **Getting to Yes: Negotiating Agreement without Giving In,** 2nd ed. New York: Penguin Books, 1991.

Secular advice for negotiation, *Getting to Yes: Negotiating Agreement without Giving In* is a useful resource for those involved in congregational decision making. The book is based on answering a common question in church work: what is the best way for people to deal with their differences? The authors suggest a process of "principled negotiation," or viewing those we are negotiating with as partners and looking for mutual gains whenever possible. The authors go on to address problems in negotiating, including what to do if those we are negotiating with are more powerful than we are or use unfair tactics, and what to do if they won't negotiate. In their last chapter, the authors list the 10 most common questions about principled negotiation and answer them in some depth.

Friedman, Edwin H. **Generation to Generation: Family Process in Church and Synagogue.** New York: Guilford Publications, 1985.

> Friedman—for 25 years a congregational rabbi, family therapist, and counselor to clergy of numerous faiths—describes in detail how families do and don't work. He applies the prism of family systems theory to both the congregational family and families in a congregation, focusing on the powerful position of clergy for enabling family development around life-cycle events and associated rituals. Friedman centers on behavior rather than on labeled individuals, and he demands our attention to process rather than to an "identified problem." Friedman's work is at the very core of understanding leadership work with both the static and the changing "family."

Friedman, Edwin H. **Reinventing Leadership** (video). New York: Guilford Publications, 1996.

> Edwin Friedman, a rabbi in the Reformed tradition and a family systems therapist, applied the insights of family systems to understanding the dynamics of congregations in his book *Generation to Generation: Family Process in Church and Synagogue.* This video presentation builds on that work by describing how communities become dysfunctional when they are gripped by anxiety and how such communities tend to sabotage healthy leadership. The video goes on to describe the qualities required in leaders in order to overcome the sabotage. The video will prove useful to leadership groups and in classes with clergy and laity who exercise leadership roles in church and society. (Duration: 40 minutes.)

May, Gerald G. **Addiction and Grace.** San Francisco: Harper & Row, 1988.

> This is a powerful and highly readable text that bears reading and rereading by both pastoral caregivers and those who come to them for guidance. Author Gerald Mays explores the forces (especially

addictions) that limit human freedom and the means for transcending them. Underlying the book is the premise that all of us have an innate longing or "sacred hunger" for communion with God. Unfortunately, this hunger attaches itself to any number of substances (drugs, food, money) or other phenomena (achievement, approval, intimacy), and the downward cycle of addiction begins. The author deftly describes the stages through which attachment becomes addiction, the factors that indicate addiction is present, and the psychological, neurological, and theological natures of addiction. He then discusses a way out of addiction—through grace. While we cannot summon or control grace, May suggests we can make room for grace to enter our lives—through prayer and by living faithfully as best we can, with a commitment to honesty, dignity, community, responsibility, and simplicity.

Parsons, George, and Speed B. Leas. **Understanding Your Congregation as a Spiritual System: The Manual.** Bethesda, MD: Alban Institute, 1993.

In this application of systems theory, congregational leaders can explore the forces at work and examine their systemic implications in six key areas: strategy, process, pastoral and lay leadership, authority, relatedness, and learning. The manual provides an overview of systems theory, complete instructions for administering and scoring the Congregational Systems Inventory (available separately), and guidance for interpreting and explaining the inventory results through the examination of sample scores. One focus of the book is to help congregations live in the tension between stability and change by encouraging adaptation to demographic and development changes without incurring too much stress and conflict.

Steinke, Peter L. **How Your Church Family Works: Understanding Congregations as Emotional Systems.** Bethesda, MD: Alban Institute, 1993.

As an accompaniment to Edwin Friedman's *Generation to Generation: Family Process in Church and Synagogue*, this book suggests that interrelatedness produces anxiety and other emotions, but that the anxiety inherent in interrelatedness provides opportunities for change and growth. Author Peter Steinke encourages leaders to be in relationships that neither diminish their own integrity nor intrude on the integrity of others. Healthy responses to congregational struggles, he says, include focusing on self, not others; strength, not weakness; process, not content; challenge, not comfort; integrity, not unity; system, not symptom; and direction, not condition. This book is a valuable resource for congregational leaders.

Steinke, Peter L. **Healthy Congregations: A Systems Approach.** Bethesda, MD: Alban Institute, 1996.

Applying the insights of systems theory to congregational life, Steinke argues that the most effective way to nurture congregational health is by shifting the focus from single individuals or issues to the way the congregation functions as a whole. The author discusses ten principles of health, how anxiety can affect a congregation, and the crucial role that leaders play in congregational functioning. In this era of emphasis on congregational growth, Steinke asserts that a declining congregation can also be healthy. Easily understandable, this book contains helpful illustrations from congregational life as well as reflection and discussion questions at the end of each chapter.

Weiser, Conrad W. **Healers Harmed & Harmful.** Minneapolis: Fortress Press, 1994.

In *Healers Harmed & Harmful,* Conrad Weiser examines the roots of misconduct among clergy, counselors, and other "healers" from the perspective of contemporary clinical psychology. The premise of this publication is that the harmful or inappropriate actions of adults are manifestations of unprocessed damage from childhood. Such damage, Weiser says, can distort perceptions of reality, create an inability to accurately distinguish one's own boundaries or those of others, and interfere with the establishment of healthy relationships. This book explores a wide range of harmful behaviors that can result from unresolved psychic wounds. While not a therapeutic how-to manual for restructuring the self, this book does provide ways for clergy to discern whether they or their colleagues are significantly wounded, how these wounds might be manifesting themselves, and whether they are at risk for misconduct.

8

To Be Paraboloni:
Congregations Serving Communities

Amy L. Sherman

In the third century C.E. a terrible plague struck the city of Alexandria, claiming many lives. The pagans of Alexandria interpreted the event as the gods' punishment. They refused to help the sick since they "deserved" their calamity. Christians in Alexandria, though, responded differently. Out of love for God they nursed the weak and buried the dead. In the process many of them were exposed to the disease and died. Their amazed Alexandrian neighbors nicknamed the Christians "paraboloni," which means "ones who take a risk."

Paraboloni is a biblical word, employed by the apostle Paul in his letter to the Philippians. He notes that his fellow worker Epaphroditus "risked his life" for the sake of the gospel. A pressing question before the church today is whether we, too, are willing and ready to earn this title of honor, to be paraboloni for the sake of Christ's kingdom. Will we engage in vigorous community outreach, compelled by the love of Christ to share grace and compassion with the least, the lost, and the left out?

Foretastes of the Kingdom

Congregations desirous of serving their communities as modern-day "paraboloni" have many resources available to them. The most important is the Bible itself. The scriptures paint the grand picture of God's redemptive story as all history moves toward the consummation of his kingdom. This story of the unfolding of the kingdom of God is the grand theological narrative into which our specific works of community outreach are embedded. We are "called and sent to represent the reign of God" here on earth.[1]

We know the characteristics of this reign. In Revelation we see that the fully consummated kingdom is a place of perfect *shalom*— no more tears, suffering, poverty, loneliness, alienation, oppression, racism, injustice, famine, abuse, destitution, hopelessness, pain, or death. God has left us sufficient evidence of what his best intentions are for humanity; we know the kind of new world he is going to bring into being one day.

This kingdom is "not yet" and will arrive in its fullness only with Christ's return. But this kingdom is also "now." We hear this good news from Jesus' lips: the kingdom has broken into our world (Luke 11:20). Even better, we see visible witness to that reality as Jesus' miraculous deeds bring a foretaste of the kingdom into the lives of those he touches. It is as though he reaches into the future, fully consummated kingdom of God and yanks a taste of it back into the present. It is as if he says, "In the future kingdom there will be no blindness, and so I give you your sight, blind Bartameas. In the future kingdom there is no death, so I say to you, Lazarus, 'Up from the grave!'" In their best form, our community ministries provide people with similar foretastes of the kingdom's healing and peace and power.

This work operates on both the individual and structural levels—that is, the church engages in kingdom work in terms of ministering to specific persons in need. But kingdom work also involves the promotion of public justice, our attempts to advocate policies that can best serve the interests of society's vulnerable members. Sometimes these twin tasks of church-based outreach have been labeled "mercy ministry" and "justice ministry." Both are needed components of effective community outreach.

The book that probably does the best job of discussing the relationship of these two tasks and offering concrete proposals for both mercy and justice work is Ronald J. Sider's *Just Generosity: A New Vision for Overcoming Poverty in America*. In his signature style, Sider starts with biblical analysis and develops a set of general principles around which he orders his policy prescriptions. Not everyone will agree with Sider's specific public policy proposals (he touches on such contentious issues as health care reform, school choice, the living wage, and tax policy) or with every point of his theological interpretation (such as how he treats the subject of the jubilee).

Nonetheless, Sider raises the right questions and helps Christians think "big picture" about the work of the church in addressing poverty in our communities. For more conservative perspectives on some of the topics Sider covers, see James L. Payne's *Overcoming Welfare*,[2] Calvin Beisner's *Prosperity and Poverty*,[3] or Robert Woodson's *The Triumphs of Joseph: How Today's Community Healers are Reviving Our Streets and Neighborhoods*.[4]

SOURCES OF WISDOM

A healthy theory of community ministry begins with the notion of such ministries being foretastes of the kingdom. Many additional sources of wisdom can help churches further refine their work "on the ground." First, specific biblical texts offer practical guidelines to undergird effective mercy and justice ministries. Second, we can glean insights for our community work from many biblical narratives—the story of Nehemiah and the parable of the good Samaritan, for instance. Third, the record of church history is saturated with accounts of saints gone before who have loved their neighbors well. Contemporary community ministers can find much practical advice, for example, in the writings of the church fathers, the Reformers, and 19th-century Christians who engaged in front-line work among the needy. Fourth, numerous books and articles written in just the last 10 years describe many contemporary models of effective church-based outreach and provide practical, step-by-step guidance for congregational leaders wanting to strengthen current outreach programs or launch new ones. Fifth, conferences for church leaders provide useful workshops and prototype models of different kinds of programs. Finally, in the age of the Internet, church leaders can also consult a number of helpful Web sites that can link them to other congregations that share their mission of transforming their communities for the sake of Christ.

BIBLICAL FOUNDATIONS FOR COMMUNITY MINISTRY

To mobilize a congregation for effective community ministry that loves and serves hurting people with humility and Spirit-dependent power—bringing a foretaste of the kingdom to distressed places—church leaders must answer two basic questions: the "why" question and the "how" question.

Parishioners need to know why it is crucial for them and their congregation to get involved in community outreach. The motivator probably needs to be more than the simple statement that there are many community needs "out there." How can leaders and members embrace the challenge of risking comforts, conveniences, time, and money for the sake of needy neighbors? Surely God himself must first work in the heart, fighting selfishness and fostering compassion. In addition, church leaders must cast a compelling vision that inspires the congregation to action.

Nonetheless, getting the why question answered is just the first step. Once inspired and motivated to do something, parishioners need how-to guidance. How does the congregation launch a new community ministry? How should it be organized? How do we practice a mercy ministry that treats poor people with dignity and that avoids the creation of an unhealthy dependency? How do we go about fighting specific instances of injustice in our community? These and many other how-to questions quickly present themselves after the fire that fuels service in the community captures the heart.

THE WHY QUESTION

Several answers can be given to the inquiry, "Why should our church engage in community outreach?" The simplest is that God commands it. Loving our neighbors in need is fundamental to the Christian faith. We know that God is passionate about the poor because over 400 scripture verses speak of his concern for the poor and needy and his desire that his followers engage in compassionate service. Jeremiah 22:16 informs us that defending the cause of the poor is what it means to know God. James 1:27 tells us that "true religion" involves visiting widows and orphans in their distress. First John 3:16 says that if anyone has material possessions and sees his brother in need but has no pity on him, the love of God is not in him. Proverbs 14:31 teaches us that "he who oppresses the poor shows contempt for their Maker, but he who is kind to the needy honors God." The prophet Amos warns us of God's fury over those who "sell the righteous for silver and the poor for a pair of sandals" and who "deny justice to the oppressed" (Amos 2:6-7). And Matthew 25:44-46 warns us that if we fail to care for the least of God's children, if we neglect the naked and poor and hungry, we will be guilty of neglecting Christ himself and our punishment will be eternal damnation.

Ron Sider's little book *For They Shall be Fed: Scripture Readings and Prayers for a Just World*[5] is perhaps the most comprehensive single-volume gathering of these scriptures. Another study examining the scripture's teaching on stewardship and God's concern for the poor is Tom Sine's *Mustard Seed vs. McWorld*.

The sheer magnitude of God's words on the subject of compassionate service among the needy is staggering, especially if the reader has heard little about these particular portions of the Bible in Sunday morning sermons. My workbook *The ABCs of Community Ministry: A Curriculum for Congregations* reviews these teachings and draws implications for our current practice of community outreach. I divide the discussion on biblical texts along the various genres of scripture, examining what the Law, the wisdom literature, the prophetic literature, the Gospels, and the epistles each have to say about God's concern for the poor and his desire that his followers imitate that concern.

Many other books offer answers to the "why question," examining the scriptural mandate for community ministry. These include: *Restoring At-Risk Communities: Doing it Together and Doing it Right*, edited by John Perkins; Carl Dudley's *Community Ministry: New Challenges, Proven Steps to Faith-Based Initiatives*; Michael Christensen's *City Streets, City People*; Cheryl Sanders' *Ministry at the Margins: The Prophetic Mission of Women, Youth & the Poor*; George Grant's *The Micah Mandate*; Tim Keller's *Ministries of Mercy: The Call of the Jericho Road*; and Eldin Villafane's *Seek the Peace of the City: Reflections on Urban Ministry*.

Beyond the call of scripture, churches can also be motivated to reach out to their communities by the desire to evangelize and increase their membership. Others start community ministries that address needs their own parishioners have personally experienced—such as a church-based program providing respite care to parents of severely disabled children that grows out of a congregation's efforts to help one of its own families who have a handicapped child. Welfare reform has stimulated many congregations to launch new ministries to single mothers, including mentoring and job training programs. Local government and social service agencies often approach the faith community for help in solving community problems. In short, the impetus for starting a new community outreach can come from many sources.

In my devotional booklet *Sharing God's Heart for the Poor: Meditations for Worship, Prayer, and Service* I discuss a further answer to the "why" question, arguing that congregations should be motivated to reach out to the local community by the recognition that hands-on, relational engagement among the needy will enrich them spiritually. We who would seek to serve and give to the needy should understand that we will also be receivers in this process, for ministry is mutually transforming. For example, we gain "the gift of agitation" through front-line involvement with suffering people. The New Testament makes it clear that the appropriate posture of the church is the posture of the longing bride, waiting at the altar for the appearance of the bridegroom. The bride is filled with a "holy discontent" over the absence of her bridegroom. The bride is keenly aware of—and acutely impatient with—the "not-yet-ness" of the kingdom of God. The bride, the church, is supposed to be crying out "Maranatha! Maranatha! Come Lord Jesus!" That's what the first century church did, in large measure because it was a persecuted church. It was a body of people keenly aware of the uncomfortableness of their "alien and stranger" status and personally experiencing much suffering and hardship.

This longing posture is not typical of many American congregations, particularly wealthier ones. Our abundance and affluence anesthetize us. We're rather content, and we're not in any big hurry for the kingdom to be consummated. But when we allow ourselves to be touched with the brokenness and pain experienced by our needy neighbors, then an oh-so-needed "holy discontent" can begin to grow within us. As we entangle our lives with those who suffer we can begin to become agitated with the ways things are. And we *should* be agitated because things are not the way they are supposed to be! If things are the way they are supposed to be, then why is the Lord Jesus coming back again to "make all things new" (Rev. 21)?

In addition to gaining an appropriate posture of urgent intercession over the brokenness of the world, we gain "the gift of the garden" from entangling our lives with the lives of those who are poor and needy. This gift is described in Isaiah 58:10-11. The passage reads:

> If you spend yourselves in behalf of the hungry and satisfy the needs of the oppressed, then your light will rise in the darkness, and your night will become like the noonday. The Lord will guide you always; he will satisfy your needs in a sun-scorched land and will strengthen your frame. You will be like a well-watered garden, like a spring whose waters never fail.

There is an important linguistic connection we should notice here. The word translated "spend" in verse 10—"if you *spend* yourself on behalf of the poor"—connotes the idea of issuing forth or pouring out. The King James version talks of "drawing out" your soul to bestow a mercy upon the recipient. We use terms like these when we talk about water. We talk about pouring out water or drawing water from a well. Here the passage asks us to spend ourselves; we've got this "water" of time, energy, heart, and soul and we are to pour it out to water others.

But isn't it our fear that by pouring ourselves out we will become empty and dry? What holds us back from spending our lives on the poor? Isn't it a fear that we won't have anything left? At this point we must be grabbed and comforted by the promise of Isaiah 58:11, which says that we take our "water" and we pour ourselves out among people who need that water. We do not run dry because God pours himself and his provision into us so that we become a well-watered garden. This is the wonderful paradox of the Christian life. When we pour ourselves out we do not become empty; instead, we become full. Engaging in hands-on ministry among those who hurt can bring this rich experience into our lives.

In mobilizing volunteers to serve on the front lines of a new church-based community ministry, it is enormously helpful to talk about these kinds of gifts. This approach—more than a "needs-based" pitch or an appeal that motivates by guilt—is the one most likely to produce humble volunteers who recognize that they will learn as well as teach through their service, that they will receive from the poor as well as give to them. An appeal based simply on need or duty can run the risk of producing a patronizing volunteer, the kind that (metaphorically) rides into a depressed community on a white horse, assuming he has all the resources and answers needed.

THE HOW QUESTION

Scripture not only presents a compelling case for why the church must reach out and serve the hurting, it also offers practical how-to advice through specific exhortations and stories. Consider, for example, the apostle Paul's advice to young pastor Timothy regarding the care of widows in 1 Timothy 5. Paul lays out realistic principles: only older widows should get help, the widows' own

families should be expected first to meet their needs, church leaders should consider the character of the supplicants so as to ensure
that help gets to where it is most needed, and so on. Proverbs, too,
is full of practical wisdom for those that conduct ministry among
the poor. We learn there of the importance of saving and of hard
work. The prophetic literature is saturated by God's concern for
justice and it reminds us in the contemporary church that we must
be educated about the injustices of our land and engaged in actions
to change public policies that violate the poor. (For an excellent discussion of some egregious policies in the United States that hinder
the efforts of low income citizens to improve their lot, see Clint
Bolick's *Transformation: The Promise and Politics of Empowerment.*)[6]

Various passages in the Old Testament also shed light on the
proper construction of benevolence activities. Two examples are of
special note. First, God had the Israelites make provision for the
able-bodied poor through the law's gleaning regulations
(Deuteronomy 24:19-22). Farmers were told to harvest their crops
just one time and to allow the able-bodied poor to glean the rest of the
produce. This system required the "haves" of society to share and provide opportunities for the poor, and it required the "have-nots" to
assume some responsibility and expend some of their own energy
in meeting their needs. Our context today is very different than the
agrarian economy of ancient Israel, but with creativity and inten-
tionality, church-based outreach programs can still practice the gleaning principle.[7] Doing so helps to preserve the dignity of the poor,
many of whom do not want to be passive recipients of charity.

Second, Isaiah 61:1-4 reveals a pattern for transforming broken
people and broken places that has relevance to contemporary community ministry. The pattern has two parts. First, God moves into
the lives of broken people. He did this most clearly through the
sending of Jesus. The scriptures tell us that Jesus was sent to bring
redemption and healing, to comfort those who mourn, and to bind
up the brokenhearted. Through the ministry of Jesus broken people
are renewed and restored. That's the first part of the pattern. The
second part is that the once-broken people—who are now transformed people—themselves become transformers, and God then
uses *them* to restore their broken communities. Think of what Isaiah
61:3-4 tells us about the people whom God meets, heals, and trans-
forms. It says that they will be "oaks of righteousness" who will
rebuild the ancient ruins and restore the places long devastated.

We have the opportunity to participate in this pattern as we minister among the poor. We are the body of Christ, and God calls us to move into the lives of the poor believing that his power can transform people into "oaks of righteousness" that he can use to advance his kingdom in the "places long devastated." Based on this scriptural pattern, we should have a very high regard for those we serve, recognizing that they may be the key change agents God will use in their community to bring renewal. It means that in our community ministries we will make intentional investments in indigenous leadership development.

Various biblical stories also shed light on key general principles that must undergird any effective outreach. From the story of Nehemiah, who not only rebuilt the wall of Jerusalem but also engaged in a spiritual reconstruction of the Israelites' hearts, we see the principle of holistic ministry in action. Distinctively Christian community ministry treats people as whole persons, attending to their physical, emotional, and spiritual needs.

Or take the story of Jeremiah and the field at Anathoth from Jeremiah 32, from which we can gain "a theology of place." [8] We find Jeremiah utterly bewildered. God has given him such a strange command! God has told him to purchase a field in Anathoth, a village on the northern outskirts of Jerusalem. Jeremiah is to buy this land and studiously execute all the legal protocols accompanying the purchase—such as having the deed signed and duly witnessed— and then to seal up the deed and "place it in a clay jar so that [it] will last a long time" (verse 14). Jeremiah faithfully obeys, but he doesn't understand what in the world God is doing because the Babylonians have laid siege to Jerusalem, and Anathoth is behind enemy lines! "Why is God asking me to make such a foolish real estate investment?" Jeremiah wonders, for it appears foolish indeed. Who spends money to buy property they cannot access, property that lies in the enemy's territory?

Jeremiah obeys, but he can't help asking God for an explanation of his strange decree. God answers in verses 27-44, reminding Jeremiah that he has brought upon Israel the judgment he had warned them about: the Babylonians have invaded and conquered. But God wants his people also to know that the time of judgment will not last forever. It will be limited. God promises to redeem Israel from her oppressors. He foretells the day when feasts and weddings will sound again in the fields of Anathoth and across Judea when he restores the fortunes of his wayward children. Simply put, God is asking Jeremiah to make a publicly noticeable investment in a place that others have given up as lost. By doing so, Jeremiah makes tangible God's future promise to reclaim and restore.

The story of Anathoth should cause us to remember that God is still in the reclamation business. He is still calling his followers to "foolish" investments. Impoverished neighborhoods in our cities are also behind enemy lines; Satan has a grip on them through drugs, crime, violence, abuse, and despair. But God has not forsaken this territory and neither should the church. Moreover, he has followers in these neighborhoods—even if they may be besieged by the destructive "street culture" that surrounds them. In accordance with "the Anathoth principle," Christians outside such troubled neighborhoods need to invest in them. We need to embrace our inner-city brothers and sisters, making visible to the watching world the reality that God remains concerned about these distressed places (they are not "God-forsaken") and that it is his desire to see his people unleashed to bring restoration and healing to them.

The well-known story of the good Samaritan instructs us as well. We notice that the good Samaritan did not toss canned goods and a religious tract at the wounded traveler from the opposite side of the street. No, he got up close and personal with the man, getting blood on his own hands from tending the victim's wounds. Often, if we are honest, our community ministries can feel sterile and clinical— we stand behind the soup kitchen line at arm's length, never really embracing those we serve. The good Samaritan displayed mercy of the sort that the church father Gregory of Nyssa had in mind when he defined true mercy as "a voluntary sorrow that joins itself to the suffering of another."[9]

In addition to the wisdom of scripture, we can also learn much from the example of the church in ages past. *Welfare Reformed: A Compassionate Approach*, edited by David Hall, includes a wonderful discussion of the community benevolence policies practiced by the churches of the Reformation. Orphans were adopted and apprenticed; the disabled elderly were given charity. The Reformers' approach to mercy ministry was flexible and personal, not a one-size-fits-all model. Hall notes that Calvin insisted that deacons visit quarterly each family that had received financial help from the church. This promoted a personal relationship between such families and the deacons, allowing the deacons to assess needs (and guard

against fraud). During the Reformation, Calvin's church also provided loans and equipment to able-bodied refugees who had fled
to Geneva under duress, enabling these individuals to restart their
former businesses or trades. Such an approach was considered far
superior to a welfare handout.

Peter Phan's book *Social Thought,* in the *Heritage of the Fathers of
the Church* series, includes quotes and teachings from the church
fathers regarding congregational outreach among the poor. Among
the practical principles penned by these saints was the realistic
charge to "let your alms grow damp with sweat in your hands until
you know to whom you are giving them." We should beware of
thinking the church fathers were coldhearted, though. They coun-
seled believers to share sacrificially. They exhorted people to give
themselves, their time, and their advice rather than simply their
money. They criticized giving "mechanistically." They also encouraged church members to serve the needy in teams. That way, each
helper could offer a little something and the need would be met
without undue impoverishment of the givers.

Saints from a period not so distant to our own time also have
wisdom to share about community ministry. Marvin Olasky's *The
Tragedy of American Compassion* identifies seven key marks of effective compassion drawn from the example of 19th-century
evangelicals who gave themselves sacrificially to serve the poor.
Like the Reformers, these 19th-century Christians categorized the
poor, providing charity in some cases, conditional aid in others, and
work opportunities in still others. These believers also emphasized
bonding—creating a personal friendship with supplicants through
which truly holistic aid could be rendered. These front-line workers reconnected the poor to those bound to help (family, parish) and
engaged in bold yet winsome evangelism to connect them to a restored relationship with their loving Heavenly Father. Such principles are as valuable for action in the 21st century as they were in
the 19th.

PRACTICE: SPECIFIC HOW TOS

While mining the treasures of the past, church leaders should also
be sure to acquaint themselves with the large variety of contemporary scholarship about church-based community development.
Many helpful resources are available today that provide more

specific "how-tos" than the general ministry guidelines discussed above.

Carl Dudley's *Community Ministry: New Challenges, Proven Steps to Faith-Based Initiatives* is a must read in this field. The book offers a short, logical, understandable plan for leading congregations in launching new community serving ministries. Dudley offers guidance for undertaking the three central tasks of such an endeavor: understanding the social context, discovering the congregation's identity, and building the organizational structure necessary to undergird the outreach programs. For each of these categories of activities Dudley offers specific step-by-step advice. For example, to gain understanding of the social context in which the congregation is located, Dudley suggests that a church committee chart the boundaries of its community, identify its anchor institutions, and learn about residents by exploring the community and studying census tract data.

In defining the congregation's unique identity, Dudley encourages leaders to consider their denomination's theology and, if applicable, statements or creeds addressing social concerns. He also suggests that church leaders review the congregation's or denomination's history of social engagement, remembering the kinds of models and programs earlier leaders from their tradition used to spread Christ's love in word and deed. Moreover, Dudley provides examples of churches that have conducted surveys of their congregations to learn of their strengths and weaknesses, assets and liabilities.

With regard to building the organizational structure needed to implement community outreach, Dudley offers advice concerning fundraising, volunteer mobilization and training, and staffing and management issues.

My *Restorers of Hope: Reaching the Poor in Your Community with Church-based Ministries That Work* also contains several "how to" chapters. It discusses strategies for overcoming the barriers to outreach; for casting vision and recruiting volunteers; for defining the outreach's mission, vision, and philosophy of ministry; for assisting churches in the transition from "commodity-based benevolence" (food pantries and clothing closets) to true relational, holistic ministry; and for launching a neighborhood-targeted ministry in partnership with local residents.

John Perkin's edited volume, *Restoring At-Risk Communities: Doing it Together and Doing it Right,* contains one chapter specifically addressing the steps for starting a new, neighborhood-targeted community development ministry. The book also includes how-to advice about specific aspects of Christian community development, including indigenous leadership development and racial reconciliation.

Several books profiling the community ministries of specific churches indirectly provide how-to knowledge (as they look at how the studied ministries began, how they operate, the challenges and changes they have managed, etc.). Included in this genre are such works as: *Upon This Rock: The Miracles of a Black Church* by Samuel Freedman (describing the work of St. Paul Baptist Church in New York City);[10] Howard Edington's *Downtown Church: The Heart of the City* (describing First Presbyterian Church in Orlando); [11] John Perkins' *Resurrecting Hope: Powerful Stories of How God is Moving to Reach our Cities* (includes many anecdotes from ministries associated with the Christian Community Development Association); [12] Andrew Billingsley's *Mighty Like a River: The Black Church and Social Reform* (the latter half looks at community outreach initiatives of several different stripes in African American churches studied onsite or through surveys);[13] Robert Carle and Louis DeCaro, Jr.'s edited volume *Signs of Hope in the City: Ministries of Community Renewal* (which includes case studies of a variety of outreach-oriented congregations—Asian, Latino, African American, and Anglo—in New York City);[14] Nile Harper's *Urban Churches, Vital Signs* (more case studies of urban ministries);[15] and *Restoring Broken Places and Rebuilding Communities: A Casebook on African-American Church Involvement in Community Economic Development* (this report, produced by the African American Church Project of the National Congress for Community Economic Development, profiles 12 congregations—including historically black denominations, mainline denominations, and the evangelical tradition—that are heavily invested in housing, real estate development, and business development in economically depressed urban communities).

Two Web sites also have gathered case study information on the outreach programs of specific congregations. The profiles of the churches include a description of their makeup (demographics, size, and ecclesiology of the congregation) and their community serving ministries (activities, mission, budget, staffing, volunteers). World Vision and other organizations sponsor the www.churchesatwork.org site; Evangelicals for Social Action sponsors the www.network935.org

Web site. The new Web site of Faith and Service Technical Education Network (www.fastennetwork.org), sponsored by the Pew Charitable Trusts, contains many how-to resources, curricula, and profiles of effective faith-based programs.

Additional books provide helpful how-to hints by describing multiple types of church-based community service. Deanna Carlson's *The Welfare of My Neighbor: Sharing Christ's Love for the Poor* includes, for example, a chapter called "Sixty-Six Ways to Love Your Neighbor off Welfare." My *Establishing a Church-Based Welfare-to-Work Mentoring Ministry: A Practical How-To Manual* helps congregations launch mentoring programs to serve families affected by welfare reform. Jeffrey Arnold's *Small Group Outreach: Turning Groups Inside Out* walks church leaders through various ways of utilizing a congregation's small groups as the front-line agents of community service. Jenell Paris and Margot Eyring's workbook, *Urban Disciples: A Beginner's Guide to Serving God in the City*, gives practical advice to short-term missions groups (composed of youth or adults) from non-urban churches seeking to help in inner city communities. Michael Christensen's *City Streets, City People* offers how-to advice for starting ministries among the homeless.

Audiotapes from workshops at various conferences on mercy and justice ministries also offer a wealth of practical advice and ministry training. The annual conferences of the Call to Renewal (www.calltorenewal.com), the Christian Community Development Association (www.ccda.org), and the Interfaith Community Ministries Network are just three examples. Denominations also sometimes sponsor their own conferences on these subjects.[16]

There are many other training programs and curricula available. Evangelicals for Social Action's affiliate, Network 9:35, has recently piloted a new training program called C2C, in which "veteran" congregations engaged in vibrant community ministries school "newcomer" congregations that want to imitate their work (see www.network935.org). In addition, Joseph Holland has created a curriculum called Holistic Hardware to aid churches in helping the homeless and other chronically unemployed individuals to gain the life and job skills necessary to break out of poverty (contact Holland at Holiware@aol.com). New Focus, a national ministry that trains churches in setting up a life skills and budgeting/mentoring program for the working poor, offers a variety of regional training summits throughout the year (contact New Focus in Michigan at

616-895-5356). The National Jobs Partnership (www.tjp.org) has pioneered an effective model for bringing together urban and suburban churches and local businesses to provide job training, mentoring, and job placement for unemployed and underemployed residents of distressed neighborhoods. Begun in Raleigh, North Carolina in 1997, the model has been replicated in over 20 U.S. cities. The National Jobs Partnership's how-to manual, *Collaborating for Employment Among the Poor: The Jobs Partnership Model*, is available through its national headquarters (phone: 919-571-8614).

PRACTICE: MODELS OF CONGREGATIONAL COMMUNITY MINISTRY

While much wisdom can be absorbed through books and tapes, sometimes the experience of visiting a ministry on site is the best catalyst for launching a new community outreach. As Carl Dudley notes in *Community Ministry*, a church committee can, on the basis of its research in the community and in the body of the congregation, develop a rough idea of the kind of ministry that would be most suitable. Once the church knows what kind(s) of ministry it might want to begin, it can learn where similar programs are already underway and interview the people involved. Dudley's book includes an appendix listing short descriptions of a variety of congregations and their community programs.

Community ministries can take a variety of shapes. Some are *population-focused*. That is, they concentrate on a specific group, such as at-risk teen girls, the homeless, women in crisis pregnancies, or gang members. Others are *school-based*. A congregation "adopts" a school or a school district and focuses its ministry efforts there. This might, for instance, involve tutoring children on site at the school. Other ministries are *issue-focused*. They target a specific issue, such as the need for affordable housing or for a health clinic. Others are *neighborhood-focused*. They target a specific community with defined boundaries and invest in the overall development of that area.

Finally, community ministries can also be categorized in terms of their organizational structure. Yvonne Dodd Sawyer, former executive director of Hope for New York, has written a helpful (unpublished) paper describing nine forms of congregational community ministries and identifying their strengths and weaknesses.[17] Some churches follow a diaconal model that utilizes trained deacons (and, where applicable, deaconesses) for mercy outreach to members of the community. Others work together in a regional association with sister congregations (for example, a presbytery), pooling money and volunteers to accomplish ministry projects in a common locality. The United Methodist Church has pioneered the "Shalom Zone" model, in which churches, community groups, and social service agencies all located in a specific area of a city covenant to work together to address comprehensively the needs of that area. Other churches spin off separate, legally incorporated nonprofit organizations (with strong or loose ties to the congregation) devoted to community ministry. Some churches join "issue coalitions," in which congregations of all sorts as well as secular nonprofits, businesses, and diverse community groups come together around a particular issue. Some congregations, such as Lawndale Community Church in Chicago and New Song Community Church in Baltimore, follow the basic model of the Christian Community Development Association (the "3 Rs" of relocation, reconciliation, and redistribution described in *Restoring At-Risk Communities: Doing it Together and Doing it Right*, mentioned earlier). Still other congregations do their work through urban-suburban partnerships aimed at wedding the resources, social networks, and talents of suburban churches with the on-site presence, credibility, local knowledge, and skills of urban churches that are actively fighting poverty in their neighborhoods.

CONCLUSION

Whatever the organizational structure or focus of ministry, the chances are that some other congregation somewhere has attempted to do something similar to what your church proposes. The membership directory of the Christian Community Development Association, which indexes ministries by their type of outreach (youth, tutoring, business development, housing, etc.) is an excellent place to find someone who's already doing what you hope to do. For Hispanic faith leaders desiring to know what their peers are doing in community ministry, visit the searchable, on-line *National Resource Directory of Hispanic Compassion Ministries* at www.hudsonfaithincommunities.org.

The use of such resources can be extremely helpful, but it is also important to realize that despite what you can learn from others, God has something unique for your church. You will need to adapt others' wisdom, experience, and lessons learned for your own context. With much prayer, study, and reliance on the guidance of the Holy Spirit, your congregation can do it—for the spiritual health of your own flock, as well as for your neighbors' good.

SOME FURTHER RESOURCES

Books/Workbooks

Sara Anne Robertson, *Helping the Hurting: A Guide to Financing Christian Social Service Ministries* (Milwaukee, WI: Christian Stewardship Association, 1996).

Theresa Rudacille, *Raising Resources: More Than Fundraising Handbook.* Available through The Empowerment Network (TEN), this is a helpful tool for faith-based and grassroots organizations to use to determine mission, strategic plan, and budget and then to find the resources to fulfill their mission. Contact Rudacille at 6109 Cordova Rd., Columbus, GA 31907 or e-mail: trudacille@aol.com.

Organizations

The Faith-Based Initiative of the National Congress for Community Economic Development. Contact: 1030 15th St. NW, Suite 325, Washington, DC 20005. Telephone: 202-289-9020. Web site: www.ncced.org.

Shalom Zone, United Methodist Church. Web site: gbgm-umc.org/programs/shalom.

Models

Best Friends (school-based teen girls program emphasizing abstinence). Contact: Monte Corbett. Telephone: 202-478-9677. Web site: www.bestfriendsfoundation.org.

Bridge of Hope (church-based mentoring of homeless families in transition). Contact: Edith Yoder. Telephone: 610-380-1360. Web site: members.aol.com/bridgepage.

Center for Urban Missions (neighborhood-targeted, whole-family ministry). Contact: Rev. Gerald Austin. Telephone: 205-252-8286. Web site: www.newcitycenter.org.

Inner City Christian Federation (affordable housing development). Contact: Jonathon Bradford. Telephone: 616-336-9333. Web site: www.iccf.org.

Kids Hope USA (school-based tutoring). Contact: Virgil Gulker. Telephone: 616-846-7490. Web site: www.goseplcom.net/ia/links/khop.htm.
Putting Families First (church-based mentoring of low-income families). Contact: Lisa Van Riper. Tel: 864-917-2001.

Notes

1. Darrell L. Guder, ed., *Missional Church: A Vision for the Sending of the Church in North America* (Grand Rapids, MI: Eerdmans, 1998), 77.
2. James L. Payne, *Overcoming Welfare: Expecting More from the Poor and from Ourselves* (New York: Basic Books, 1998).
3. E. Calvin Beisner, *Prosperity and Poverty: The Compassionate Use of Resources in a World of Scarcity* (Westchester, IL: Crossway Books, 1988).
4. Robert L. Woodson, Sr., *The Triumphs of Joseph: How Today's Community Healers are Reviving our Streets and Neighborhoods* (New York: Free Press, 1998).
5. This is a revised version of Sider's earlier book, *Cry Justice* (New York: Paulist Press, 1980).
6. Clint Bolick, *Transformation: The Promise and Politics of Empowerment* (Oakland, CA: ICS Press, 1998).
7. For some concrete examples, see George Grant's *Bringing in the Sheaves: Transforming Poverty into Productivity* (I.C.E. Free Books, 1985).
8. Mark R. Gornik and Noel Castellanos, "How to Start a Christian Community Development Ministry," in *Restoring At-Risk Communities: Doing it Together and Doing it Right,* edited by John M. Perkins (Grand Rapids, MI: Baker Books, 1995), 217-218.
9. Quoted in Peter C. Phan, "Social Thought," from *Heritage of the Fathers of the Church* (Wilmington, DE: Michael Glazier, Inc., 1984), 129.
10. Samuel Freedman, *Upon this Rock: The Miracles of a Black Church* (New York: Harper Collins, 1993).
11. Howard Edington, *Downtown Church: The Heart of the City* (Nashville: Abingdon Press, 1996).
12. John Perkins, *Resurrecting Hope: Powerful Stories of How God is Moving to Reach Our Cities* (Ventura, CA: Regal, 1995).
13. Andrew Billingsley, *Mighty Like a River: The Black Church and Social Reform* (New York: Oxford University Press, 1999).
14. Robert Carle and Louis DeCaro, Jr., eds., *Signs of Hope in the City: Ministries of Community Renewal* (Valley Forge, PA: Judson Press, rev. ed., 1999).
15. Nile Harper, *Urban Churches, Vital Signs: Beyond Charity Toward Justice* (Grand Rapids, MI: Eerdmans, 1999).

16. My own, the Presbyterian Church in America, held national conferences on mercy ministry in March 2001 and March 2003 in Atlanta. For a list of topics covered (e.g., ministries to the disabled, the homeless, prisoners) and information on ordering tapes, go to www.pcanet.org/cep/Training/Mercy-ministry-report-3-01.htm.
17. For a copy of the paper, contact Ms. Sawyer at FcfcFL@aol.com.

BIBLIOGRAPHY

Arnold, Jeffrey. *Small Group Outreach: Turning Groups Inside Out.* Downers Grove, IL: Intervarsity Press, 1998.

Beisner, E. Calvin. *Prosperity and Poverty: The Compassionate Use of Resources in a World of Scarcity.* Westchester, IL: Crossway Books, 1988.

Billingsley, Andrew. *Mighty Like a River: The Black Church and Social Reform.* New York: Oxford University Press, 1999.

Bolick, Clint. *Transformation: The Promise and Politics of Empowerment.* Oakland, CA: ICS Press, 1998.

Carle, Robert, and Louis DeCaro, Jr., eds. *Signs of Hope in the City: Ministries of Community Renewal,* rev. ed. Valley Forge, PA: Judson Press, 1999.

Carlson, Deanna. *The Welfare of My Neighbor: Sharing Christ's Love for the Poor.* Washington, DC: Family Research Council, 1999.

Christensen, Michael, Paul Moore, and Steve Webber. *City Streets, City People: A Call for Compassion.* Nashville: Abingdon Press, 1989.

Clemetson, Robert A., and Roger Coates, eds. *Restoring Broken Places and Rebuilding Communities: A Casebook on African-American Church Involvement in Community Economic Development.* Washington, DC: National Congress for Community Economic Development, 1992.

Dudley, Carl. *Community Ministry: New Challenges, Proven Steps to Faith-Based Initiatives.* Bethesda, MD: Alban Institute, 2002.

Edington, Howard. *Downtown Church: The Heart of the City.* Nashville: Abingdon Press, 1996.

Freedman, Samuel. *Upon This Rock: The Miracles of a Black Church.* New York: Harper Collins, 1993.

Gornik, Mark R., and Noel Castellanos. "How to Start a Christian Community Development Ministry" in *Restoring At-Risk Communities: Doing it Together and Doing it Right,* edited by John M. Perkins. Grand Rapids, MI: Baker Books, 1995.

Grant, George. *Bringing in the Sheaves: Transforming Poverty into Productivity.* I.C.E. Free Books, 1985.

———. *The Micah Mandate: Balancing the Christian Life.* Nashville: Cumberland House Publishing, 1999.

220

Guder, Darrell L., ed. *Missional Church: A Vision for the Sending of the Church in North America*. Grand Rapids, MI: Eerdmans, 1998.

Hall, David, ed. *Welfare Reformed: A Compassionate Approach*. New York: Covenant Foundation, 1994.

Harper, Nile. *Urban Churches, Vital Signs: Beyond Charity Toward Justice*. Grand Rapids, MI: Eerdmans, 1999.

Keller, Tim. *Ministries of Mercy: The Call of the Jericho Road*, 2nd ed. Phillipsburg, NJ: P&R Publishing, 1997.

Olasky, Marvin. *The Tragedy of American Compassion*. Washington, DC: Regnery Publishing, Inc., 1995

Paris, Jenell, and Margot Eyring. *Urban Disciples: A Beginner's Guide to Serving God in the City*. Valley Forge, PA: Judson Press, 2000.

Payne, James L. *Overcoming Welfare: Expecting More from the Poor and from Ourselves*. New York: Basic Books, 1998.

Perkins, John. *Resurrecting Hope: Powerful Stories of How God is Moving to Reach Our Cities*. Ventura, CA: Regal, 1995.

———, ed. *Restoring At-Risk Communities: Doing it Together and Doing it Right*. Grand Rapids, MI: Baker Book House, 1996.

Phan, Peter. *Heritage of the Fathers of the Church*. Wilmington, DE: Michael Glazier, Inc., 1984.

Robertson, Sara Anne. *Helping the Hurting: A Guide to Financing Christian Social Service Ministries*. Milwaukee, WI: Christian Stewardship Association, 1996.

Rudacille, Theresa. *Raising Resources: More than Fundraising Handbook*. Washington, DC: Empowerment Resource Network, 2000.

Sanders, Cheryl. *Ministry at the Margins: The Prophetic Mission of Women, Youth & the Poor*. Downers Grove, IL: InterVarsity Press, 1997.

Sherman, Amy. *The ABCs of Community Ministry: A Curriculum for Congregations*. Charlottesville, VA: Hudson Institute, 2002.

———. *Establishing a Church-Based Welfare-to-Work Mentoring Ministry: A Practical How-To Manual*. Charlottesville, VA: Hudson Institute, 1999.

———. *Restorers of Hope: Reaching the Poor in Your Community with Church-Based Ministries that Work*. Wheaton, IL: Crossway Books, 1997.

———. *Sharing God's Heart for the Poor: Meditations for Worship, Prayer, and Service*. Charlottesville, VA: Hudson Institute and Trinity Presbyterian Church, 1999.

Sider, Ron, ed. *For They Shall be Fed: Scripture Readings and Prayers for a Just World*. Richmond, VA: ESA Books, 1997.

Sine, Tom. *Mustard Seed vs. McWorld*. Grand Rapids, MI: Baker Book House, 1999.

Villafane, Eldin. *Seek the Peace of the City: Reflections on Urban Ministry.* Grand Rapids, MI: Eerdmans, 1995.
Woodson, Sr., Robert L. *The Triumphs of Joseph: How Today's Community Healers are Reviving our Streets and Neighborhoods.* New York: Free Press, 1998.

Resources on Community Ministry from the Congregational Resource Guide

Bos, A. David. **A Practical Guide to Community Ministry.** Louisville: Westminster John Knox Press, 1993.

> Community ministry, in which congregations of different denominations form an alliance to serve their locality, is unique in that it responds to both community and congregational needs. This book gives direction on assessing local community needs and on starting and developing a ministry. Believing that the strength of directors is the most influential entity in directing the ministry's vision, the author presents a model for orienting and training the board. He also gives advice on staffing and funding sources. Pastors, lay leaders, and congregational board members will gain practical insights and ideas as they reach out to other denominations and pool their resources to serve local needs.

Dudley, Carl S. **Community Ministry: New Challenges, Proven Steps to Faith-Based Initiatives.** Bethesda, MD: Alban Institute, 2002.

> *Community Ministry* is a book for the members and leaders of any congregation seeking to engage in community ministry. Carl Dudley begins this readable and practical resource with a frank look at recent social and political changes that have created both challenges and opportunities for churches working to establish social ministries in the U.S. today. He then outlines the product of his 25 years of work with congregations—a four-part model for effectively realizing the goal of sharing God's love in practical ways in the community. Rather than a set of hard and fast rules, the process Dudley outlines is one that encourages—even requires—a congregation to consider its own uniquenesss. Through a series of simple steps, Dudley guides readers through a process designed to

help them better understand their own community's character and needs, enhance their awareness of their congregation's strengths, discover their calling, and build relationships with other organizations who share a similar mission or vision. Dudley rounds out this practical manual with checklists, sample questions, and lists of printed resources and Web links for those wishing to learn more.

Faith Into Action Resource Guide
www.faithintoaction.org

The downloadable Faith Into Action Resource Guide covers six leading-edge social ministry categories: economic development, criminal justice, health, leadership development, diversity, and positive identity formation—all topics that active congregations and communities are dealing with across this nation. The resource guide provides an overview of the current state of these ministry topics. In the guide you will find best practice models for each theme.

Faith and Service Technical Education Network
www.FASTENnetwork.org

Offers a variety of resources for faith-based organizations seeking to strengthen their organizations, their relationships, their programs, and their fundraising practices.

Harper, Nile, ed. **Urban Churches, Vital Signs: Beyond Charity Toward Justice.** Grand Rapids, MI: Eerdmans, 1999.

Each of the 28 urban churches whose stories appear in this book has been rejuvenated into a community ministry center by launching social service and economic development projects and by taking political action to achieve justice for marginalized groups. Each story is accompanied by a list of learnings—such as the value of strong pastoral leadership, the power of local congregations to affect larger society, and the ways we can build on our church's history. One of the churches described operates a complex of buildings devoted to shelter for homeless women, spiritual recovery, health care, skills training, and housing. Another, after its building was destroyed by fire, rebuilt for maximum service to the community. Other churches will find inspiration in these stories and important suggestions for new ministry.

Jacobsen, Dennis A. **Doing Justice: Congregations and Community Organizing.** Minneapolis: Fortress Press, 2001.

Doing Justice is a primer on the theology of, and rationale for, congregation-based community organizing for urban ministry. It covers such topics as the roles of power, money, and self-interest in these organizations and explores how to build and sustain ministries that promote justice. It also includes an index of organizations involved in congregation-based community organizing and a study guide for use by groups. *Doing Justice* is long on theology and stories and a bit short on concrete practical advice for setting up a congregation-based community organizing effort, but it would be helpful to congregations exploring the possibility of doing such organizing.

National Congress for Community Economic Development

The National Congress for Community Economic Development (NCCED), the association and advocate for the community-based development industry, represents over 3,600 community development corporations (CDCs) and in early 1999 published a comprehensive, annotated bibliography on faith-based community economic development. This internet-accessible bibliography (www.ncced.org/fbi/articles/anbibcover.htm) features faith-based examples of development and sections on the history, practices, policies, and products of community economic development. It also includes a section on religious resources specifically aimed at community economic development issues.

Queen, Edward L., II, ed. **Serving Those in Need: A Handbook for Managing Faith-Based Human Services Organizations.** San Francisco: Jossey-Bass, 2000.

There is much discussion of the role of faith-based organizations (FBOs) in the provision of social services. This discussion needs to include not just whether FBOs and congregations should take on this role, but how they should manage their responsibilities having done so. This edited book includes such chapters as "Religion and the Emerging Context of Service Delivery," "Funding the Dream," and "Developing Financial Accountability and Controls." The book is meant not just for FBOs but also for congregations. Clergy, laity, and nonprofit executives will benefit from this book.

Sanders, Cheryl J. **Ministry at the Margins: The Prophetic Mission of Women, Youth and the Poor.** Downers Grove, IL: InterVarsity Press, 1997.

> Women, minorities, and youth have often been the objects rather than the agents of Christian mission. But this challenging book demonstrates how ministry can be revitalized when it is not just ministry to, but ministry by, oppressed peoples seeking justice. Cheryl Sanders begins by outlining key ethical principles: accountability ("the fear of the Lord"), compassion ("the kingdom mandate"), and empathy ("the Golden Rule"). Subsequent chapters examine the prophetic ministries of women, children, and youth, Concluding with an exploration of "mission and ministry in multicultural perspective," the book urges readers to take the next steps toward reconciliation among all of God's people.

Sherman, Amy L. **Restorers of Hope: Reaching the Poor in Your Community with Church-Based Ministries that Work.** Wheaton, IL: Crossway Books, 1997.

> This book tells the stories of seven church-based or parachurch ministries that have helped transform communities and lives. It describes the programs and why they work, provides how-to advice to congregations wanting to begin their own ministries, and examines both the benefits of pitfalls of collaboration with government agencies. It is an important book often cited in discussing the efficacy of faith-based solutions to social problems.

9

PREACHING TODAY: SORTING IT OUT

G. Lee Ramsey, Jr.

The busy preacher who pauses to survey current preaching theory and practice discovers a rich yet bewildering array of resources. Since the publication of Fred Craddock's *As One without Authority* in 1971, the church of North America has witnessed a flood of material that, like abundant fresh wine, offers new zest for preaching yet tempts overindulgence. In form and content, preaching now enjoys a renaissance of interest. This renewal has led to more theologically thoughtful and pastorally effective preaching, but the danger is real that the conscientious preacher who wants to stay abreast of these new directions will either become inebriated from taking in too much too fast or become surfeited by the array of homiletical options and decide to back away from the feast. The challenge is to sort out these new directions and resources in a way that invigorates our preaching.

NEW OPTIONS IN PREACHING: OVERVIEWS

A good place to begin is with several studies that summarize the "new homiletic" over the past 30 years. In *A New Hearing: Living Options in Homiletic Method*, Richard Eslinger provides a thorough review of the turn to narrative preaching in the work of Charles Rice, Henry Mitchell, Eugene Lowry, and Fred Craddock and in the phenomenological approach of David Buttrick. He evaluates the theory of each of these teachers, then concludes each chapter with one of their own sermons. Although the book is now out of print, it is worth a trip to the closest seminary library or a request through interlibrary loan. Eslinger has updated his review of the current state of homiletics in *The Web of Preaching: New Options in Homiletic Method*. This work builds upon the previous but takes a closer look at the categories of narrative and imagination as they continue to influence contemporary preaching.

Lucy Rose's *Sharing the Word* offers a different sort of overview. Rather than focusing upon select figures in recent preaching, she identifies three distinctive emphases that developed throughout twentieth-century preaching. She categorizes preaching as traditional persuasion, kerygmatic event, and transformational encounter. While her categories might strike some as too narrow, her typology highlights crucial distinctions in purpose, content, and method that many preachers will find useful. Rose's own proposal, preaching as "communal conversation," puts preaching in dialogue with feminist and postmodern theologians, and it opens up new ground to consider preaching as a collaborative event between preacher and congregation.

In *Creative Styles of Preaching*, Mark Elliott sketches nine different styles of preaching and then couples two sample sermons with each style. He draws some of the sermons from well-known preachers who have written about the particular approach. For example, he links Fred Craddock with narrative preaching, Samuel Proctor with African American Preaching, and Barbara Brown Taylor with imaginative preaching. The book provides a snapshot of many of the major emphases in preaching today. As with all surveys, the brevity of the presentation does not allow for satisfactory exploration. For example, Elliott gives a scant one page to Fred Craddock's inductive approach to preaching. This is inadequate unless the reader has some prior understanding of inductive method. This might be a good book to read first, but it should be followed by one of the other studies mentioned above and then by the original works themselves.

Finally, John McClure collects a group of suggestions for preachers in his edited volume *Best Advice for Preaching*. McClure summons to the discussion table a diverse group of preachers and teachers around topics ranging from the calling of the preacher and getting a message to polishing the sermon and coordinating with the rest of the service. The advisors include John Claypool, Joanna Adams, Walter Burghardt, James Harris, Barbara Lundblad, Thomas Troeger, Henry Mitchell, and others. A final chapter on essential resources for preaching is markedly practical. This smorgasbord of best advice, along with the theoretical overviews already mentioned, adds up to an appetizing first course for those who wish to dine at the homiletics table today. From here on, the fare thickens and deepens.

The Source and Content of the Sermon

The first year of weekly preaching within a congregation drives home one unmistakable point: Sunday always comes. Ready or not, every seventh day the preacher will stand and attempt to answer the congregation's question, "Is there any word from God?" The relentless regularity of preaching pushes the minister deep into the soil of Christian faith. The preacher will either emerge on a weekly basis with an honest semblance of a sermon or will slowly become buried by the weight of the task. Perhaps most pressing for the preacher is the question—what to preach?

We can sort the source and content of the sermon among several categories. These include scripture, theology, the life of the congregation, the life of the preacher, and the world. While each of these influences the other, a sermon typically begins and revolves around one or the other of these home bases. Many preachers will return every week to the same source—scripture, for example—because of theological convictions, denominational tradition, or habit. Some preachers, however, prefer a variety of starting points for preaching, convinced that God's revelation is not limited to any one location, book, or event. Either way, early on the preacher has to clarify where a sermon begins and what the sermon is about.

Scripture and Preaching

Scripture has been the normative source for preaching in the Christian tradition. Most Protestant denominations give priority to sacred scripture as the place where the church most consistently encounters God, Jesus Christ, and the Holy Spirit.[1] While approaches to scriptural interpretation vary and often lead into complex theories of hermeneutics, the scriptural principle remains consistent. Hence, the church and preacher turn repeatedly to the Bible.

Resources for biblical preaching tumble off the shelves. They attempt to aid the preacher in biblical interpretation that leads to an *expository* sermon. Historical criticism of the Bible, while continuing to be important for preaching, has been augmented by various forms of literary criticism, narrative criticism, reader-response, feminist, and liberationist approaches to scriptural interpretation. The preacher who wants to brush up on these recent arrivals could consult an introductory article, such as Carl Holladay's "Contemporary Methods of Reading the Bible," or a more thorough study, such as David Bartlett's *Between the Bible and the Church*, then move toward any number of recent applications of these approaches to preaching from scripture (Jacobsen, McKenzie, Newsom and Ringe, O'Day, Ourisman, or Turner). David Buttrick's article "The Use of the Bible in Preaching" outlines many of the twists and turns in the relationship between preaching and scripture as does Ronald Allen's reliable text, *Interpreting the Gospel*. Paul Scott Wilson's *Four Pages of the Sermon* provides practical help for moving from biblical text to sermon on a weekly basis.

Once the preacher decides to take scripture as the point of departure, he or she must still decide which part of scripture to engage from week to week. This challenge can be met in several different ways. The preacher may opt to jump willy-nilly from one scriptural passage to another based upon his or her own inclinations. This random approach taxes the preacher who feels compelled each week to "get a new sermon" by plucking scripture and sermon direction out of thin air. It becomes tedious for the congregation, whose members are forced to hear the preacher repeat the same message in various disguises because he or she has no other principle of text selection than personal preference. Often preachers who use such free selection unconsciously limit their choice of scripture to those that are comfortable for themselves and the congregation. Hence, they avoid the prophetic call of God through the scriptures. A wide open approach to scripture selection has less to commend than caution, and it should be used sparingly when the preacher wants to intentionally break out of confining patterns.

Some preachers take a thematic approach to scriptural selection. Such sermons incorporate various scriptural passages to explore themes such as vocation, forgiveness, stewardship, covenant, and discipleship. This approach allows preacher and congregation to experience the breadth of theological meaning throughout the entire Bible. Preachers can develop individual thematic sermons or series. I know one preacher who regularly preaches from the lectionary but during the summer months develops a series of sermons based upon one or more scriptural themes. This gives everyone a needed change of pace, but—more importantly—it allows for sustained theological reflection on the chosen themes. One fine example of this use of scripture is Ronald Allen's *Preaching Luke–Acts.*

One of the most significant developments over the past 30 years takes us into scriptural selection based upon the lectionary. While designated readings have been a part of the Catholic liturgy for centuries, the Protestant church has only recently given widespread acceptance to the lectionary. The most widely followed lectionary today is the Revised Common Lectionary, compiled by an ecumenical group of biblical teachers and preachers. This table of select readings for each week of the year is composed of four lessons (Hebrew Scripture, Psalm, Gospel, Epistle) that are coordinated with the principle seasons of the Christian year (Advent, Christmas, Epiphany, Lent, Easter, and Pentecost). The readings change over a three-year cycle before beginning afresh.[2]

Many preachers use these selected readings as a basis for sermon and worship planning. There are many benefits to the approach. The lectionary steers preachers and congregations toward a more thorough use of scripture than they might otherwise choose. Difficult passages challenge the church to grapple honestly with the complexity of biblical interpretation. The lectionary provides a consistent backbone for the preacher to build upon over time, and it frees the minister from the tyranny of having to decide each week what to preach. Some preachers find it helpful to plan out an entire year's worth of preaching based upon the lectionary.

Commitment to the lectionary generates enormous preaching and worship resources. The quickest way to locate these is through the World Wide Web (search for "lectionary"). One of the most comprehensive sites is The Text This Week (textweek.com). It includes weekly commentary on the revised common lectionary passages and links to other sites, and coordinates scriptural passages with movies and works of art. As for print material, one quality resource among the many available is *Preaching through the Christian Year* (Craddock, et. al). The series combines dependable biblical scholarship with helpful suggestions for preaching.

The preacher must decide whether the lectionary provides enough of a theologically valid approach to scriptural selection to become a basis for weekly preaching. Some cautions are in order. We should not allow any approach to the sermon to tyrannize pulpit or pew. The lectionary does not address every concern within the church and world. Some events loom so large that a preacher must be free to move away from the lectionary to engage the topic at hand. Cataclysmic social events such as September 11, 2001 may or may not be best addressed through preaching from the given lectionary passages for the day. Furthermore, the ecumenical selection committee uses various principles of selection that may not accord with those of individual preachers and congregations. For example, the lectionary does not consistently select passages emphasizing social justice, and the entire cycle is weighted more toward New Testament passages than Hebrew scriptures. Overall, the lectionary helps orient preaching and worship, but we should probably give it, as David Buttrick says, "two cheers and some questions."[3]

Theology and Preaching

The days of preaching entire sermons as doctrinal exposition may be gone forever, and to that more than a few preachers and hearers will say, "Amen." Rarely do preachers, Protestant or Catholic, stand and deliver entire homilies on the atonement or sanctification, and certainly not in the style of earlier generations. Nevertheless, theology matters in preaching. Indeed, preaching that does not attend to theology can become vapid, wrapped in unexamined piety and the mutability of human experience. Some voices are calling for a recovery of theology in preaching that can help correct, on the one hand, a propensity of biblicism in contemporary homiletics and, on the other hand, a dangerous drift towards subjectivism.[4] Theology is present in all preaching whether the preacher is conscious of it or not. A careful review of one's own theological convictions and those of the congregation can help the preacher develop sermons that are challenging and nourishing for the congregation. Listeners of preaching hunger for sermons that help them make God-sense out of their lives and the events of the world. In *Claiming Theology in the Pulpit*, Burton Cooper and John McClure help preachers identify the theological roots of their own preaching in order to strengthen the place of theology in the pulpit. They suggest a theological typology that can be broadly applied to most preaching. Preachers who want to "locate" themselves and their congregations theologically will find concrete help in this new offering. Sermons with greater theological clarity and depth may follow.

Another equally helpful resource is Ronald Allen's *Preaching Is Believing*. Allen provides a clear discussion of the relationship between preaching and systematic theology. He demonstrates the link between interpreting scripture and theological meaning making in the congregation. Clearheaded theology in preaching helps the congregation think more faithfully and clearly about the claim of the gospel upon its life. This book invites preachers who ordinarily look to scripture as the primary source for preaching to look again at the role of theology.

Congregation as Source for Preaching

Good sermons often grow right out of the soil of the congregation. Since Christ forms the church, it makes sense for preachers to listen carefully to the actual congregation for the sounds of revelation. Readiness to do exegesis of the congregation as well as scripture is one of the compelling features of preaching today.

This means that the preacher must learn to "read" the congregation. We read the people pastorally with care for who the people are and what God is doing among them. In *Preaching as Theology and Folk Art,* Leonora Tubbs Tisdale offers refreshing guidance for pastors who believe that the sermon should attend to the congregation as well as scripture. Drawing from the field of congregational studies, Tisdale shows how to listen for the embedded theology of the congregation, then more accurately attune the sermon to the life of the people. The preacher who takes the time to listen to the congregation before speaking will preach *for* the people rather than *at* them.

My own work in pastoral preaching overlaps that of Tisdale. In *Care-full Preaching: From Sermon to Caring Community,* I show how pastoral preaching shapes the congregation as a pastoral community. We help the congregation see itself in the sermon as a *care-full* people who share God's care among themselves and the world. The sermon can help cultivate such care in very specific ways through the use of imagery, stories, and actual events from the life of the congregation. Sermons should regularly turn the spotlight upon the congregation and its ministry of care, trusting that such congregational compassion is a reliable source for sermon material. Of course, we do not rely solely upon the congregation for the sermon since Christ cannot be reduced to our own experience. But if we can, however dimly, discern the outlines of the suffering and resurrected Christ among the caring ministry of the congregation, then we should point it out in our sermons on a regular basis.

World and Sermon

Early in the twentieth century Karl Barth drew a line in the sand between church and world that deepened into a canyon. Preaching is an act of proclamation of the unique revelation of God through Jesus Christ attested to most completely in scripture. Preachers need not concern themselves with the revelation of God in the world; rather, they should simply preach from the scripture and rely upon the Word of God contained therein. At one point, Barth wrote that "the sermon will be like the involuntary lip movement of one who is reading with great care."[5] Countering Barth, theologians and preachers have claimed that God's revelation is also experienced within culture. While we surely attune our ears to scripture for the sound of Jesus Christ, we dare not ignore the sound of revelation in the world.

This basic tension continues in preaching today. Many say that homiletics has abandoned the Barthian project and opted for liberalism's emphasis upon human experience and the life of the preacher as the basis for the sermon. John McClure summarizes that for this generation of preachers "there is far more emphasis on the humanity of the preacher and the existential and numinous qualities in preaching."[6] From within postliberalism, Charles Campbell objects strongly to this direction in contemporary homiletics. Campbell argues in *Preaching Jesus* that the modern pulpit's turn to human experience has written Jesus Christ out of the sermon. Preaching has become captive to world and culture. Sermons have substituted self and cultural narratives for the real narrative of Jesus Christ revealed in scripture. He calls preachers to turn to scripture, the primary language of the church, in order to be formed into the Christ-shaped body that God intends for the Christian community.

Preachers may be taken with the postliberal homiletic and its call for countercultural Christianity. But the position raises serious questions. A postliberal approach to preaching can overlook the activity of God outside of the church. Revelation seems to be completely contained within scripture, church, and proclamation. This is problematic because God creates and redeems both inside and outside of Israel and the official church. Jesus, though concerned for the salvation of Israel, clearly does not limit his own proclamation to the synagogue, and he readily names kingdom analogies gleaned from the created order. Postliberal homiletics does raise important cautions for a pulpit that has grown too cozy with culture, but it would be foolish for the church to assume that it is now time to renounce our commitment to the world.

Preachers today will continue to point toward the grace-filled action of God within church *and* world. Mary Catherine Hilkert makes a strong theological claim for just such preaching in *Naming Grace: Preaching and the Sacramental Imagination.* This is an especially significant work for Protestant preachers who wish to understand the sacramental orientation within Catholic preaching that sees the world through the lens of the sacred. The "world," part of God's good creation, can't be shut out of the church any more than the church can be removed from the world. When you get right down to it, the church is in the world because that's where God wants the church to be. Preaching today will continue to be responsive to church and world, scripture and human experience.

The Life of the Preacher as Source of the Sermon

If you want to get up a good argument about preaching, all you have to do is ask another preacher whether he or she thinks personal experiences are appropriate material for the sermon, then take the opposing stance. Obviously, the life of the preacher impacts the sermon since preachers cannot shed their own skins before climbing into the pulpit. Barbara Brown Taylor explores this connection in *The Preaching Life.* We are embodied selves, and every aspect of preaching—from choice of material, to organization of the sermon, to the tilt of the head and twitch of the knees—is in one way or another filtered through self.

Preachers fill contemporary sermons with personal experiences. Some claim that such material establishes identification with the listeners, while others believe that personal experience, like the testimonial, is revelatory. Through personal experience the preacher conveys directly to the congregation how he or she has witnessed God. The experiential events are as varied as life itself—from a trip to the grocery store to an exotic family vacation to a heated conflict in a committee meeting. All personal experience is potentially revelatory for those who open their eyes; therefore, many argue that such experience can be claimed for proclamation.

On the other hand, others assert that while personal experience is one way that we know God, such experiences should not be directly relayed from the pulpit because they shift focus from God to the preacher. David Buttrick sums up his opposition to the use of personal experience in the sermon this way: "All in all, we are a poor substitute for the Gospel."[7] We can learn from personal experience, he says, but we shouldn't focus upon it in the sermon.

The issue is tricky and as old as classical rhetoric. What part does the *ethos*, the character, of the speaker actually play in the speech event? What marks appropriate and inappropriate use of self in preaching? What are the theological implications of referring to oneself (or one's family, friends, or church members) in the pulpit while attempting to point toward Christ? For those who want to pursue the concern, Andre Resner's *Preacher and Cross* rewards careful reading. Resner claims that self-reference in preaching must be measured against the Pauline theological criteria of Jesus Christ as self-emptying. If the preacher's personal experiences can point toward the wise folly of the cross, then it might be appropriate to include them in the sermon. Otherwise, it must be left out. A fresh publication by John McClure and Ronald Allen, *Speaking of Preaching*, explores how listeners of sermons respond to preaching, and how they assess the importance of the classical rhetorical appeals of *ethos, pathos,* and *logos.* Many listeners interviewed in this study indicate that clergy character is crucial for establishing authority in the sermon.

Preachers should commit to some theological criteria for gauging the use of personal experience in preaching. Without such criteria, personal experience in the sermon can become ego preening or a thinly veiled attempt at self-therapy in the pulpit. Here the preacher uses the congregation as a mirror to shore up the weak self or as a therapist for his or her own confused self. There is no room for such misuse of the self in the pulpit. Theologically aware preachers will always ask, "Who is being lifted up when I refer to myself in this sermon? What is the best way to use this personal experience to point towards God, Jesus Christ, and the mission of the church in the world? Is it through direct reference to the personal experience, or is there another way?" For example, can the preacher alter the situation, come at the situation from another person's point of view, or use the experience to enter imaginatively into an analogous story or character?

Preachers may decide to judiciously employ personal experience in the sermon. If we do, we should heed Barbara Brown Taylor's caution that Jesus "did not star in his own stories."[8] As far as we know, Jesus does not say, "The other day when I was standing by the Sea of Galilee...." Two resources can be very helpful at this point. Tom Long lists several criteria for the use of personal illustrations in *The Witness of Preaching*, and Joseph Webb gives extended treatment to the use of personal stories in *Comedy and Preaching*. Preachers will find these guides instructive. Congregations will appreciate the effort.

THE FORM OF THE SERMON

How to preach? The form of the sermon has undergone nothing short of a revolution since the early work of David Randolph in 1969 (*The Renewal of Preaching*) and Fred Craddock in 1971 (*As One without Authority*). Responding to suspicion of authority within church and culture and finding fresh impetus for preaching based upon the biblical school of the New Hermeneutics, Randolph and Craddock opened new avenues for preaching.

A key rhetorical assumption underneath this "new homiletic" is that language is performative. The language of the sermon does not convey objective truth. Rather, language creates meaning in the very act of preaching. Rhetoric, often understood as the scaffolding of a sermon, now becomes part and parcel of its meaning. Hogan and Reid explain this rhetorical turn in preaching in *Connecting with the Congregation*. This active view of language and rhetoric leads to two important shifts in preaching form.

First, form and content should be wedded in the sermon. Sermons are not logical vehicles designed to convey rational propositions, as in earlier preaching forms (the "old homiletic"). Rather, the sermon seeks to enact among the hearers the very message that the preacher proclaims. In other words, sermon form should align with sermon intent. For example, the sermon that seeks to help the congregation praise God can be organized and delivered as a doxology; the sermon that announces grace can reflect joy and freedom in tone and organizational patterns.

Teachers apply this same insight to biblical study and preaching. Tom Long's *Preaching and the Literary Forms of the Bible* is a clear example of this approach. Long demonstrates how to move from a biblical literary genre such as a psalm or parable to a sermon constructed along the same literary lines. Mike Graves's *The Sermon as*

Symphony outlines a similar approach, which he supplemented with sample sermons.

Second, Craddock found widespread support for his call to replace the deductive logic of earlier preaching with inductive organization and movement. Inductive sermons move from the particulars of human experience to the general experience of the Gospel. Sermons unfold in narrative fashion like stories with a beginning, middle, and end and with surprising twists along the way. Rather than stating the meaning at the beginning of the sermon, preachers lead members of the congregation to draw their own conclusions at the end of the sermon. This heightens listener participation and ownership of the message. As Craddock says, "If *they* have made the trip, then it is *their* conclusion."[9]

This new homiletic method shares the room with biblical study's interest in narrative. Teachers variously treat the sermon as narrative, from Edmund Steimle's *Preaching as Story* and Eugene Lowry's *The Homiletical Plot* to David Buttrick's *Homiletic*. For each of these homileticians, narrative means something slightly different. Especially distinctive, Buttrick's approach offers a theology and form of preaching that yields narrative-like moves and sequences within the sermon. For Buttrick, perhaps the dramatic play—with changing scenes, spotlights, and points of view—is a more apt literary genre than narrative. Nevertheless, Buttrick also raises some reservations about preaching as narrative. While preaching helps the Christian congregation find its own story within God's story, Jesus Christ "stands out from the story and is a 'living symbol' to the Christian community."[10] In other words, Jesus Christ, the central character in the Christian story, cannot be limited to the biblical narrative and should not be reduced to a cipher of our own stories. While embracing narrative preaching, Buttrick pushes preachers to remain open to the surprising transformation that God enacts in the world "outside" of the biblical narrative.

Narrative in preaching isn't new to many traditions, though the additional theoretical focus has heightened awareness and attention to form. African American preaching has often taken a storied approach to scriptural interpretation. Perusal of the sermons of Gardner Taylor (*The Words of Gardner Taylor*) or the sermons collected by Ella Mitchell (*Those Preaching Women*) will bring out some of the many ways that preaching in the African American tradition employs narrative. Susan Bond offers insightful commentary upon narrative in African American preaching in *Contemporary African American Preaching*.

Stress upon all of these elements of the new homiletic—heightened awareness of language, the uniting of form and content, inductive movement, and deeper exploration of literary forms in preaching, particularly narrative forms—might suggest that the "old homiletic" has been buried for good. In fact, a great deal of preaching today is still propositional in nature and deductive in form. Many sermons are a hybrid of various forms. Ronald Allen suggests in *Interpreting the Gospel* that at least one of four basic forms undergirds every sermon. Many preachers, from Sunday to Sunday, will shift from one form to another depending upon the focus of the sermon, the implications of the biblical text, or the nature of the situation. As Tom Long says, "Left to our own devices, most of us who preach would fall into a numbing monotony . . . too easily slipping into the habit of pouring this week's gelatin into last week's mold. . . . Our sermon planning, then, must provide not only for a variety of themes and issues but also for a variation in sermon styles and forms."[11] This is sound advice. Even though the preacher may initially find it difficult to vary preaching forms, over the long haul such periodic changes will invigorate preacher and congregation. You will find many suggestions and sample sermons with a variety of forms in Long's *A Chorus of Witnesses* and Ronald Allen's *Patterns of Preaching*.

BEYOND THE NEW HOMILETIC

Preachers are beginning to raise questions about the new homiletic, now roughly 30 years old. For one thing, the experiential focus of these newer methods—that sermons seek to create an event for listeners—is theologically suspect. Must sermons always engender experiences of God for the hearers? If so, does this mean that preaching is really more focused upon the inward experience of the listener than the nature of Christ, say, or the call to discipleship? Has the new homiletic, with its roots in theological liberalism, unintentionally exchanged theology for anthropology? If the preacher intends to create an experience for the listener, then isn't the preacher really attempting to "control" the experience of the hearers rather than share with them the responsibility for the message? In this case, how different then is the new homiletic from the old insofar as both already know the outcome of the sermon? The questions pile up.

A second concern is that the new emphasis in preaching has been more intent upon the methods of preaching than theologies of preaching. As David Lose claims, we have eagerly agreed with Marshal McLuhan that the medium is the message, but we have been less willing to say the inverse that the message is the medium.[12] We have cried buckets over how to preach but barely broken a sweat over what to preach. Maybe it is time for preachers to be honest about the theology that informs our preaching. These are only a few of the questions that beckon us into the next generation of preaching.

THE MANY VOICES OF PREACHING TODAY

Finally, the postmodern stress upon social context, mutuality, and multiple sources of authority challenges preaching today.[13] New interest clusters around Lucy Rose and John McClure's images of preaching as conversation in a "roundtable pulpit" within a "roundtable church." How can preachers rethink a theology and practice of preaching that opens up the sermon as shared conversation without losing the ethical imperatives of gospel faithfulness?[14] Preaching as conversation certainly builds upon the work of the new homiletic and so remains faithful to preaching tradition, but the model remains more a vague outline than a clear picture. We need more theological thoughtfulness and more practice of "sharing the word" to grasp its significance.

The conversation broadens within preaching. Numerous voices gather around the postmodern preaching table to help create a multilingual conversation. For example, Kathy Black's *A Healing Homiletic: Preaching and Disability* calls us to think about how preaching includes or excludes persons with disabilities. Women, whose speech has been muted by the church, are slowly finding their voices within the academy and parish. Other women have picked up Christine Smith's early work on feminist-informed preaching (*Weaving the Sermon*). Mary Lin Hudson and Mary Donovan Turner's *Saved from Silence* is an excellent study of the gifts that women bring to preaching and the challenges that women undergo to find their own voices within the pulpit. Jana Childers' collection on women's preaching, *Birthing the Sermon*, moves the discussion forward. Susan Bond's *Trouble with Jesus* offers a cogent review of feminist theology's struggle with Christology. She proposes a "Christology of salvage" that is uncannily relevant for post-September 11 preaching.

The genius of African American preaching now has numerous presenters who make this powerful preaching tradition more available to the church at large. One should certainly read Henry Mitchell's *Celebration and Experience in Preaching* for a foundational statement about black preaching, but many other fine studies provide additional explanations of the tradition, including works by Cleophus LaRue, Evans Crawford, and Teresa L. Fry Bown. The broad African American preaching tradition is regularly explored in the quarterly journal *The African American Pulpit*.

The Western church is hearing insights from Asian Christianity that enriches our understanding of preaching. For example, Korean homiletician Eunjoo Kim's *Preaching the Presence of God* explores the uniqueness of Asian congregational spirituality and then develops an approach to preaching that is commensurate with the cultural reality of the Asian congregation.

For those preachers who want to engage questions of cultural pluralism, two good studies are Joseph Webb's *Preaching and the Challenge of Pluralism* and James Nieman and Thomas Rogers's *Preaching to Every Pew*. These books honestly assess our cultural heterogeneity and offer suggestions for preaching when theological, ethnic, and social diversity is assumed.

PREACHING TODAY: SUMMING IT UP

Preaching today draws from a deeply rooted and newly flourishing tradition brimming with possibility and alive to the changing shape of the postmodern church and culture. Attention in preaching to the current social and ecclesial situation is not a matter of "political correctness." It is simply a fact that the church of today must, as always, be honest about and responsive to the very culture in which it is located. Preachers today are especially challenged to proclaim the gospel with enough clarity and engaging conviction to be heard as voices counter to all the other truth claims that squawk for attention.[15] This calls for steady homiletical focus upon biblical text, theology, congregational reality, and the varieties of forms that give flesh to sermons. The preacher who wishes to faithfully proclaim the gospel in the twenty-first century will have to learn more than toleration of others. Rather, we will learn to delight in the presence of others who, like ourselves, come to sanctuary and pulpit bearing gifts, eager and prepared to continue the task of preaching the gospel. Granted, preaching within a culture marked by religious pluralism and cultural diversity stretches the conscientious pastor almost to the homiletical breaking point. But what else can the caring preacher do but attempt to find a way to preach with open arms to all who might hear while remaining centered in Jesus Christ?

NOTES

1. For a discussion of how various traditions approach preaching, see Richard Lischer and William H. Willimon, eds. *Concise Encyclopedia of Preaching* (Louisville: Westminster John Knox Press, 1995).
2. For the full table of readings, see "Consultation on Common Texts," *The Revised Common Lectionary* (Nashville: Abingdon Press, 1992).
3. David Buttrick, "Preaching the Lectionary: Two Cheers and Some Questions," *Reformed Music and Liturgy* 28 (Spring 1994): 77-81
4. See Thomas G. Long, Edward Farley, eds. *Preaching as a Theological Task* (Louisville: Westminster John Knox Press, 1996).
5. Karl Barth, *Homiletics*, trans. G.W. Bromily and D. E. Daniels (Louisville: Westminster John Knox Press, 1991), 76.
6. John S. McClure, ed., *Best Advice for Preaching* (Minneapolis: Augsburg Fortress, 1998), xv.
7. David Buttrick, *Homiletic: Moves and Structures* (Philadelphia: Fortress Press, 1987), 106.
8. Barbara Brown Taylor, *When God Is Silent* (Cambridge, MA: Cowley Publications, 1998), 114.
9. Fred Craddock, *As One Without Authority* (Nashville: Abingdon Press, 1979 [1971]), 57.
10. David Buttrick, *Homiletic*, 14.
11. Thomas G. Long, "Patterns in Sermons," in *Best Advice for Preaching*, John S. McClure, ed. (Minneapolis: Fortress Press, 1998), 37.
12. David J. Lose, "Medium and Message Reconsidered: Thoughts on Preaching the Gospel and Teaching Such Preaching," in *Annual Papers*, The Academy of Homiletics (2001), 402-406.
13. See Ronald J. Allen, Barbara S. Blaisdell, and Scott B. Johnston. *Theology for Preaching: Authority, Truth, and Knowledge of God in a Post-modern Ethos* (Nashville: Abingdon Press, 1997) and David J. Lose, *Confessing Jesus Christ: Preaching in a Postmodern World* (Grand Rapids, MI: Eerdmans, 2003).

14. See Charles L. Campbell, *The Word Before the Powers: An Ethic of Preaching* (Louisville: Westminster John Knox Press, 2002).
15. See Martin B. Copenhaver, Anthony B. Robinson, and William H. Willimon, *Good News in Exile: Three Pastors Offer a Hopeful Vision for the Church* (Grand Rapids, MI: Eerdmans, 1999).

BIBLIOGRAPHY

African American Pulpit. Valley Forge, PA: Judson Press, published quarterly.

Allen, Ronald J. *Preaching Luke–Acts.* St. Louis: Chalice Press, 2000.

———. *Interpreting the Gospel: An Introduction to Preaching.* St. Louis: Chalice Press, 1998.

———, ed. *Patterns of Preaching: A Sermon Sampler.* St. Louis: Chalice Press, 1998.

———. *Preaching is Believing: The Sermon as Theological Reflection.* Louisville: Westminster John Knox Press, 2002.

Allen, Ronald J., Barbara S. Blaisdell, and Scott B. Johnston. *Theology for Preaching: Authority, Truth, and Knowledge of God in a Post-Modern Ethos.* Nashville: Abingdon Press, 1997.

Bartlett, David. *Between the Bible and the Church: New Methods for Biblical Preaching.* Nashville: Abingdon Press, 1999.

Black, Kathy. *A Healing Homiletic: Preaching and Disability.* Nashville: Abingdon Press, 1996.

Bond, Susan L. *Trouble with Jesus: Women, Christology, and Preaching.* St. Louis: Chalice Press, 1999.

———. *Contemporary African American Preaching: Diversity in Theory and Style.* St. Louis: Chalice Press, 2002.

Buttrick, David. *Homiletic: Moves and Structures.* Philadelphia: Fortress Press, 1987.

———. "The Use of the Bible in Preaching," in *The New Interpreter's Bible,* vol. 1. Nashville: Abingdon Press, 1994.

Campbell, Charles L. *Preaching Jesus: New Directions for Homiletics in Hans Frei's Postliberal Theology.* Grand Rapids, MI: Eerdmans, 1997.

———. *The Word Before the Powers: An Ethic of Preaching.* Louisville: Westminster John Knox Press, 2002.

Childers, Jana, ed. *Birthing the Sermon: Women Preachers on the Creative Process.* St. Louis: Chalice Press, 2001.

Cooper, Burton Z., and John S. McClure. *Claiming Theology in the Pulpit.* Louisville: Westminster John Knox Press, 2003.

Copenhaver, Martin B., Anthony B. Robinson, and William H. Willimon. *Good News in Exile: Three Pastors Offer a Hopeful Vision for the Church.* Grand Rapids, MI: Eerdmans, 1999.

Craddock, Fred, et. al. *Preaching through the Christian Year.* Harrisburg, PA: Trinity Press International, 1992.

———. *As One without Authority.* Nashville: Abingdon Press, 1979 [1971].

Crawford, Evans C., and Thomas H. Troeger. *The Hum: Call and Response in African American Preaching.* Nashville: Abingdon Press, 1996.

Elliott, Mark B. *Creative Styles of Preaching.* Louisville: Westminster John Knox Press, 2000.

Eslinger, Richard. *A New Hearing: Living Option in Homiletic Method.* Nashville: Abingdon Press, 1987.

_____ *The Web of Preaching: New Options in Homiletic Method.* Nashville: Abingdon Press, 2002.

Fry Brown, Teresa L. *Weary Throats and New Songs: Black Women Proclaiming God's Word.* Nashville: Abingdon Press, 2003.

Graves, Mike. *The Sermon as Symphony: Preaching the Literary Forms of the New Testament.* Valley Forge, PA: Judson Press, 1997.

Hilkert, Mary Catherine. *Naming Grace: Preaching and the Sacramental Imagination.* New York: Continuum, 1996.

Hogan, Lucy Lind, and Robert Reid. *Connecting with the Congregation: Rhetoric and the Art of Preaching.* Nashville: Abingdon Press, 1999.

Holladay, Carl R. "Contemporary Methods of Reading the Bible," in *The New Interpreter's Bible,* vol. 1, edited by Leander Keck. Nashville: Abingdon Press, 1994.

Hudson, Mary Lin, and Mary Donovan Turner. *Saved from Silence: Finding Women's Voice in Preaching.* St. Louis: Chalice Press, 1999.

Jacobsen, David S. *Preaching in the New Creation: The Promise of New Testament Apocalyptic Texts.* Louisville: Westminster John Knox Press, 1999.

Kim, Eunjoo Mary. *Preaching the Presence of God: A Homiletic from an Asian American Perspective.* Valley Forge, PA: Judson, 1999.

LaRue, Cleophus J. *The Heart of Black Preaching.* Louisville: Westminster John Knox Press, 2000.

Lischer, Richard, and William H. Willimon, eds. *Concise Encyclopedia of Preaching.* Louisville: Westminster John Knox Press, 1995.

Long, Thomas G. *Preaching and the Literary Forms of the Bible.* Philadelphia: Fortress Press, 1989.

———. *The Witness of Preaching.* Louisville: Westminster John Knox Press, 1989.

Long, Thomas G., and Cornelius Plantinga. *A Chorus of Witnesses: Model Sermons for Today's Preacher.* Grand Rapids, MI: Eerdmans, 1994.

Long, Thomas G., and Edward Farley, eds. *Preaching as a Theological Task: World, Gospel, Scripture.* Louisville: Westminster John Knox Press, 1996.

Lose, David J. *Confessing Jesus Christ: Preaching in a Postmodern World.* Grand Rapids, MI: Eerdmans, 2003.

Lowery, Eugene. *The Homiletical Plot.* Nashville: Abingdon Press, 1980.

McClure, John S. *The Roundtable Pulpit.* Nashville: Abingdon Press, 1995.

———, ed. *Best Advice for Preaching.* Minneapolis: Augsburg Fortress, 1998.

McClure, John S., and Ronald J. Allen. *Speaking of Preaching.* St. Louis: Chalice Press, 2004.

McKenzie, Alyce M. *Preaching Proverbs: Wisdom for the Pulpit.* Louisville: Westminster John Knox Press, 1996.

———. *Preaching Biblical Wisdom in a Self-Help Society.* Nashville: Abingdon, 2002.

McLuhan, Marshall. *The Medium is the Message.* New York: Random House, 1967.

Mitchell, Ella Pearson. *Those Preaching Women,* vol. 2. Valley Forge, PA: Judson Press, 1988.

Mitchell, Henry H. *Celebration and Experience in Preaching.* Nashville: Abingdon Press, 1990.

Newsome, Carol, and Sharon Ringe, eds. *The Women's Bible Commentary* (expanded). Louisville: Westminster John Knox Press, 1998.

Nieman, James R., and Thomas G. Rogers. *Preaching to Every Pew: Cross Cultural Strategies.* Minneapolis: Fortress Press, 2001.

O'Day, Gail R., and R. Alan Culpepper, "Luke–John," in *The New Interpreter's Bible,* vol. 9, Leander Keck, ed. Nashville: Abingdon Press, 1995.

Ourisman, David J. *From Gospel to Sermon Preaching Synoptic Texts.* St. Louis: Chalice Press, 2000.

Ramsey, G. Lee, Jr. *Care-full Preaching: From Sermon to Caring Community.* St. Louis: Chalice Press, 2000.

Randolph, David J. *The Renewal of Preaching.* Philadelphia: Fortress Press, 1969.

Resner, Andre, Jr. *Preacher and Cross: Person and Message in Theology and Rhetoric.* Grand Rapids, MI: Eerdmans, 1999.

Rose, Lucy. *Sharing the Word: Preaching in the Roundtable Church.* Louisville: Westminster John Knox Press, 1997.

Smith, Christine M. *Weaving the Sermon: Preaching in a Feminist Perspective.* Louisville: Westminster John Knox Press, 1989.

Steimle, Edmund, Morris J. Niedenthal, and Charles L. Rice, *Preaching the Story.* Minneapolis: Fortress Press, 1983.

Taylor, Barbara Brown. *The Preaching Life.* Cambridge, MA: Cowley Publications, 1993.

Taylor, Gardner. *The Words of Gardner Taylor: Quintessential Classics, 1980-Present*, vol. 3, compiled by Edward L. Taylor. Valley Forge, PA: Judson Press, 2000.

Tisdale, Leonora Tubbs. *Preaching as Local Theology and Folk Art*. Minneapolis: Fortress Press, 1997.

Turner, Mary Donovan. *Old Testament Words: Reflections for Preaching*. St. Louis: Chalice Press, 2003.

Webb, Joseph M. *Comedy and Preaching*. St. Louis: Chalice Press, 1998.

———. *Preaching and the Challenge of Pluralism*. St. Louis: Chalice Press, 1998.

Wilson, Paul Scott. *The Four Pages of the Sermon: A Guide to Biblical Preaching*. Nashville: Abingdon Press, 1999.

Resources on Preaching
from the Congregational Resource Guide

The African American Pulpit. Valley Forge, PA: Judson Press.

The African American Pulpit is a quarterly journal focused on African American preaching. Each issue has a theme and features sermons by African American preachers, an article on homiletic method, reviews of resources useful for pastors, and interviews with outstanding African American preachers and leaders. *The African American Pulpit* can help preachers become more reflective and intentional about their own preaching style and content by comparing their own practice to the variety of approaches and styles presented in the journal. All Christians will find this journal instructive for enhancing their own preaching and for gaining increased understanding of African American culture and faith traditions.

Childers, Jana. **Birthing the Sermon: Women Preachers on the Creative Process.** St. Louis: Chalice Press, 2001.

Jana Childers has collected proposals that describe the preaching processes utilized by experienced women preachers. This book explores the diverse paths taken by these preachers as each outlines her own process. The authors affirm that preaching is a lonely and challenging task, and some say it can take years of preaching for women to find their own voice in proclamation. Women preachers will find affirmation of the diversity of preaching style among the authors, and all experienced preachers will be challenged through these authors to renew their commitment to prayer, study, culture and practice in their sermon preparation.

College of Preachers
www.collegeofpreachers.org

> The College of Preachers, located in Washington, DC, is a center of continuing education serving those called to Christian proclamation. On its Web site, the College lists its many conferences, workshops, and pilgrimages, and posts sermons, book reviews, reading lists, lectures, and essays to assist preachers in their work. Also featured are links to over 60 other Web sites, including divinity schools, seminaries, consortia, study centers, online resources specifically for preachers, and a variety of denominational Web sites.

Graves, Mike. **The Sermon as Symphony: Preaching the Literary Forms of the New Testament.** Valley Forge, PA: Judson Press, 1997.

> Examining ten literary forms in the New Testament, the author proposes that sermons be prepared as "regenerations of the textual event." The thesis: form-sensitive sermons, unlike traditional sermons, should seek to be more experiential than expository. Key questions: What is the text saying? What is the text doing? How can the sermon *say* and *do* the same thing? Replete with exercises, the volume illustrates the use of literary forms in sermons by some of today's best-known preachers: Eugene Lowry, Barbara Brown Taylor, Thomas Long, William Willimon, Frederick Buechner, Thomas Troeger, and Donald Musser. This work will serve those seriously interested in creative and faithful biblical preaching.

Long, Thomas G. **The Witness of Preaching.** Louisville: Westminster John Knox Press, 1989.

> In this book, Long presents the vocation of the preacher as one of witnessing to God's presence in scripture. However, the author says, the preacher does not stand over and against the community but goes to the scripture on behalf of the community and shares with the whole community, the preacher included, what he or she has witnessed. This book offers a wealth of information on how to construct a sermon, with discussion of the statement of focus, the statement of function, beginnings, endings, connections, images, illustrations, and some of the mechanics of delivery. Long's treatments are always helpful and reasonable.

McClure, John S., ed. **Best Advice for Preaching.** Minneapolis: Fortress Press, 1998.

> In this immensely practical book on the art of preaching, editor John McClure presents the counsel of 27 outstanding Christian preachers. In each chapter, a different author guides the dialogue. William Sloane Coffin and Walter Burghardt discuss theological reflection. J. Philip Wogaman and Barbara Brown Taylor advise an annual retreat to plan sermons for the year. Fred Craddock and Joanna Adams tell how they organize their material. Barbara Lundblad and Virgilio Elizondo describe how they polish a sermon. David H. C. Read and John Vannorsdell explain how the sermon fits into the whole worship experience, and Thomas Ridenhour explores the range of resources available when constructing a sermon. Each chapter includes instructions, advice, and frequently asked questions.

Nieman, James R., Thomas G. Rogers. **Preaching to Every Pew: Cross-Cultural Strategies.** Minneapolis: Fortress Press, 2001.

> Homiletics professors James Nieman and Thomas Rogers weave the voices of preachers with insights from the social sciences to present a practical theology for preaching in multicultural contexts. Having interviewed pastors who serve in multicultural congregations, the authors discuss what it means for preachers to be neighbors to the rest of the community. They present a case for exploring culture through four frames: ethnicity, class, displacement, and beliefs. Using illustrative narratives, Nieman and Rogers organize their learnings into practical preaching strategies. Most of what they share can enable preachers in every pulpit to touch the hearts of all God's people.

Taylor, Barbara Brown. **The Preaching Life.** Boston: Cowley Publications, 1993.

> Popular speaker, writer, and Episcopal priest Barbara Brown Taylor has written a two-part exposition on the art of preaching. Part One, in chapters with titles such as *Imagination, Worship,* and *Bible,* uncovers the author's approach to creating a sermon. The chapter on preaching spells out her approach: "I do not want to pass out knowledge from the pulpit; I want to share in an experience of

God's living word." It is a worthy goal for any preacher, and the
sermons included in Part Two both share God's living word and
illustrate the ideas explicated in Part One. *The Preaching Life* gives
us some of the finest preaching of today and the opportunity to
explore sermon creation with an excellent writer.

The Text This Week
Textweek.com

> This Web site provides upcoming Revised Common Lectionary
> passages with links to resources for study and liturgy for each,
> along with links to study resources relating to specific passages.
> Also featured is an index of artwork by biblical theme and a list of
> movies indexed by spiritual theme.

Tisdale, Leonora Tubbs. **Preaching as Local Theology and Folk Art.**
Minneapolis: Fortress Press, 1997.

> Leonora Tisdale says preachers need to be adept at exegeting their
> local congregation and its context. Knowing local language, images,
> metaphors, and rituals produces proclamation that is relevant and
> transformational. Careful and creative steps guide the reader into a
> method of exegeting the preacher's context. Following Tisdale's
> process invites the preacher to speak as both poet and prophet,
> weaving together the Gospel and local experience into new images
> and symbols that transform the imaginations and hearts of the
> hearers. The preacher/prophet measures the adequacy of local
> stories and understandings in light of the bigger Gospel message.
> All preachers will gain useful tools from this work.